How Ideas Shape
Urban Political Development

THE CITY IN THE TWENTY-FIRST CENTURY

Eugenie L. Birch and Susan M. Wachter, Series Editors

A complete list of books in the series
is available from the publisher.

How Ideas Shape Urban Political Development

Edited by

Richardson Dilworth

and

Timothy P. R. Weaver

UNIVERSITY OF PENNSYLVANIA PRESS

PHILADELPHIA

Published by University of Pennsylvania Press
Philadelphia, Pennsylvania 19104-4112
www.upenn.edu/pennpress

Printed in the United States of America
on acid-free paper
10 9 8 7 6 5 4 3 2 1

A Cataloging-in-Publication Record is available from the Library of Congress
ISBN 978-0-8122-5225-5

CONTENTS

PREFACE

Urban Political Development and the Politics of Ideas

Robert Henry Cox and Daniel Béland

Constructivist social scientists take it as self-evident that human societies are constructed by the people who inhabit them. The physical world does not prescribe a particular way that any society should be ordered, its order coming instead from the choices made by the people who comprise these societies.

Cities are also historically and socially constructed, not natural creations. This is the basic message of this volume and makes a compelling case for the value of a constructivist approach to understanding urban political development. At a time when constructivism is growing across the social sciences, Richardson Dilworth, Timothy P. R. Weaver, and the other contributors to this volume have made a strong case for understanding why ideas have been the real drivers behind urban political development and why a constructivist understanding is more persuasive than conventional approaches.

What distinguishes constructivist from conventional approaches is that these approaches see the social world as analogous to the natural world, therefore requiring the same manner of investigation to reveal its secrets. Constructivists, by contrast, assume that a big difference between the natural and the social world is that human beings shape their social orders by imbuing them with meaning. There are physical and biological elements to any social order. Families have biological relationships; safety and security can be enhanced by living in close proximity; and we have the ability to construct durable shelter. All these things we can investigate using conventional methods of analysis.

An urban space can be described in terms of its physical characteristics, but it also has a meaning to the people who inhabit it. Open plazas can be spaces for relaxation and contemplation or for commerce and exchange. Some buildings can provide spaces for various rituals, ranging from spiritual to hygienic. The buildings can be described in terms of their physical characteristics and the functional needs they serve, but the description is incomplete without also explicating their meanings to the actors who built and inhabited them.

Explicating the meaning and significance of social spaces requires allowing actors to speak about their own subjective meanings. This in turn requires that researchers appreciate those subjective meanings as being constitutive of the social order they wish to understand. Conventional approaches take the opposite approach. In a conventional inquiry, the investigator begins by defining terms, looking for evidence of those terms, and refining her or his understanding following a test of the terms in situ. All the thinking and acting is done by the researcher.

The approach advocated in this volume, by contrast, is to not construct a priori definitions of terms, preferring instead to embrace the ideas—and the meanings they evoke—as they are used by the actors themselves. The objective is to reveal how humans think and reason about the urban spaces they create.

Another important difference is that constructivists are concerned with shared meanings. It matters to know what a key decision maker thinks, but it also matters to know what ideas have resonance with a broader group of people. Understandings of the world, like cities themselves, are built by people who create and reproduce common meanings for their surroundings. For conventional views, by contrast, the meaning that matters is the one constructed by a solitary researcher who devises his terms and outlines the relationships among them. The conventional researcher seeks conceptual precision, theoretical elegance, and simplicity of causes. Constructivists, by contrast, assume that the world is a messier place and seek to explain how humans strive to navigate and make sense of its complexity. Needless to say, we get much richer and more textured understanding from a constructivist approach.

We see this point illustrated when we consider the role of interests in social science research. As the editors of this volume point out, the notions of interests are dominant in depictions of how actors influence urban development. But the concept of interest often employed by conventional scholars of urban political development is one that is devised by the researcher and ascribed to the actors. Indeed, the only way we could say that people act against their own interests is by having a notion of their interest that is independent of what they think themselves. A constructivist, on the other hand, takes it as a given that people act in their own interests (if that is what they say they are doing) but then seeks to explore why they define their interests in the way they do. The key issue is to find out what their interests are to them, not to compare them to some objective standard of interest.

This remark does not mean that interests are purely subjective or unrelated to material and institutional factors. What it means is that actors define their interests by interpreting their surroundings in certain ways, which might be grounded in particular historical and cultural meanings. From a constructivist standpoint, in other words, interests are complex and changing and do more than simply reflect the seemingly objective economic status of actors.

The same can be said for institutions. For the past thirty years, institutional analyses have been pervasive across the social sciences. Institutions are most commonly formulated as constraints; obstacles that savvy actors learn to maneuver around as they pursue their interests. Institutions are furthermore assumed to provide stability, forcing actions to follow a logic of incremental adjustment and preventing dramatic departures from the status quo. Institutions make change difficult. However, institutionalists recognize that change does happen, though they include it in their models as exogenous forces or shocks, such as unforeseen events.

Constructivists take a different view of institutions. Yes, institutions are stable forces that discourage dramatic change and lend predictability to social outcomes. And yes, they can be disrupted by exogenous forces. But they also can be disrupted by autonomous actors who envision alternatives to the status quo. For a constructivist, institutions matter until they don't. The purpose of research is not to prove the constraining force of institutions but instead to identify when institutions exercise this power and when actors decide to change their institutions. Institutional stability and change are treated as an empirical question, not a theoretical assumption.

Both interests and institutions, like cities, are constructed by human actors. Consequently, they too are inspired by the ideas held important by those actors. This is what we mean by the power of ideas. The real drivers of social change are ideas about how the world works. These ideas are generated by creative individual and collective actors, and influential actors can realize their ideas through their actions. Their ideas can form their interests and also inspire their efforts to build new or transform existing institutions. These are formulations that make the ideas more permanent and help to disseminate those ideas more broadly. Consequently, we can see in interests and institutions the ideas that inspired their architects.

This point is illustrated by focusing on many of the ideas detailed in the empirical chapters of this volume. Blight, urban renewal, and urban crisis, to name a few, are ideas developed by specific actors to advocate certain courses of action. They describe discomfort with the status quo and frame the problem they identify. Their ideas are more successful when they are formulated in such a way as to generate broad appeal. In doing so, they give dimension to vague feelings that others might also have but had not found the ideas to express. Thus, ideas are more successful when they are formulated in such a way as to appeal to shared understandings of the world.

The shared meanings evoked by ideas are fluid. They often lack precise definition. This is why, as Sally Ford Lawton points out in Chapter 3, the idea of blight evokes a common sense of an undesirable state of affairs, but its imprecision allows actors to attach it to many different situations, some of which may not fit a technical or legal definition.

This fluidity of an idea opens it to contest over its relevance. Actors can debate whether the idea describes the situation accurately and whether it is defined correctly by the person invoking it. Such contests over the meanings of ideas and the situations to which they apply are at the heart of politics. Considered in this light, politics is more than the contest over who gets what, when and how, as Harold Lasswell famously put it. Politics is also about what is just, fair, and legitimate.

Clearly, ideas are an integral part of political battles, and different types of actors deploy these ideas to define and advance their cause. For example, in Chapter 4, Marcus Anthony Hunter shows how activists in Philadelphia used ideas to frame their opposition to the proposed Crosstown Expressway that threatened their communities. Conversely, in Chapter 11, Timothy P. R. Weaver focuses on the role of policy entrepreneurs in promoting the idea of enterprise zones in the United States and the United Kingdom. Here the focus is not on grassroots activists but instead is on experts and ideologues who try to sell their policy ideas to both business and government officials. What these two examples suggest is that within the politics of ideas, many different actors can move to the front stage to wage ideational battles over urban policy.

Another lesson from this volume is that the constructivist perspective associated with the study of the role of ideas in politics applies equally well to advanced industrial societies and to countries located in the Global South. The presence of case studies about Chile, China, India, and Africa in this volume is important because it shows how the constructivist perspective is applicable to different parts of the world and how domestic and transnational processes may interact. For instance, this interaction is central to Chapter 15, in which Vanessa Watson examines how urban design ideas from other parts of the world are adapted to African urban settings.

Finally, this volume offers historical perspectives that allow us to grasp the development and spread of ideas over time and their interaction with changing economic and political landscapes, including perceived crises, that may disrupt the status quo to various degrees, thus increasing the potential influence of new ideas. Taking into account these crises and variations enriches our understanding of both urban political development and the role of ideas in politics and public policy.

The authors of the chapters in this volume recognize the multifaceted and historically constructed character of urban politics and embrace it as an effort to bring meaning to the urban spaces we inhabit and the political struggles we witness and take part in. The contribution they make is not only to apply a focus on ideas to the study of urban political development but also to show us how our cities have been shaped and reshaped by the ideas that we and others have about what matters and how we wish to live together. More broadly, this volume considerably enriches our empirical and analytical knowledge of the politics of ideas more generally, something that could inspire constructivist social scientists who are located in other research areas. Because ideas are central to politics in general, the chapters of this volume contribute to our broader understanding of politics as much as to our knowledge of the more specific topic of urban political development, which illustrates perfectly why social scientists must pay close attention to ideas in their research about politics and public policy.

CHAPTER 1

Ideas, Interests, Institutions, and Urban Political Development

Richardson Dilworth and Timothy P. R. Weaver

Ideas, interests, and institutions are the "holy trinity" of the study of politics. Of the three, ideas are arguably the hardest with which to grapple and thus, despite generally broad agreement of their fundamental importance, the most often neglected or treated in an ad hoc manner. This is nowhere more true than in the study of urban politics and urban political development.[1] In this chapter we discuss the existing major theoretical approaches to the study of urban politics, consider how those approaches have neglected the role of ideas, define what we mean by "urban political development" and explain how the chapters in this book contribute to that definition, and provide some preliminary thoughts and a preliminary model, building from the chapters, regarding how urban political development is shaped by ideas.

Ideas, Interests, and the Study of Urban Politics

Far more than ideas, interests and institutions have served as the primary analytical tools in the study of urban politics. Interests and ideas are of course not mutually exclusive categories; individuals and groups consciously define their wants and needs, and those definitions might be considered a special category of ideas.[2] Yet some interests are not ideas in the sense of being consciously constructed and instead are things that everyone would want and thus axiomatic, such as Rawlsian primary goods.[3] The ability to define some human wants and needs as axiomatic has no doubt made interests rather than ideas one of the fundamental building blocks in the social sciences.

Interests have also served as the primary building blocks of the social sciences because they provide simple and often reasonably accurate means of dividing individuals into groups. The assumption that interests could be derived from group membership was at the core of the community power debate and also serves as one of the basic premises of "regime theory" in the study of urban politics.[4] Whereas the community power debate revolved around the relative power of various groups in local politics, with the assumption being that groups wanted power so as to satisfy their interests, regime theory starts from the premise that various groups cooperate in order to build governing coalitions, and in the process of coalition building various group interests, particularly business interests, are satisfied. While each account differed on the question of whose interests tended to be advanced and why, both schools of thought assumed that group interests flowed from class, ethnic, racial, or similar positions.

While the participants in the community power debate and regime theorists typically satisfied themselves by deducing interests from group membership and paying little attention to ideas, scholars working in neo-Marxist traditions typically seek to deduce interests from the deeper social structure, from which they can more affirmatively dismiss ideas as largely being strategies used in the struggle between labor and capital, with no real ability to alter these fundamental material interests. Thus, for instance, sociologists John Logan and Harvey Molotch argued that the conflict between labor and capital in cities was reflected in the conflict between those who use the city primarily as a place of residence and others who use it as a place of investment. The role of ideas enters into this conflict only insofar as investment interests are able to inculcate into the residential population the ostensibly false belief that progrowth policies are to the benefit of the entire city population.[5]

Focused as it was more on coalition building and governing capacity, regime theory was similar to the contemporaneous but almost wholly separate move, starting in the 1980s, to "bring the state back in" that shaped many historical institutionalist studies and generally suggested that the state, nationally or locally, was not simply a receptacle of interests but also had interests of its own.[6] Thus, Ted Gurr and Desmond King argued in *State and the City* (1987) that the national state has an interest in such things as "maintaining public order and authority" and "securing public revenues" while the local state has an interest in autonomy from the national state, and none of these things are reducible to the interests of any specific groups.[7]

The turn toward the state and away from groups led ultimately to definitions of "political orders" as constellations of actors, ideologies, and interests that formed identifiable clusters but also contained "frictions" that were the source of "endogenous," significant, and durable changes.[8] Rogers Smith has argued that ideas are especially important in defining a political order, since such an order "*must* have some defining overarching purposes that are expressed in the rules, policies, and roles it promulgates."[9] Drawing on the work of Vivien Schmidt,[10] Smith suggested that ideas function as the unifying elements that work to smooth the frictions within political orders by providing the "coordinative discourses" that operate to build coalitions and "communicative discourses" deployed to persuade the public to support these coalitions.[11] In addition to providing coherence, stability, and agency to a given political order, however, ideas may also exacerbate existing frictions within a political order or provide the raw materials for actors to construct rival political orders, as in the classic example of "cross-cutting issues" that have played such a key role in explaining electoral shifts.

Despite increasing scholarly attention to the role of ideas in political development, there is little consensus about what an "idea" is. As Sheri Berman points out, "a common objection raised to the study of ideas is that they are simply too vague and amorphous to be used in rigorous analysis and indeed many ideational scholars are quite sloppy in this regard."[12] To add more rigor, Berman distinguishes between *beliefs*, *norms*, *cultures*, and *ideologies*.[13] Beliefs "are views or opinions held by political actors that are relatively limited in scope or relative to relatively circumscribed areas of politics."[14] By contrast, norms, cultures, and ideologies are "collective and relatively durable." Norms, for example, emerge as beliefs that become collectively held and shape behavior in predicable ways, cultures involve the adoption of norms held by particular (often ascriptively defined) groups, and ideologies are central to the creation of communities that congeal around political projects.

Another important ideational variable, associated with Vivien Schmidt's work, is *discourse*, meaning "not just ideas or 'text' (what is said) but also context (where, when, how, and why it was said). The term refers not only to structure (what is said, or where and how) but also to agency (who said what to whom)."[15] Thus, discourses involve beliefs and the communication of beliefs involved in coalition building (coordinative discourses) or garnering support from a broader audience (communicative discourses).

Daniel Béland and Robert Cox define ideas as "causal beliefs"—that is, products of cognition that enable us to posit the relationship between people and material objects and provide "guides for action."[16] However, as Weaver has noted, the notion that ideas are exclusively concerned with causation may be overly restrictive, since it appears to "rule out normative or categorical beliefs."[17] For our purposes, we therefore adopt a broad definition of ideas as "normative, categorical, or causal beliefs" that form the raw material of the other ideational variables that Berman and Schmidt have identified.

Ideas, Interests, and Institutions

In order to advance their interests, social groups construct institutions, which in turn define social roles for the groups to which individuals belong. It is thus through institutional roles that specific interests can be ascribed to individuals. In this sense, institutions are (as William Riker long ago defined them) "congealed preferences" that, once congealed, further structure and define preferences and interests.[18] In the absence of institutional roles, the only ability to define interests is through abstract forces such as capitalism that leave much to be explained; there is, for instance, a wide range of potentially conflicting policy preferences that might be consistent with promoting capital accumulation. Hence, a strictly materialist account of interests can only focus on basic human needs that do not go much beyond providing a small number of axioms, or the infinite and incomparable ways in which individuals might define their own unique interests.[19]

In order to avoid the chaos of assuming that individuals define their wants and needs sui generis, institutional roles are used to define individual interests. And the synthesis of interests from multiple institutional roles suggests at least some approximation of agency. In the study of city politics, one of the clearest expressions of interests deduced from institutional roles is provided by Paul Peterson:

> Although social roles performed within cities are numerous and conflicting, all are structured by the fact that they take place in a specific spatial location that falls within the jurisdiction of some local government. All members of the city thus come to share an interest in policies that affect the well-being of that territory. Policies which enhance the desirability or attractiveness of the territory are in the city's interest, because they benefit all residents—in their role as residents of the community. Of course, in any of their other social roles, residents of the city may be adversely affected by the policy.

> The Los Angeles dope peddler—in his role as peddler—hardly benefits from a successful drive to remove hard drugs from the city. On the other hand, as a resident of the city, he benefits from a policy that enhances the attractiveness of the city as a locale in which to live and work.[20]

The city residents imagined by Peterson might be described as "situated subjects" in the sense that their subjectivities result from their being situated at unique intersections of multiple ascribed institutional roles, namely drug peddler and resident.[21] Allowing for the possibility of multiple, overlapping, and interacting institutional roles is a more sophisticated way of discerning interests than assuming that all individuals can be placed in one of a few competing groups. Moreover, the uniqueness of each intersection of institutional roles ostensibly provides individuals with distinctive sets of motivations that describe the extent and nature of their agency. Crucially, ideas serve to unify multiple intersecting roles into cohesive identities that become carriers of those ideas. In doing so, ideas are creative reimaginings of ourselves that go beyond the notion of agency[22] and provide for a degree of inherent unpredictability. As Orion Lewis and Sven Steinmo have suggested, the role of ideas in political change might be conceived of as the equivalent of the role that random mutations play in evolution.[23]

Yet Peterson's apparent assumption that specific interests deriving from specific institutional roles can be discerned in individuals suggests that individuality is more an aggregation than a synthesis of roles, with agency accordingly attenuated. Indeed, though Peterson hinted at a sophisticated means of deriving individual agency from situated city subjectivities, he was instead concerned with isolating from those multiple identities a simplistically unitary "city interest" from which he argued that the policy options of cities are uniquely constrained.

The multiple roles played by every city resident might lead in a very different direction than what Peterson took—to one that attempts to capture the reality of individuals embedded in multiple institutions that are often an opaque mix of explicit directives and implicit norms as reflected in both formal codes and informal behaviors, some of which may very well contradict one another or are at least subject to multiple interpretations. The attempt to theorize this multiplicity and irreducible messiness leads us not to the chaos of incomparable individual interests but instead to the study of political development.

Urban Political Development

Urbanization is one of the key phenomena that has shaped and is shaping the modern and contemporary world, reflected in the United Nations' finding in 2014 that 54 percent of the world's population lived in urban areas, a proportion set to rise to 66 percent by 2050.[24] As we use the term here, "urban political development" refers to processes by which political and governmental institutions have caused, accommodated, or otherwise responded to urbanization, at least to the extent that those processes might qualify as "durable shifts in governing authority."[25] As Jack Lucas points out, institutional changes relatively specific to North American cities—for instance, the shift from at-large to ward-based council elections, boundary changes through annexations or consolidations, and the imposition of supraurban institutions such as financial control boards—offer a "concrete approach to the study of shifts in political authority."[26] While such institutional shifts provide a useful yardstick for urban political development, an exclusive focus on institutions risks overlooking crucial forces that drive institutional transformation not least in the realm of ideas, which provide institutions with their purposes, define the interests of key political actors, and offer political entrepreneurs the tools with which to construct coalitions and win power.

Similar to Robert Lieberman's notion of friction within political orders, Karen Orren and Stephen Skowronek have suggested that shifts in governing authority are almost always partial, resulting in "multiple orderings of authority whose coordination with one another cannot be assumed and whose outward reach and impingements, including on one another, are inherently problematic."[27] Defined as such, the study of political development relies on carefully crafted case studies that uncover frictions and multiple orderings.

Thus, each chapter in our book provides a case study. The first four case studies focus on how specific cities in the United States have served as the focal points for paradigm shifts and as breeding grounds for new metaphors and ideas that give greater weight to certain policy options and serve to bring together new coalitions that can drive political development. In Chapter 2, Joel Rast traces paradigm shifts in housing policy in Chicago from the paradigm that stressed strict housing regulations, and thus an adversarial relationship between real estate interests and government, to the paradigm of "slum clearance" and urban renewal, which emphasized a collaborative relationship between business and government. In Chapter 3, Sally Ford Lawton focuses on how the idea of blight became a powerful metaphor in city planning by shifting the focus of municipal policy from people to places that could be "cured" through the kind of "containment and elimination" strategies that defined postwar urban renewal. Marcus Anthony Hunter in Chapter 4 looks at the opposite side of the coin: how activists in Philadelphia fighting against the destruction of their communities deployed powerful metaphors in order to build coalitions that thwarted urban renewal projects, most notably a proposed expressway. And finally, Jason Hackworth in Chapter 5 examines how the kind of Rust Belt urban distress, experienced most acutely in Detroit, has been deployed by conservative activists against Keynesian policies and in favor of the rollout of neoliberal policies that emphasize the disciplining function of markets.

The next four chapters shift the focus to urbanization as a broader social and demographic process that extends beyond specific cities and creates the basis for new ideas, arguments, coalitions, and policies at broader scales. Thus, Lester K. Spence in Chapter 6 continues Hackworth's discussion of the "neoliberal turn" from Chapter 5 but looks more broadly at how racial ideas and identities have been fundamental to that turn especially in the definition of racially defined spaces, particularly black cities and city neighborhoods, as specific targets of neoliberal disciplinary practices. Thomas Ogorzalek continues with the discussion of race in Chapter 7 but moves back in time to examine the paradox of members of Congress who were active supporters of civil rights legislation in the 1950s and 1960s yet came from big-city political machines that were hardly liberal when it came to questions of race in their home districts. These dissonant ideas regarding race could be sustained because both relied on ideas of pluralism similar enough that they could coexist so long as they were not pushed too hard. Ogorzalek demonstrates the role of cities in creating friction, and thus the potential for change, within the political order that supported and pushed for national civil rights legislation.

In Chapter 8, Douglas S. Reed examines the intersection of national education policy, local school politics, and the politics of immigration. He looks specifically at "ideas about culturally relevant pedagogies for English-language learners (ELL) and immigrant students" and how those ideas were implemented in public schools in Alexandria, Virginia, and Tucson, Arizona. In contrast to Alexandria's relatively conservative approach of creating an "international academy" that provided resources for ELL students as it also segregated them, Tucson created an innovative and progressive Mexican American Studies (MAS) program that sought to teach students about not only their heritage but also its meaning in the broader distribution of social and political power. Ultimately, the MAS program fell victim to the increasingly militant stance against immigration in the state and to conflicts between the relatively liberal population of Tucson and the relative conservativeness of Arizona. Thus, the Arizona legislature passed and Governor Jan Brewer signed HB2281, popularly known as the "ethnic studies ban" and aimed specifically at the Tucson MAS program. The law prohibited, among other things, any instruction "designed primarily for pupils of a particular ethnic group" or that advocated "ethnic solidarity instead of the treatment of pupils as individuals."

Finally, in Chapter 9 Amy Widestrom examines the tensions inherent in the Community Reinvestment Act (CRA), the purpose of which is to increase access to credit in underserved mostly poor and minority neighborhoods. The tools provided in the CRA are generally too weak to achieve the goals of the legislation, in large part because genuine progress in providing greater access to credit would entail a massive ideational shift away from free-market banking. In addition, the effective formulation and implementation of the CRA was stymied, like so many other community-based federal policies from the 1960s and 1970s, because it challenged traditional understandings of the responsibilities of national, state, and local governments and of the proper role of the executive and legislative branches at the federal level. In short, Widestrom argues that the CRA was part of a political order that created "friction" but also represents a paradigm shift that never happened.

Part III of our book expands beyond the US case to look at how national urban policies have taken different shapes in countries similar in many respects to the United States, namely Canada and the United Kingdom. Mara Sidney in Chapter 10 compares the construction of immigrant identities in the United States and Canada and, more specifically, in Newark, New Jersey, and Ottawa, Ontario. She argues that national-level immigration policies and discourses that conceive of immigrants as largely part of economic policy in Canada lead to a correspondence between national and local policy so that in both contexts there is a focus on integration, with immigrants viewed as clients. By contrast, in the United States, where immigration is understood more as an issue of law enforcement and there are limited integration policies, there is a greater potential divergence between national policy and local conceptions of immigrants. In the case of Newark, many immigrants become rights-claiming political actors, sometimes as parts of preexisting racial and ethnic groups.

Similar to what Reed found in the case of the MAS program in Tucson, Sidney thus finds that in the US context, cities serve as the test beds for constructing immigrant identities that create tensions and frictions, with alternate images constructed through state and national policies. In the case of Newark there exists a political order apparently capable of accommodating multiple and conflicting immigrant identities, while Tucson is part of a larger political order in which multiple immigrant identities could not coexist.

In Chapter 10 Timothy P. R. Weaver examines the rollout of enterprise zones under Prime Minister Margaret Thatcher's government in the United Kingdom and their eventual diffusion to the United States. Not surprisingly, the Westminster system allowed for rapid deployment of enterprise zones that adhered closely to the original neoliberal ideas embedded in the policy, whereas the federal system of separated powers in the United States stymied enterprise zone legislation at the national level even as enterprise zones proliferated throughout the states, ultimately becoming a largely bipartisan policy tool. More surprisingly, Weaver found that though enterprise zones were clearly designed to appeal to business, organized business interests in both the United States and the United Kingdom were generally suspicious of or lukewarm to the idea; their diffusion depended on promotion by policy entrepreneurs and intellectual ideologues who believed in the power of the idea by itself.

The final four chapters in the book provide case studies of city-based political development in Chile, China, India, and Africa, thus extending our analysis to areas of the world that have experienced a more recent form of urbanization, with deep and intimate ties and similarities to urban political development in the Global North, that is occurring at a broader scale and thus with greater potential for major disruptions and shifts in governing authority. As Jeremy Wallace has pointed out in the case of China, for instance, contemporary urbanization presents a major opportunity for development and economic growth but also a major threat to governing regimes.[28]

Of the Global South regions covered in this book, Latin America was the first to experience massive urbanization, followed by India and China and now Africa. In Chapter 12 Eleonora Pasotti examines how a neighborhood group in Santiago built a political coalition to thwart plans for redevelopment and expanded that coalition into a national movement around the construction of an inclusive notion of neighborhood identity and its preservation in the face of real estate interests promoting new development and gentrification. In Chapter 13 William Hurst provides a sweeping history of Chinese urban development since the 1949 revolution, tracing the evolving conception of urban citizenship, as institutionalized in the *hukou* household registration system, through the early market reforms of the 1980s and the ongoing push for massive urbanization. Hurst argues that Chinese urbanization is unique, especially in the Global South, as a state-led project while at the same time reflecting a paradigm shift similar to the neoliberal turn elsewhere as the central government has groped and muddled its way through the convulsions inherent in combined processes of urbanization and market-based reforms. In Chapter 14 Debjani Bhattacharyya uses a history of slums and homelessness in Kolkata to suggest a new "politics of dwelling" in which more informal claims to living spaces might be recognized alongside more formal systems of property and ownership. And Vanessa Watson in Chapter 15 examines how foreign ideas of high-status city designs travel to Africa as they are promoted by prominent architecture and development firms and how those ideas are adapted to the African context. Yet their depiction of working and living spaces, imagined as replete with sleek glass high rises accompanied by marinas and other luxuries, contradicts the reality in many African countries that contain widespread poverty, public spaces used as traditional and informal markets, and unreliable energy sources. Embedded in the boosterish modernization fantasies of these new city designs is thus a motive for the displacement of traditional populations and practices.

As this precis suggests, although we see the urban level as especially fertile ground for uncovering the dynamics of ideationally driven political development, this book combines stand-alone urban-level case studies with those that view the city as being embedded in a series of different contexts, many of which are multiscalar. Examples would include policy diffusion across scales (Watson, Weaver) and domains (Reed), cross-country comparison (Sidney), and multilevel environments (Hackworth, Ogorzalek). Taken together, the case studies herein therefore avoid the trap of what Neil Brenner has called "methodological localism."[29]

Ideas in Urban Political Development

Collectively, the chapters in our book tell an urban history that covers the transition, especially in the United States, from the period immediately after World War II, defined by low immigration and political orders in which policies such as urban renewal and segregated public housing traveled in dynamic tension with support for civil rights, through the "urban crisis" years of black in-migration to central cities, white out-migration to suburbs, riots, deindustrialization, the decline of northeastern Rust Belt cities, the rise of Sunbelt cities, and the "white backlash" that underwrote the Reagan revolution and neoliberalization; and continuing in the urban resurgence starting in the 1990s, which has been fueled by an immigration boom in the Global North, a resurgence of anti-immigrant sentiments, and massive rural-to-urban migrations in the Global South that have simultaneously promoted ambitious development plans and the large shanty towns that provoked Mike Davis to define the twenty-first century as one of a "planet of slums."[30]

Embedded within this urban history are a host of past and potential critical junctures, shifts in governing authority, and other forms of significant change and disruptions to status quos, some unique to specific cities, regions, and countries and some of global impact. Such moments of political development provide unique points of entry for new ideas. As Mark Blyth has shown, new ideas are most likely to have the greatest impact under conditions such as economic crises, when the circumstances are so unique that actors are unable to rely on materialistic rationales to order their preferences.[31] The basic relationship between ideas and moments of stability and change can thus be summarized as in Table 1.1. Status quo periods of stability are defined by policy paradigms and political orders in which new ideas have minimal, typically incremental, influence. Major disruptions to the status quo have the potential to delegitimize policy paradigms and disrupt political orders and thus may present windows of opportunity for new ideas to define new status quos, especially if the disruption to the status quo also disrupts the link between the perceived interests of groups and specific institutional arrangements; as groups seek to reformulate their interests they will grasp for new ideas, leading them to support new institutional arrangements.

If groups maintain a clear understanding of their interests during a disruption of the status quo, they will more likely stick to old ideas and seek to reestablish institutions as they had existed prior to the disruption. Thus, for instance, the disruption of the "separate but equal" system of racial segregation initiated by *Brown v. Board of Education* (1954) did not disrupt whites'

Table 1.1. Likelihood of ideationally led political development

		Strength/Coherence of Material Interests	
		High	**Low**
Disruption to Status Quo	**High**	medium	high
	Low	low	medium

perceived interests as they were embedded in the ascriptive tradition of racial hierarchy, as evidenced by "massive resistance," and the spatial reinscription of that racial hierarchy through white flight to the suburbs (reinforced by *Milliken v. Bradley* in 1974), redlining in cities, and the punitive practices of neoliberalism as described by Spence in this volume. In other instances, deeply disruptive shocks might dislodge previously settled assumptions about group interests, yet there will be no new ideas present to redefine interests. Thus, Kathryn Newman has found that the fall of communism in Eastern and Central Europe led many formerly state-owned enterprises to not innovate or adopt new ideas; instead, the transformation was so fundamental that many organizations could only respond by falling back on traditional routines.[32]

New ideas serve both as catalysts in the transition from an old to new status quos brought about by some significant change and as the key agents that render such changes as "durable shifts," because ideas operate as emulsifiers that allow actors to blend otherwise disparate and potentially incompatible elements into a definition of a new world defined by new institutional arrangements. In the absence of new ideas, changes will be more incomplete as actors are forced back into defending reflexive interests or continuing with old routines. Thus, at least somewhat in contrast to accounts of political development that seek to define changes as always incomplete, leading to layered political orders rife with contradictions and frictions, ideas are precisely the ingredient that smooths contradictions and frictions and provides the language of the future world that explains changes as more complete and definitive breaks from the past.

Ideas, in other words, have causal power because they are key to constructing new realities. As Béland and Cox have put it, "Ideas help us to think about ways to address problems and challenges that we face and therefore are the cause of our actions."[33] Perhaps the most radical advocate of this "constructivist" position is Colin Hay, who has argued that actors' "desires, preferences, and motivations are not a contextually given fact—a reflection of material or even social circumstance—but are irredeemably ideational, reflecting a normative (indeed, moral, ethical, and political) orientation toward the context in which they will have to be realized."[34] In a similar vein, speaking specifically of the potential for empowering US cities during the height of the urban crisis era and echoing something similar to Anthony Giddens's notion of structuration, Gerald Frug argued that "our ideas make the current status of the city seem such a natural and inevitable feature of modern society that any attempt to find, as a matter of law, a 'local' function to be protected from state control, or to find, as a political matter, a way to decentralize real power to cities, seems defeated from the start. Changing our way of thinking about cities has become a necessary, although by no means sufficient, ingredient in increasing the power of cities."[35]

The chapters in our book suggest that metaphor is a particularly powerful means by which new ideas have influence. In only one or a few words, metaphors have the potential to introduce an entirely new paradigm into a discussion and thereby alter the direction of that discussion and of the resulting policy outcomes. Thus, for instance, vacant and dilapidated urban housing could be depicted as "blight," which defined the problem away from issues of race and economic inequality; an expressway project in Philadelphia could be defined as a new "Mason-Dixon Line," thus inserting the language of racial division and hierarchy into a discussion that expressway proponents wanted to be about efficiency and transportation; and neighborhoods and entire cities can be defined by racial classifications—a "black neighborhood" or a "black city"—that justify the imposition of austerity policies and other disciplinary measures. As Hackworth demonstrates, the simple word "Detroit" has been crafted to serve as an expression of the idea that Keynesian-style government policies lead to dependence, inefficiency, and profligacy.

It is not sufficient to assume, as we do in Table 1.1, that new ideas are omnipresent and will simply automatically fill in the spaces of "flux" opened up by some significant change to the status quo—a sort of pathogenic model suggested by the language of "diffusion" that is common to discussions of the spread of ideas.[36] Certainly ideas have a foundational and constitutive quality that makes them somewhat free-floating; not driven by the motive forces of individual or group ambitions since they define those ambitions, in that respect ideas are vaguely similar to pathogens. Yet for ideas to be present at the right place and time so as to have an impact at moments of significant change, we need to have in place systems and institutions that serve as incubators for new ideas and thus sustain what John Kingdon called the "primordial soup" from which policy entrepreneurs can draw. Cities clearly serve an important and unique role in sustaining this primordial soup, because they serve as the generators of new problems (e.g., the combination of concentrated poverty and substandard housing that served as the definition of "blight" in the United States and is now so prominent in the shanty towns of Global South cities) and new solutions (e.g., new housing regulations, Tucson's MAS program, and new forms of historic preservation in Santiago) that are often then replicated in other places.

There are numerous examples of policy ideas that have originated in individual cities and then been replicated—or "diffused"—elsewhere. This was the case, for instance, with mental health courts in the United States, first established in Florida's Broward County, which then served as the model for a US Department of Justice program to fund the establishment of similar courts elsewhere. In Santiago, as Pasotti demonstrates in this volume, neighborhood preservation as developed by Vecinos por la Defensa del Barrio Yungay also became a model for neighborhood groups throughout Chile. Much earlier, in 1900 in Galveston, Texas, a devastating storm created the opportunity for business-oriented Progressive reform interests to build on the electoral advantages they had found in at-large elections and create the commission form of city government that was then rapidly replicated in other cities.[37] As Woodrow Wilson noted, "No single movement of reform in our governmental methods has been more significant than the rapid adoption of the so-called commission form of government in the cities of the country."[38]

The case of Galveston highlights the role that an exogenous shock unique to a specific city can play in creating a localized critical juncture that makes the city a test bed for new ideas that policy entrepreneurs are poised to replicate elsewhere. This was also the case with enterprise zones, as described by Weaver, though the exogenous shock in that instance was broader than a single storm and involved the disinvestment and abandonment in cities as a result of deindustrialization. Similarly, as Hackworth notes, Detroit's uniquely acute financial crisis made it an inadvertent proving ground for neoliberal austerity policies. And Bhattacharyya in Chapter 14 suggests that the *bastis* in Kolkata might serve as an opportunity to reconceptualize property rights and ownership.

Thinking of cities as sites of new idea generation and thinking of localized critical junctures that might make them serve as test beds for ideas that come from elsewhere—in both instances as sites for the diffusion of new ideas—provides the material for refining the conceptual diagram in Table 1.1 so that it becomes a framework for theorizing about the impact of ideas specifically in urban political development, as described in Table 1.2. While the assumption in Table 1.1 was that disruptions to the status quo were uniform, Table 1.2 allows for the fact that such disruptions will vary in severity from place to place.

A full extension of Table 1.1 that divided the extent of disruption (high or low) and the cohesion of material interests (high or low) by whether they were uniform across a given territory or varied spatially would give us at least a 4x4 grid with sixteen potential outcomes, which would provide a false sense of

Table 1.2. Likelihood of ideationally led urban political development

		Strength/Coherence of Material Interests	
		High	**Low**
Disruption to SQ	**High**	A. Cities/urban areas more likely to serve as testbeds for ideas that originated elsewhere.	B. Cities/urban areas more likely to serve as the sites for generating ideas that then diffuse elsewhere.
	Low	C. Cities/urban areas likely to serve as sites for generating ideas that have limited diffusion.	D. Cities/urban areas likely to serve as sites for generating ideas that may diffuse, creating the potential for disrupting the status quo.

specificity given our admittedly imprecise and indistinct initial categories. We have instead assumed in Table 1.2 that cities and urban areas are always sites of unique disruption in which there are always new ideas being generated. This is, of course, not true for all cities at all times but is most likely true for at least some cities most of the time. Thus, in Table 1.2 the main categories that define the matrix refer to larger-scale disruptions and material interests as in Table 1.1, but within the cells in Table 1.2 we have included brief explanations of the variable roles that cities might play in each of the four outcomes.

In scenarios where there has been some broad significant change and thus a disruption to the status quo, we would expect new ideas to play a greater role in political development. In the case where material interests remain strong and coherent, we would expect there to be policy entrepreneurs poised to use the moment of change to promote new ideas to their advantage (and thus ideas in this scenario would carry somewhat less weight than interests), as in the case of the neoliberal policy entrepreneurs who were keen to use Detroit as an example that promoted their policies of choice (as reflected by possibility A in the top left of Table 1.2). In these cases, localized but well-publicized disruptions to the status quo, such as Detroit's financial crisis, signal to these entrepreneurs a potentially fruitful test bed for their ideas. Indeed, given the regularity with which cities undergo major disruptions, often in the form of disasters or redevelopments,[39] and the seemingly immanent state of "urban crisis,"[40] the urban scale appears distinctive in the degree to which it is the site of ideationally driven political development.

In a case where there has been a significant disruption to the status quo that has rendered material interests weaker and less coherent, we would expect to see a broader search for new ideas. In such an instance, cities and other urban areas will serve less as the test beds for new ideas developed elsewhere and more as the sites for generating new ideas that may be adopted in other places (possibility B). For instance, the massive changes and disruptions wrought by rural-to-urban migration and the rapid growth of cities in much of the Global South has in many instances destabilized existing incentive structures, possibly reflected, for instance, in the case of Africa, where developmental responses have largely involved mimicking the designs of other cities.

In periods of general stability cities will serve to maintain the primordial soup of new ideas, since they will still experience localized critical junctures and thus moments of flux when new ideas will likely play an important role, and they will still serve as important test beds for policy entrepreneurs looking to push new ideas. Yet we would also expect lower levels of diffusion during such periods (possibility C). Such was possibly the case in Tucson, which was forced into a critical juncture because of a desegregation court decree, leading ultimately to the MAS program. At the state level, immigration was certainly an important issue, though relatively moderate immigration rates (at least in percentage terms) suggest that it was hardly a disruptive shock to the status quo. Immigration was significant enough an issue to arouse an anti-immigrant sentiment in a relatively conservative state and a slate of politicians willing to serve that sentiment. In such a context a new idea such as the MAS program could not be expected to spread very far from its originating city, where it was in fact ultimately snuffed out by the statewide ethnic studies ban.

Finally, in periods of general stability, there may be some lack of coherence in terms of material interests (possibility D). The late 1990s, for instance, was a period of economic growth and general stability but also in many respects a moment of flux in material interests with the advent of the information age, reflected in the buildup and burst of the dot-com speculative bubble. This was also a unique moment when city-generated ideas had unique influence as evidenced, for instance, in the fracturing of the traditional highway-dominated federal transportation policy monopoly and the introduction of "new urbanist" ideas that included an emphasis on planning, the environment, and alternative means of transit.[41] In this instance, then, when material interests enter a period of flux amid an otherwise stable environment, cities most likely serve to generate ideas that will be disruptive to that stability.

These are all very rough distinctions and constitute a highly speculative conceptual framework. For instance, the actual distinction between external ideas tested in cities by policy entrepreneurs and ideas that originated in cities and diffused elsewhere is hardly clear: external ideas will become unique to some cities as they are adopted in response to local circumstances and may then resemble internal ideas that diffuse elsewhere. Our hope is only that these distinctions and the framework that those distinctions define point in a direction for further discussion and conceptual refinement. The chapters in this book provide an initial down payment on that conceptual refinement.

The Future

The size, density, and complexity of cities has traditionally served as the basis for their role as hubs of freedom, innovation, and the generation of new ideas. Cities clearly still play that role and are often celebrated as such, yet there are significant looming threats. First is the recent rise of populist-fueled authoritarianism and the new technologies of surveillance and control available to authoritarian regimes. A case in point is the city of Urumqi in the Xinjiang Uyghur Autonomous Region of northwestern China, where "security checkpoints with identification scanners guard the train station and roads in and out of town. Facial scanners track comings and goings at hotels, shopping malls and banks. Police use hand-held devices to search smartphones for encrypted chat apps, politically charged videos and other suspect content. To fill up with gas, drivers must first swipe their ID cards and stare into a camera."[42] Though this sounds like an extreme example fueled by recent ethnic clashes and riots, Urumqi also clearly reflects the darker, more general potential of all "smart cities" that are so often celebrated and promoted throughout the world.

Second, as Daniel Drezner has argued, the rise of economic inequality, ideological and partisan polarization, and declining trust in prestigious institutions has led to the declining influence of "public intellectuals," whose primary job was to serve as critics, and the increasing prominence of "thought leaders," who operate more as evangelicals with "their own singular lens to explain the world" and "proselytize that worldview to anyone within earshot."[43] Certainly the impacts of such thought leadership are evident in the rush to develop "smart" and "eco" cities in Africa and in attempts to attract the "creative class" in the United States. Indeed, cities are excellent targets for thought leaders (often in the form of consultants) because there are so many of them, and their officials are often looking for new solutions that have already been legitimated through marketing and mass media campaigns and might thus have popular appeal.

There is, of course, hope that the realities of big cities are an antidote to the potential and relatively obvious connections between authoritarianism, high-tech surveillance, disciplinary practices, and a cadre of thought leaders who work mostly in the service of the upper class. There are real struggles and conflicts in cities that cannot be wished away by new high-rises, sports stadiums, arts districts, marinas, smart streets, and convention centers. There are progressive mayors pursuing radical redistributive policies throughout the world, seeking to create a force against the rising tide of economic and social inequality, and there are urban neighborhoods pursuing identities of inclusive diversity rather than exclusive homogeneity. The cities that define our urban world are focal points of human suffering, folly, and potential and thus serve as anchors for generating meaningful ideas, even in a "post-truth" world.

PART I

Ideas in American City Political Development

CHAPTER 2

How Policy Paradigms Change

Lessons from Chicago's Urban Renewal Program

Joel Rast

An important way that ideas matter in urban political development is by serving as the conventional wisdom in a given policy area. Intuitively, we know this to be true. Policy makers, when considering how best to respond to pressing urban problems such as crime and poor educational attainment, do not start from scratch. Rather, their thinking is informed by widely shared ideas about what sorts of policies and programs are appropriate, politically viable, and likely to be most successful. Such ideas are typically inscribed in "best practices," disseminated among public officials, leaders of nonprofit groups, and other stakeholders through professional training, conferences, publications, networking, and social media. As the conventional wisdom changes and evolves, so do the attitudes and behavior of policy makers and interested groups. Consider, for example, the shift by transportation planners in recent years to better incorporate public transit, cycling infrastructure, and pedestrian amenities into urban and regional transportation planning. To be sure, these changes came about in part because key interests demanded them. However, they are also the result of changes in the beliefs and attitudes of planners themselves. A set of ideas that once privileged automobility to the exclusion of nearly everything else has given way to new approaches emphasizing the need for greater balance among multimodal forms of transportation.

Ideas that serve as the conventional wisdom in a given policy domain are examples of what scholars have termed policy paradigms.[1] Such ideas are shared conceptual frameworks through which actors understand societal problems and develop solutions, setting boundaries around "what is thinkable, possible, or acceptable."[2] Paradigms thus serve as a kind of policy lens, allowing actors to "see" certain kinds of policy solutions but not others. Not only do paradigms serve as screening devises in this fashion, selecting for policy ideas that are consistent with paradigmatic assumptions, but they do so in ways that are largely invisible to the general public and, in many cases, to policy makers themselves. As political scientist Peter A. Hall puts it, "Like a *Gestalt*, this framework is embedded in the very terminology through which policy makers communicate about their work, and it is influential precisely because so much of it is taken for granted and unamenable to scrutiny as a whole."[3]

While there is considerable scholarly agreement that policy paradigms shape attitudes and behavior in this way, paradigms also change, leading in some cases to dramatic shifts in the conventional wisdom within a given policy domain. Yet the process through which this takes place—whereby old ideas are exchanged for new ones—is not well understood. In this chapter I consider the question of paradigm change, using evidence from housing policy in twentieth-century Chicago—in particular, the city's engagement with slum and blighted areas—to identify mechanisms of change that go beyond those that certain other scholars have emphasized.

The most influential perspective on paradigm change remains Hall's seminal 1993 case study of Britain's shift from Keynesianism to monetarism during the 1970s and early 1980s. According to Hall, a series of economic disruptions that the Keynesian paradigm "could neither fully anticipate nor explain" led to a crisis of confidence in Keynesian thinking that advocates of monetarism were able to successfully exploit.[4] With support from Conservative Party politicians, including newly elected prime minister Margaret Thatcher, monetarism was institutionalized as the new policy paradigm for macroeconomic management in Britain, replacing countercyclical deficit spending with tax cuts and balanced budgets. Change, according to Hall, was both abrupt and discontinuous, leading in relatively short order to the replacement of one set of ideas for managing the economy with vastly different ones.

Hall's view of paradigm change was inspired by Thomas Kuhn's famous treatise on scientific revolutions, which uses the concept of scientific paradigms to develop an argument about how scientific understanding develops over time. According to Kuhn, most scientists spend their careers performing what he uncharitably describes as "mopping-up operations"—efforts to reconcile existing paradigms with observations that do not fully align with theoretical assumptions or expectations.[5] Through ad hoc modifications and refinements of scientific paradigms (what Kuhn calls "normal science"), theory and observation are brought once again into sync. On occasion, however, anomalies resist explanation, challenging paradigmatic expectations to the core. At such times, openings exist for the emergence of new paradigms in which the formerly anomalous becomes the expected. When a new paradigm surfaces that convincingly resolves the existing crisis in scientific understanding, equilibrium is restored and the process of normal science can resume once again.

Borrowing from Kuhn, Hall operationalizes paradigm change as what he calls first-, second-, and third-order change. First- and second-order changes are defined as incremental adjustments to policy instruments and their settings—akin to Kuhn's notion of "normal science" in which practitioners limit their activities to the articulation and refinement of existing paradigms. For example, in the housing policy domain, Section 8 housing choice vouchers are a type of policy instrument that can be used to provide shelter for low-income residents, while the dollar amounts of rent subsidies are the settings for such instruments. Third-order changes, by contrast, represent changes to "the overarching goals that guide policy in a particular field."[6] In housing policy, the shift from conventional public housing to housing vouchers and other public-private partnerships is an example of third-order change. According to Hall, only when first- and second-order change is accompanied by fundamental departures in policy goals (third-order change) can it be said that a change in policy paradigm has in fact occurred.

Kuhn's "punctuated equilibrium" view of scientific progress, featuring extended periods of stability disrupted on occasion by moments of extraordinary change, is also a feature of Hall's model of paradigm change. As he writes in his assessment of the British case, "Policy displayed a specific kind of trajectory. The presence of a policy paradigm generated long periods of continuity punctuated occasionally by the disjunctive experience of paradigm shift."[7] What were the causes of these dramatic shifts in policy and policy understanding? For Hall and others who share this view of paradigm change, change is nearly always seen as being driven by exogenous disturbances of some kind, pressures from outside the policy system itself. In Hall's case, it was the twin pressures of inflation and economic stagnation—developments that, according to Keynesian logic, should not have occurred simultaneously. Economic crisis was the trigger that paved the way for paradigm change, undermining confidence in the conventional economic wisdom and emboldening challengers. As Dilworth and Weaver point out in chapter 1 of this volume, exogenous events of this kind are often viewed in the literature on policy ideas as key turning points, moments when extraordinary change is suddenly possible.[8] As John Campbell argues, "When shocks, crises, and other disturbances create policy problems for which prevailing paradigms provide little guidance, policy makers search for new ones that help them envision new policy solutions, especially if they believe that there is evidence that the new one will work."[9]

Kuhn's argument has been deservedly praised for its elegance and parsimony. Still, such qualities, admirable as they are, can become problematic when observation reveals behavior to be more idiosyncratic than routine. While Hall's use of Kuhn's framework and its punctuated equilibrium view of change seems to fit the case he describes, it is not clear that paradigm change always or even routinely conforms to this pattern. A key question is whether policy paradigms can be seen, for the most part, as reflecting some kind of ideational equilibrium. If so, then exogenous disturbances of the kind Hall and others point to may need to be invoked to explain how such stable patterns are disrupted. If, however, factors can be identified that call the stability of paradigms into question independently of external shocks or disruptions, then a more complex model of change that takes into account endogenous as well as exogenous factors may be necessary.

In fact, we do not need to look far to find arguments that call into question assumptions about the stability of policy paradigms and ideological patterns more generally. For example, scholars of American political development (APD) have long criticized models of political systems that view equilibrium and order as the normal state of affairs.[10] A key question that has animated APD scholarship is the alignment, or "fit," between policy ideas and goals and institutional arrangements.[11] In this perspective, institutions are sometimes seen as "selecting" for policy ideas, creating fertile environments for certain kinds of ideas and policy goals, while throwing up barriers to others.[12] If the fit between a policy paradigm and institutional arrangements is a poor one, resulting in failure to advance policy goals, a search for new ideas may ensue. The paradigm, in other words, is unstable and susceptible to change. As Robert Lieberman argues, such instances may not be unusual. Since the policy ideas and institutions through which governance takes place develop over time, driven by different interests and societal problems, there is no reason to presume that they will routinely be "connected with each other in any coherent and functional way." Instead, they may "collide and chafe," leading to frustration with existing arrangements and a search for alternatives.[13]

In addition to the fit between ideas and institutions, we should also consider the impact of policy paradigms on organized interests, particularly when paradigms are newly emerging and not yet fully institutionalized. As scholars have long recognized, public policies generate "feedback effects" that influence interest group activity. Policies may cause certain groups to mobilize or may lead to the formation of new groups that become active either in support of or in opposition to a given policy or policy agenda. Theda Skocpol argues that "public social or economic measures may have the effect of stimulating brand new social identities and political capacities, sometimes groups that have a stake in the policy's expansion, sometimes groups that seek to repeal or reorient the policy in question."[14] Newly emerging policy paradigms may also generate feedback effects of this nature, particularly if they are accompanied by more concrete programmatic ideas. The key question is whether interest group activity works to reinforce or impede the current trajectory of the paradigm. Paradigms may prove to be unstable to the extent that they stimulate interest group activity that pushes in alternative directions.

Finally, scholars have also examined the properties of paradigms themselves, focusing on whether paradigmatic ideas and goals are internally consistent. As Vivien Schmidt points out, "any program is the result of conflicts as well as compromises among actors who bring different ideas to the table," meaning that policy goals and ideas may have competing impulses.[15] To the extent that paradigm goals clash with one another, actors will encounter obstructions, and the paradigm itself may be vulnerable to change, particularly when the pursuit of one paradigm goal undermines the achievement of another.

In sum, while Hall's punctuated equilibrium perspective has certain advantages, it seems far from clear that the model reliably captures the full set of mechanisms through which paradigm change may be effected. In seeking to reproduce the parsimony of Kuhn's model of scientific progress, Hall presents what is arguably an oversimplified and incomplete model of change. His approach cannot explain, for example, why such major economic disruptions as the Great Recession of 2008–2010 sometimes lead to paradigm change and other times not. While many expected that particular crisis to pose a significant challenge to neoliberal policies and ideas, the effects proved to be short-lived. Careful examination of endogenous factors may help us better understand the conditions under which crises of this nature are likely to produce consequential and lasting ideational shifts.[16]

In the remainder of this chapter, I draw on evidence from Chicago's urban renewal program of the 1950s and 1960s and the previous policy approach of restrictive housing regulations to show how policy paradigms for addressing the problem of slums and blighted areas grew unstable over time. As I will demonstrate in the pages ahead, economic crisis was a factor in the shift from one paradigm to the next, but the instability of both paradigms made them each prone to change. In the former case, the poor fit between policy ideas and the city's institutional arrangements made policy goals largely unachievable; in the latter case, paradigm goals turned out to be mutually contradictory. In both cases, endogenous factors played key roles in undermining confidence in the conventional wisdom and creating openings for policy ideas of a very different kind.

Renewing the City

Chicago's postwar urban renewal program was by no means the city's first effort to rid itself of slum districts. Organized action to address slum conditions began during the late nineteenth century, when Progressive Era housing reformers began mobilizing around policy initiatives to promote slum rejuvenation. Inspired by new research documenting the squalor in which many of the city's least fortunate residents were living, housing reformers successfully pressed for new housing regulations that would create a rigid set of standards for the construction and maintenance of buildings.[17] For housing reformers at the time, two goals were paramount: the elimination of slums wherever they existed and the provision of safe and sanitary housing for the residents of slum districts. These goals were to be achieved through the creation of stringent housing and building regulations accompanied by effective enforcement mechanisms. The relationship between the public and private sectors in housing policy was therefore adversarial: the job of government was to require property owners, using the full force of the law if necessary, to provide safe and sanitary housing.

This set of ideas served as the conventional wisdom—the policy paradigm—for addressing problems of slums and blight in early twentieth-century Chicago. Substandard housing would be eliminated through the actions of building inspectors and other enforcement officials, empowered by strict new building regulations that imposed harsh penalties for noncompliance. Yet passing new housing laws was one thing; enforcing them was quite another. Like other cities at the time, Chicago was governed through machine-style institutional arrangements in which rampant corruption on the part of public officials was the norm. As new regulations went into effect, the quid pro quo relationships of machine politics soon called enforcement mechanisms into question. Exemptions to the new building laws were routinely approved by aldermen at the request of politically connected developers and building owners, while building inspectors—badly paid and generally working alone—were susceptible to bribery.[18] Even honest inspectors found themselves at times ensnared in the workings of the machine. As one city newspaper complained, "It is known that in many cases where the inspectors appear to have done all that lay in their power, action has been staid by the order of their superiors or at the request of aldermen."[19] Reformers pushed for stronger enforcement, but their actions worked against the grain of the city's institutional arrangements. Instead of stability and equilibrium, the result was frustration and a continuous drive for change.

Despite these challenges, those pressing for solutions to Chicago's housing problems generally sought to perfect the existing policy approach rather than pursue new directions in housing reform. In Kuhnian terms, they sought to articulate and extend the existing paradigm, not replace it with a radically different alternative. However, the collapse of housing markets that accompanied the Great Depression of the 1930s created openings for new policy ideas. In particular, the construction of several new public housing projects in Chicago through the New Deal's Public Works Administration housing program introduced the prospect that government, rather than the private sector, might take the lead in rehabilitating slum areas.[20] Fearful that a government-sponsored housing program would intrude on their turf, real estate interests mobilized around an alternative set of ideas for attacking the slums. Insisting that slums could be rebuilt by private enterprise if the right tools were made available, real estate interests endorsed a legislative proposal that under certain conditions would provide private developers with eminent domain powers that could be used to assemble slum properties for redevelopment. Substandard buildings would be demolished, replaced by good modern housing. The law was passed in 1941 but sparked little interest within the development community. No projects were initiated using the new legislation.[21]

The 1930s and 1940s were decades of significant experimentation and political contestation in housing reform in Chicago and other cities. The old policy paradigm of restrictive housing regulation had lost credibility and support, yet no alternative set of ideas had surfaced as a clear successor. By the late 1940s, however, the basic ideas behind what would become Chicago's urban renewal program were being articulated by a number of civic leaders. The gist of these arguments was that neither government nor the private sector on its own could rid the city of its slum districts. Instead, the solution would require a collaborative effort between public and private actors—a public-private partnership for rebuilding the city's blighted areas. Government's role would involve assembling slum properties, demolishing existing buildings, and offering the land to developers at below-market prices. Government would also build public housing to rehouse families displaced by slum-clearance projects. Developers, lured to blighted areas by generous public subsidies and the potential for lucrative profits, would rebuild the slums with new modern housing.[22] Urban renewal would be the program through which the new paradigm of public-private collaboration would be initiated.

With its emphasis on business-government cooperation, urban renewal represented a fundamental reworking of the division of labor between state and market in housing policy. Gone was the adversarial relationship that distinguished the previous paradigm of restrictive housing regulation whereby government acted principally to hold private initiative in check. With urban renewal, the real estate community and other business leaders came to view city government in a much different way: as a force that created rather than curbed opportunities for profit. In Hall's terms it was third-order change, a reordering of policy goals to be pursued through new sets of policy instruments.

Urban renewal became state law in Illinois with the passage of the Blighted Areas Redevelopment Act of 1947 and a companion bill providing funds for the construction of public housing for displaced slum residents. Two years later, passage of the federal government's Housing Act of 1949 provided additional resources for slum clearance and public housing, further institutionalizing the new paradigm of public-private cooperation. It took several years, but by the mid-1950s several major renewal projects were under way in Chicago. Ground was broken for the first of these new developments, the one hundred–acre Lake Meadows apartment complex, in 1952. By 1957, the partially completed project located within the city's South Side Black Belt was being trumpeted in the media as a "showpiece" for urban renewal, attracting visiting planning and development experts from around the globe.[23] By the time the last building was completed in 1960, the project's developer had invested $35 million in a location described by the *Chicago Tribune* as "a vast, rotted, and seemingly irreparable slum."[24] Just north of Lake Meadows was the 1,710-unit Prairie Shores residential development, which began renting in

1958. The $20 million project, built mainly to house doctors, students, nurses, and other staff at nearby Michael Reese Hospital, filled quickly, further generating confidence in the viability of former slum property for middle-income residential development.[25]

These projects and others like them inspired considerable optimism among the city's civic and political leaders that a successful formula for attacking the slums had at last been devised. Testifying before a House subcommittee in January 1959, Chicago mayor Richard J. Daley made the first of what would be a series of promises to eliminate slums in Chicago, arguing that a federal commitment of $500 million to $600 million per year in housing and redevelopment funds would be sufficient to "remove slums from the cities of America in the next decade or two."[26] By 1962, Daley had grown more optimistic. Insisting that "renewing Chicago's neighborhoods and communities" was his administration's highest priority and emboldened by new US census data showing that substandard housing in Chicago had declined from 65,447 units in 1950 to 30,926 units in 1960, Daley pledged that the city's slums would be eliminated within five to six years.[27] By 1966, he was poised to declare victory. Campaigning for passage of a bond issue to provide the local contribution for the next round of federal urban renewal funds, Daley claimed that the program would allow the city to "revitalize every neighborhood in Chicago, removing every slum and blighted building by the end of 1967."[28]

Yet even as Daley repeated such promises to end slums in Chicago, there were signs already by the early 1960s that the city's renewal program might not be up to the task. New developments such as Lake Meadows and Prairie Shores were celebrated by many as key milestones in Chicago's campaign against the slums, yet for the most part they did not provide shelter for displaced residents of these areas. The average rent paid by nonwhite families for substandard units in Chicago was $67 monthly at the time Lake Meadows began renting. Of a total of 55,078 families living in substandard housing units at the time, only 1,794 paid $120 or more in rent. Yet rentals at Lake Meadows for two-bedroom apartments began at $137 per month. At Prairie Shores, two-bedroom units started at $148 monthly, and at the Carl Sandburg Village renewal project north of the Loop, apartments of this size rented for a whopping $240 per month and higher.[29] Although displaced residents received priority in the application process for apartments in the new developments, few could afford the rents. Most of the new occupants were in "professional or managerial occupations," with incomes in the "middle- to upper-income brackets."[30] As the project manager for Lake Meadows joked,

"We have enough physicists in Lake Meadows to build our own H-bomb."[31] Priced out of the market for the new high-rise apartments built on the ruins of their former homes, most of the existing residents of these areas would have to find somewhere else to go.

By the early 1960s, complaints that urban renewal was producing "luxury housing" unaffordable to present slum dwellers had become widespread.[32] Yet the fact that projects took this form is far from surprising, given the content of urban renewal legislation and the actors spearheading Chicago's new redevelopment projects. Urban renewal had two principal goals, one of which—the elimination of slums citywide—was carried forward from the previous paradigm of restrictive housing regulation. The other main goal of that period—to provide safe and sanitary housing for slum residents—largely fell by the wayside. In its place was a very different objective: achieving the highest and best use of land. In this new approach, the developer rather than the housing regulator occupied center stage; slums would be eliminated by creating favorable conditions for profit-seeking investors to initiate projects in blighted areas. The market, in other words, would drive the redevelopment process. Despite some dissenting voices, urban renewal policy largely incorporated this maxim. Through the creation of public-private partnerships and the privileged position of developers in the renewal process, the principle of highest and best use was institutionalized. For developers and city officials, it was a mutually beneficial arrangement. Developers would maximize profits, and city officials would maximize property tax receipts.

Of course, the principle of highest and best use did not in itself imply that housing produced through the urban renewal program would be limited to high-rent developments. This principle simply meant that where such projects were viable, this was the form that redevelopment should take. The reality, however, was that the vast majority of the city's new urban renewal projects were unaffordable to those residents—mostly African Americans—whose homes had been demolished to make way for the projects. Some found refuge in the new high-rise public housing projects on the city's South and West Sides. Others, however, were left to fend for themselves. Excluded from most white areas of the city by racial prejudice and unable to find housing within the city's already overcrowded Black Belt, many displaced residents moved to transitional areas on the edges of the ghetto, where the combination of white flight and building owners seeking to profit from racial succession soon created new slum conditions. As white tenants fled such areas, unscrupulous landlords converted buildings, illegally in most cases, to create additional dwelling units. In relatively short order, overcrowding and deferred maintenance by landlords turned formerly stable residential units into new slum housing.[33]

Had race not been a factor in the rehousing of slum residents, the outcome might have been different. Displaced persons would have had access to the full Chicago housing market, where vacancies in white areas of the city could have accommodated them.[34] As it was, however, the highest and best use of land paired with a dual housing market—one for whites and the other for blacks and other nonwhites—proved to be a toxic combination. Displaced residents found themselves caught up in a game of musical chairs where the ability to find a seat was determined by race and income, both of which worked against them. Instead of eliminating slums, urban renewal produced what one report called a "rolling ghetto" where the revitalization of one area produced conditions that were directly implicated in the decline of another.[35]

By the late 1960s, the attack on the slums had begun winding down. Both urban renewal and public housing were by this time politically unpopular. Neither program had achieved its intended results or showed promise of doing so in the near future—far from it. The high-rise public housing projects of the 1950s and early 1960s were now widely viewed as unmitigated social disasters. Within a few years the infamous Pruitt-Igoe public housing development in St. Louis would be dynamited, only sixteen years after its completion in 1956. And despite hundreds of millions of federal dollars spent for slum clearance and redevelopment, slums had not been eliminated in Chicago or any other major city.

As a set of ideas for addressing slum conditions, urban renewal's public-private partnership revealed itself as a fundamentally flawed and inherently unstable policy paradigm. The layering of new goals (achieving the highest and best use of land) onto old ones (eliminating slums) produced contradictory imperatives that could not be reconciled. The maximization of land values—a condition attached to urban renewal by the central role of real estate developers in the renewal process—meant that high-rent housing, not housing for moderate-income families, would be the default scenario for many slum-clearance projects. By uprooting existing slum residents and pushing them into transitional areas, such projects were instrumental in the creation of new slums and the extension of the ghetto into formerly stable areas. And as long as housing markets remained segregated, there seemed to be no way to disrupt this pattern. Mired in contradictions, urban renewal collapsed partly of its own weight, setting the stage for the emergence of new ideas about how the city should be rebuilt and how the problem of slums and blight should be addressed.

Conclusion

What does this case tell us about policy paradigms and how such ideas change? To begin, the events described here are somewhat at odds with the punctuated equilibrium view of change advanced by both Hall and Kuhn. Two policy paradigms for addressing the problem of slums and blighted areas were considered: restrictive housing regulations and the public-private partnership approach of urban renewal. Neither was particularly stable. The housing regulations advocated by progressive housing reformers of the early twentieth century clashed with the city's machine-style institutional arrangements, creating severe enforcement problems. And as we have just seen, the goals of urban renewal were internally contradictory; efforts to pursue certain objectives of the program directly undermined the ability to achieve others. These two endogenous factors—lack of alignment between the paradigm and institutional arrangements in the former case and internal inconsistency of paradigmatic ideas and goals in the latter—contributed to the suboptimal outcomes experienced during both periods. As policy solutions failed to meet expectations, pressure for change mounted.

Still, it would be a mistake to argue on the basis of the evidence here that an endogenous model of paradigm change is sufficient in itself to explain the outcomes in this case. In the case of restrictive housing regulations, incongruities between policy ideas and institutions help explain the disappointing performance of this approach and its susceptibility to change. However, it was economic crisis in the form of the Great Depression that ultimately paved the way for the introduction of radically different ideas about how housing reform should proceed. Absent these (exogenous) crisis conditions and their effects on housing markets, it is unclear that the conventional wisdom for addressing slum conditions would have departed so abruptly from the existing approach to take the path it did. In short, endogenous factors created instability and propensity for change, while exogenous factors produced the breaking point that made new ideas politically feasible. Both are important parts of the explanation in this case. Whether this is true more generally—that paradigm change routinely occurs through endogenous and exogenous developments acting in concert—requires additional investigation. However, the evidence here suggests that at a minimum, scholars examining paradigm change should be alert to possible endogenous causes.

Finally, this case shows that ideas matter—but so do interests.[36] The public-private partnership approach to eliminating slums emerged as a policy paradigm in large part because of the support it received from powerful real estate interests. New ideas about how to address slum conditions in postwar Chicago were not simply free-floating. They were tethered to interests, and those ideas that achieved prominence owed their success in large part to the distribution of power in place at the time. Yet interests alone cannot explain the form this paradigm took. Years of failed experiments with slum-rejuvenation programs left powerful interests unclear about how to proceed. Uncertain how to best realize their interests, these actors looked to ideas for guidance. Interests mattered, but these were interests who were feeling their way through trial and error, choosing solutions that they hoped would benefit them but knowing full well that they might be wrong. Hugh Heclo's words are instructive: "Politics finds its sources not only in power but also in uncertainty—men collectively wondering what to do. Finding feasible courses of action includes, but is more than, locating which way the vectors of political pressure are pushing. Governments not only 'power' . . . they also puzzle. Policy-making is a form of collective puzzlement on society's behalf."[37] Such an argument may hold more generally, but it seems to capture particularly well the uncertainty and openness to new ideas and experimentation that typically accompanies the shift from one policy paradigm to another.

CHAPTER 3

The Idea of Blight in Baltimore

Sally Ford Lawton

This story begins in January 2016 on a block in Baltimore's Sandtown-Winchester neighborhood. Seven months earlier, this same block witnessed a rebellion[1] protesting the murder of Freddie Gray, who died while in police custody. To salvage the reputation of both the neighborhood and the city, Baltimore mayor Stephanie Rawlings-Blake and Maryland governor Larry Hogan stood at a podium to announce plans to improve Sandtown-Winchester by tearing down structures they had identified as "blighted." As Hogan explained, "Fixing what is broken in Baltimore requires that we address the sea of abandoned, dilapidated buildings infecting entire neighborhoods."[2] According to Hogan's evaluation, the vectors for disease in poor neighborhoods are most importantly not insects, rats, underemployment, poverty, or access to quality food. The primary danger is buildings. Hogan's blight rhetoric reflects a long-standing justification for building clearance, increased powers of eminent domain, tax incentives designed to encourage development, and public-private partnerships. According to this justification, blighted structures represent a threat to public health, and in certain cases they represent a threat to economic health as well.[3] As a result, municipal governments must eliminate blight for the public good.[4]

Governor Hogan's reference to blight as the cause of urban ills reflects the history of an idea that began just before the Great Depression and continued afterward. Urban planners and municipal officials deployed urban blight as a way to both describe the decay of districts that resulted from the poverty of the 1930s and suggest remedies for that decay.[5] More than a metaphor, blight is a powerful idea. I argue that blight reveals three factors in urban political development. First, blight as a concept highlights how ideas contribute to municipal institutional development. Second, blight provided part of the justification for increased institutional capacity sought by interests in the form of planning and zoning commissions. Third, blight narrowed the available policy debates and solutions by convincing political participants that things are one way and not another.[6] Namely, blight assigned biological characteristics to inanimate objects, especially black housing, which allowed new routines of management and spatial organization.

The Idea of Blight and Historical Institutionalism

Institutionalists study history in part by exploring how rules and routines constrain actions.[7] They seek to identify the conditions for order and change, including the intercurrence of old, concurrent, and developing ideas, institutions, and interests.[8] Scholars deploy historical institutionalism as a method to account for and describe the expansion of the American state, the development of bureaucracy, the emergence of the carceral state, and the formation of the industrial economy.[9]

As scholars such as Timothy Weaver and Robert Lieberman assert, historical institutionalists tend to overplay the hand of stability and underplay the hand of change.[10] One strategy for counteracting this tendency is to place more emphasis on the role of ideas. Ideas go further to explain change than do purely institutionalist accounts, because ideas lie at the origin points of breaks in the institutional order. Ideas enter political and policy lexicons and, if given the right institutional soil watered with earnest interests, flourish into enduring features on the political landscape.[11] A purely institutional approach cannot explain the explosion of new municipal institutions during the first half of the twentieth century, when ideas about the city underwent a powerful evolution. This chapter focuses on one idea—blight—and traces its influence on emerging municipal institutions.

The political story of twentieth-century American cities can be told several ways. Clarence Stone's regime theory emphasizes informal coalitions of public and private actors who had the capacity to accomplish policy goals.[12] Paul Peterson emphasizes the city's place in a competitive system, where without the far-reaching power of a national government, municipalities were compelled to create business-friendly environments.[13] By contrast, the story of blight begins not with informal coalitions or with city competition but instead with the development of a new idea originating out of the "ecological school" of the sociology department at the University of Chicago that just so happened to align with existing political goals, especially those of planners, public health advocates, and realtors.

The ecological school argued that spatial relations are the basis of any urban system, that human beings find their ecological niche in the city, and that land must be put to its best ecological use. Hence, banks should be in the center of town in order to serve the most customers, residential districts should be separate from business and industry, and people ought to live where they will help the ecological system thrive. Elements of the built environment come to find their niche through competition for the land best suited to them. Once each organism finds its suitable habitat, it should remain in its niche.

The ecological school served as the guiding principle for urban planning and conservation in the twentieth century.[14] Human ecologists conceived of cities as natural systems that included moments of growth, invasion, decay, and renewal. By mapping out the natural pattern of cities, ecologists and city planners claimed the power to predict land-use patterns. Under the ecological model, city problems such as blight and slums resulted from poor scientific management and incongruous patterns of human settlement.[15] The vocabulary developed by the ecological school and implemented in city institutions remains in circulation, although it is no longer strictly part of the original movement. As recently as the November 2016 election, a municipal bond issue on the ballot in Baltimore proposed "the elimination of unhealthful, unsanitary, or unsafe conditions, lessening the density, eliminating obsolete or other uses detrimental to the public welfare or *otherwise removing or preventing the spread of blight*."[16] Since its deployment, blight remains a powerful idea and metaphor that gestures toward a specific set of policy decisions.

The ecological school is important to the study of urban institutional development because it demonstrates how ideas about how spaces ought to be managed spread among policy entrepreneurs and organized interests and ultimately contributed to the formation of critical municipal institutions. The ecological school put the built environment front and center. While people certainly play a role—the Waverly renewal program in Baltimore, one of the first to use ecological principles for renewal, notes that one of the neighborhood's strengths was its primarily white residents—it is maps and references to "species" such as businesses and homes that are emphasized. Spaces are "invaded" and then "die." This emphasis on the ostensibly ecological characteristics of the built environment set the trajectory that shaped and defined zoning, slum clearance, and neighborhood conservation.

Blight represents what Deborah Stone calls "reasoning by metaphor and analogy. It is trying to get others to see a situation as one thing rather than another."[17] According to Stone, metaphor is more than a literary device and is used extensively to advocate for policy.[18] Policy metaphors create a "normative leap" by setting out both the policy problem and the implied solution. Policy metaphors are everywhere once you know to look: "slippery slope," "drain the swamp," and "the melting pot" are just a few of the more popular ones. By saying that "a" is like "b," policy makers presume that the solution is to treat "a" as you would treat "b." Blight is a fast-spreading disease that in farming is usually handled by destroying the diseased crops. As Stone explains, disease metaphors, of which blight is one, imply a struggle with dangerous germs and calls for frequently harsh containment and elimination strategies. The diseased object is automatically "bad," while those seeking to eliminate the disease are inherently "good."

As a metaphor, blight transforms common city problems into a tidy narrative. All cities confront issues of housing, public safety, and public health. There are *many* policy solutions to these problems. For example, cities could simply improve housing, enforce code, give money for repairs, etc. However, the impulse is to eliminate parts of the city entirely. Blight narrows the policy choices—if the poor housing stock is diseased and highly contagious, then the solution is to borrow from the public health playbook on highly contagious epidemics.

"Blight" as a legal term has multiple meanings in different places. It might mean a dilapidated structure that is not up to code, or it might mean a property that does not match its ideal land value.[19] In 1981 the entire town of affluent Coronado in California declared itself blighted in order to secure additional state funding for schools.[20] Well-to-do and attractive areas of Chicago such as the glitzy central loop have been declared blighted in order to secure tax abatements.[21] Contemporarily, blight is deployed to assemble land through eminent domain, to demand improvements to structures, and to underwrite land-development projects.[22]

The term "blight" as applied to city space emerged in the early twentieth century to respond to the urban crisis that followed the Great Depression. Citizens, politicians, and urban planners faced cities with collapsed land values, crowded tenements, and dilapidated built environments. "Blight" described an area in either physical or economic decline.[23] The publication of Mabel Walker's *Urban Blight and Slums* emphasized the economic decadence of blight, a definition that remains. The notorious *Kelo vs. City of New London* decision argues that economic blight is sufficient reason for taking land.[24]

Although Walker and jurisprudence emphasize the economic aspects of blight, the term "blight" also assigns biological characteristics to space. Definitions of "blight" nearly always employ descriptions of physical and moral disease.[25] According to Walker, features of blight include housing that is a threat to health and morals.[26] Blight is also an "insidious malady," a festering sore that endangers adjacent districts, an infection, and an "economically 'sick'" area.[27] Contemporaries of Walker described blight as a "civic cancer" for which there is no cure but "the knife."[28] In 1943 architect and planner Eliel Saarinen illustrated how blight contributes to slum growth by comparing it to dying cell tissue.[29] Contemporary blight regulation and court decisions continue to reflect fear of contagion. For example, one initiative in Baltimore seeks to reduce liquor stores because they contribute to blight and corresponding moral decay.[30] In *Young v. American Mini Theatres, Inc.* the US Supreme Court upheld a municipality's right to zone against adult entertainment establishments because these buildings are frequently patient zero in the creation of a blighted district.[31]

Blight and Baltimore

Baltimore is an especially appropriate place in which to examine how the idea of blight was used in municipal policy. First, in 1910 the city was the first to pass and implement a housing segregation law, setting a precedent for the geographical separation of black from white living space.[32] Second, Baltimore is a border city, possessing characteristics of northern working-class towns such as Chicago and Detroit while also demonstrating characteristics of the former slaveholding states of the South.[33] Third, Baltimore is a majority black city, having had a significant black population since the 1930s.[34] Combined, Baltimore's political formation highlights a diverse set of conditions present in many cities, allowing broad application of this study.

The term "blight" entered Baltimore's city code in 1946, defining areas "in which a majority of the buildings have declined in productivity by reason of obsolescence, depreciation, or other causes to an extent that they no longer justify fundamental repairs or adequate maintenance."[35] Today the technical definition of blight in Baltimore is a parcel subject to a tax lien or a property that is "distressed" and "has deteriorated to the extent that the dwelling unit or other structure constitutes a serious and growing menace to the public health, safety, and welfare." Blighted buildings are subject to immediate taking.[36]

Blight justified the establishment of Baltimore's redevelopment commission in 1946, which eventually became the Department of Planning. While blight drops out of the official justification of the planning department, the department's responsibilities reflect the 1946 charter's emphasis on promoting health, order, safety, and morals.[37] Aside from functioning to define certain geographical areas in the city and to establish a new department, blight also functions to skirt issues of ownership in order to justify takings.[38]

Blight, Zoning, and Renewal

Zoning codes set the rules about where certain buildings may go. Aside from being a thorn in the side for developers, zoning influences the shape and population of a city. For example, zoning for only single-family dwellings can ensure that an area has mostly homeowners, which drives the poor and people of color to other areas of the city. In Baltimore a zoning board did not exist until 1927.[39] Zoning as it developed in the late 1920s could not exist without in part inventing the menace of blight.[40]

The idea of blight also facilitates the creation of urban renewal agencies, most of which were established in the 1940s in response to housing vacancies and central city land devaluation precipitated by suburbanization, white flight, overcrowded housing, and the overall desire to beautify city space. Today in many cities, including Baltimore, renewal agencies have been transformed into conservation and planning agencies.[41]

While blight was not the only idea contributing to municipal development in the 1920s, archival work demonstrates its significant influence. Blight frequently emerges in the same discussions that called for zoning because blight results from improper land use. According to "A Catechism of Zoning," published with an audience of city planners in mind, zoning helps prevent fires and contagion and avoids "invasion" of city areas by inappropriate buildings. In explaining zoning against multifamily dwellings, the catechism warns that apartment homes lead to disease, smoke, immoral practices, and dark, stuffy living quarters.[42] Thus, zoning proposes that certain types of buildings are public health threats, especially when placed in good neighborhoods, and that cities must plan for where certain types of homes and businesses may be built.

In addition to underwriting new agencies, blight deployed existing agencies in new ways, especially public health and police departments. When discussing how to identify blight, the National Association of Real Estate Boards (NAREB) said that it simply asked the health department in a given city what is blighted.[43] Unsafe buildings do of course pose a real threat to public health, and an emphasis on public health indicators continued to appear in efforts to fight blight. A 1964 survey of residential blight in Baltimore uses structural indicators and rates of tuberculosis and hepatitis A.[44] This data eventually influenced the proposal written for Baltimore's 1967 application to the Model Cities program.[45] Police and fire departments also expanded their responsibilities in order to address blight. As "blight" shifted in meaning to highlight land devaluation, the board of estimates and tax officials also evolved capacity to address blight.

The ecological school also helped professionalize city planners and other real estate professionals by transforming their work into a scientific conservation effort similar to the management of natural resources.[46] Professionalism swathed in ecological science provided authority and legitimacy to real estate interests and contributed to the creation of both the planning profession and the need to appoint planners in congruently emerging municipal institutions, such as zoning and renewal agencies.

In like manner, realtors also organized to reform and influence municipal institutions. The Urban Land Institute (ULI), founded in 1936 as the research arm of NAREB, explicitly sought to cure blight through private enterprise. As a letter to the NAREB board of directors argues, "The cities of the country are anxious for help and guidance in curing blight and in solving the real estate problems that confront them."[47] To that end, ULI's first publication aimed to correct blighted areas through the creation of municipal land commissions having the power of eminent domain "with authority to recover properties for private redevelopment."[48] ULI actively sought to make blight part of the municipal lexicon and lobbied at both the local and national levels to encourage blight-control efforts.

With the encouragement of ULI and NAREB, local governments created blight-elimination committees. In 1937, Baltimore mayor Howard Jackson named a committee of engineers, builders, and realtors with the purpose of mapping blight and developing policies to combat it, primarily through land clearance.[49] The committee's primary criteria for determining blight were tax-foreclosed property and vacant property.[50] Notably, blight as a product of an unfair economy or racist housing practices did not enter into the imaginations of city planners, though it certainly played a role in how planners interpreted blight.[51]

At the national level, ULI played an active role in drafting the 1949 Federal Housing Act.[52] ULI's primary success in the legislation was Title I, which allowed for city government acquisition of blighted land and for city governments to sell the land to private developers.[53] Thus, "blight" became a term deployed by real estate interests that created a policy designed to improve urban land markets. Its urgency as a public health menace allowed ULI and NAREB to urge the government to use its police powers to protect public health, thus creating a new vision for urban space.

The idea of blight explains one aspect of the flowering of muscular municipal institutions in the mid-twentieth century. Additionally, the idea of blight was a new issue around which to mobilize urban interests, including realtors and the emerging planning profession. Combined, cities transformed their executive structure to reflect menaces to the built environment. As I will explain in the next section, blight and the institutions it developed also flattened space to topographic indicators in a way that both acted as a dog whistle for race and ignored the interests of those living in so-called blighted space.

So-Called Blight

A *Baltimore Sun* article from 1907 warns of a "Negro Blight" and the "invasion" of neighborhoods by people of color.[54] The cause of this concern? A white landlord posted a sign asking for black tenants, allegedly in retaliation against another white landlord who had poached one of the first landlord's white tenants. It seems that the first landlord's revenge frightened white folks out of the neighborhood. A 1948 article in the *Afro-American,* Baltimore's main black newspaper, argued that realtors considered blacks "blights."[55] Without too far a leap, one can guess that areas described as blighted generally housed poor black people living in multifamily dwellings. As a stand-in for "black," "blight" shifted the focus from people to the built environment, thereby largely denying the experiences or interests of those who lived in the environment and foreclosing policy alternatives.

For instance, the Baltimore Commission on Government Efficiency and Economy in 1943 identified several factors that indicated so-called blight:

a decline in taxable property value, a dwelling constructed in or before 1899, any unit requiring major repairs, homes with no private flush toilets, occupied dwelling units with no central heating, declining value of owner-occupied homes, declining rent of tenant-occupied units, population density, and public welfare cases.[56] These data points find health and economy operating together as blight indicators. Flush toilets and population density were of concern in maintaining public health, with the toilets representing sanitation and density representing the likelihood of disease transmission, especially of tuberculosis.[57] Unspoken is just who had less access to modern plumbing. To position blight without people and as only a matter of plumbing or epidemiology detracts from real questions of economic and racial inequality.

While physical indicators and human disease indicated blight, city planners who favored the ecological school were busy reinventing cities as natural systems that include moments of growth, invasion, decay, and renewal. The ecologists drew city models based on ecological maps of natural areas, such as those that depicted plant succession around a lake.[58] The concentric models appear not just in academic papers but also in municipal planning documents. For example, *Architectural Forum* distributed the pamphlet *Planning with You* to encourage city councils to think of cities as ecosystems.[59] As ecosystems with predictable patterns of growth and decay, planners could also identify threats and, in the case of blight, invent diseases in need of treatment.

Blight was used primarily among white professionals and in publications aimed at primarily white audiences, including pamphlets produced by planners and realtors and newspapers such as the *Baltimore Sun*. Black communities did not widely adopt the term as a way to describe the built environment. A search of the *Afro-American* between 1910 and 1970 shows "blight" more commonly used to describe actual gardening issues for the home gardener than insufficient or poor housing. Writers in the *Afro-American* also used "blight" to describe the continued marginalization of blacks by institutions. In place of "blight," blacks used a broad range of terms to describe the same issues that blight is meant to evoke. Complaints by blacks included protesting an overabundance of saloons in primarily black neighborhoods, absent landlords who did not make repairs, and lack of city services (especially lagging trash removal).[60] The contrast between white and black interpretations of blight reflects how the construction of the idea creates and forecloses different interpretations of city and social problems, especially when one considers that black people were (and are) more likely to experience the unhealthful and dilapidated conditions described by blight. Whereas white interlocutors of blight encourage beautification, clearance, and single-family homes, blacks argue for equitable city services, economic justice, and dispelling the myth that black entertainment areas were hotbeds of immorality and disease.[61]

Two resources demonstrate, first, how blacks used a different language to describe their built environment and, second, how that language gestured to policy alternatives foreclosed by the metaphor of blight. The first resource is a survey of the *Afro-American,* a newspaper founded in Baltimore in 1892 that featured news stories, sensationalist stories, coverage of black high society, and commentary, often with a black liberation bent. At the time of the emergence of the term "blight" in the 1930s, the *Afro-American* was the third-largest black newspaper in the United States and the most widely circulated in the Northeast.[62] The second resource is a series of interviews conducted as part of the Baltimore Neighborhood Heritage Project. Between 1978 and 1980, a team of academic and citizen researchers collected more than two hundred oral histories with longtime Baltimore residents. Respondents were recruited through a city lunch program geared toward senior citizens.[63] These interviews are useful for three reasons: respondents are from a variety of classes, the transcripts do not change the language of the respondents to more "correct" English, and respondents were moving to Baltimore and setting up house with families at the precise time that the language of blight began to change municipal policy regarding neighborhoods. I focus on black respondents living in Sandtown-Winchester because the neighborhood experienced the commencement of blight in Baltimore and continues to experience the ongoing story of blight there. Moreover, all respondents living in this neighborhood were black.

In both the *Afro-American* and interviews, Baltimore blacks specified not blight but instead equitable distribution of city services and fair enforcement of the municipal building code. In order to draw attention to this, the *Afro-American* spearheaded a clean-block campaign, a summer program led by neighborhood youths aimed at beautifying neighborhoods. Begun in 1935, the program involved youth-organized teams who picked up trash, cleaned stoops, and whitewashed fences, among many other beautification projects. While the *Afro-American* highlighted the civic pride of clean-block clubs, the project also drew attention to municipal institutional issues. Summarizing the first clean-block campaign in 1935, the newspaper observed that "soon they [the youth leaders] found that they had many difficult problems to solve. Landlords were not willing to make repairs; people were on relief and not able to put their property in proper condition; there were others who really preferred to be untidy."[64] The article goes on to explain how block leaders pressured city leaders to require landlords to meet code. Meanwhile, block leaders held fund-raisers to buy paint for those on relief who might not otherwise have afforded it.

An interview subject involved with the Baltimore Neighborhood Heritage Project describes working to clean his block during this time. The resulting trash collection led to refuse "stacked story high." He goes on to explain, "But it so happened that we were told, 'Don't do this anymore. Call and go through this in a different way.'"[65] And so he did and found trash collection to happen more robustly on his block. The point here is that organizing to clean a block is one way to ask not for clearance of "unclean" blocks but instead for the city to follow through on municipal trash removal in a way that benefits all neighborhoods.

Blacks also sought to dispel the myth that their neighborhoods were diseased to begin with. Two cases highlight how blacks countered the language of blight with stories of safe, healthy neighborhoods. First, an *Afro-American* writer observed that on a Sunday morning on Pennsylvania Avenue, the worst he saw was a dog run into the street, to the distress of the owner. The author argues that because Pennsylvania Avenue is one of the most attractive streets in the city, it attracts a range of people, good and bad, but its attractiveness means that it is "blamed for violations of which it is not guilty."[66] Note that Pennsylvania Avenue between the 1910s and urban renewal was the center of black life in West Baltimore, with a theater that featured the biggest black entertainers of the day, corner soda shops, and department stores where blacks were allowed to shop. White media, however, determined Pennsylvania Avenue "blighted" and denigrated central black social institutions such as the Royal Theatre.

Thus, black responses to the built environment sought to use the same municipal institutions, such as zoning and code enforcement, but in such a way as to also help black neighborhoods. However, they did not use the term "blight." Instead, blacks specified policy initiatives such as better trash collection and requiring landlords to improve housing. This is different than using a metaphor such as "blight," because rather than saying "A" must be treated as "B," the residents required a specific reaction. Moreover, blacks recognized that reduced city services in their neighborhoods contributed to interpretations of their spaces as being blighted. Blacks also fought the interpretation of black space as being blighted. Pennsylvania Avenue, according to reporters at the *Afro-American*, was no less criminal than a white business center. Indeed, Pennsylvania Avenue was unfairly targeted because it was black.

Policy without the metaphor of blight suggests a different type of city. We might imagine, sans blight, a more equitable distribution of city services, including trash collection and education. In his essay on zoning, legal scholar David Schleicher imagines "city unplanning" and suggests what a city would be like without the sort of regulations to which the language of blight contributed. First, cities would have lost one tool in the segregation toolbox. Most important for Schleicher, the rules of the development and political economy of land would change dramatically. For one, cities would no longer be able to artificially inflate land prices while decreasing land value in other areas, yet another blow to segregationist dog whistles. Second, city unplanning would make separating so-called blight nuisances from their location much more difficult. This might contribute to a more robust economy within neighborhoods, thus improving outcomes for residents.[67] This is not to say that no other policy metaphor would have existed, nor does this suggest that Baltimore would have treated black neighborhoods better than the residents did; however, without the policy limitations of blight, Baltimore might look different than it does today.

Conclusion

This chapter has argued that the idea of blight set into motion the formation of new municipal institutions, including zoning and redevelopment, that endure. Moreover, the term "blight" gathered such power because it evokes public health crisis *and* comes to be a stand-in for African American housing. What is more, the idea of blight continues to be utilized. While other words such as "decay" and "dangerous" might have entered the lexicon, "blight" as a word made it easier to attach housing to concepts of disease and race. Moreover, the term "blight" collapses issues of health and fair economy to a single indicator. In doing this, so-called blight obscures the needs and desires of lived reality, particularly for Baltimore blacks. Finally, the idea of blight demonstrates how ideas help account for unspoken aspects of municipal institutions. This work is important because ideas such as blight remain in active circulation, and understanding the development of the idea and its work in and on institutions reveals another layer of friction.

First, the idea of blight layers over space, changing how people view and manage the built environment. As such, blight unpacks how ideas function not just as justifications for political action, such as the establishment of new institutions, but also as tools by which interests and institutions can transform space from above in ways that sometimes contrast with the lived experience of those on the ground. In other words, blight explores the multilevel function of an idea across its temporal progression in meaning and how that meaning is different among people across both time and space.

CHAPTER 4

How Ideas Stopped an Expressway in Philadelphia

Marcus Anthony Hunter

"Philadelphia is a city of neighborhoods. We cherish our communities and our community leaders," remarked recently reelected Mayor W. Wilson Goode at an awards ceremony held at City Hall to honor Alice Lipscomb in January 1989. As the city's first black mayor and longtime friend of Lipscomb, Goode spoke glowingly: "Alice Lipscomb has spent the last 34 years of her life helping to forge a better community in the Hawthorne area. . . . Not far from Independence Hall, Alice Lipscomb fought her own battle of independence in the 1950s. She fought for tenants' rights and formed the Hawthorne Community Council as a response to the Code Enforcement Program and the relocation of families who had to leave due to urban revitalization during that time." Noting Lipscomb's prominent role in defeating a proposed expressway that would have cut through the city and her neighborhood, Goode reminded the audience of her importance as a black activist and leader and her historic role as a member of the Redevelopment Authority (RDA),[1] established in 1946 as one of the city's first agencies to take responsibility for "urban renewal," meaning the clearing and redevelopment of "blighted" areas and the resettlement of residents who had previously lived in those areas.

Having appointed her to the RDA following his being elected Philadelphia's first black mayor in 1983, Goode had come to rely on Lipscomb's leadership as a central feature of his administration's efforts to revitalize black neighborhoods across Philadelphia.[2] The ceremony held for Lipscomb reflected the convergence of the political efforts of black Philadelphians in the years following the 1964 Civil Rights Act. Once disenfranchised from the local political scene, both Goode and Lipscomb standing together are symbolic of the successful electoral strategies enacted by black residents, leaders, and activists in post–civil rights Philadelphia.

Alice Lipscomb was part of a cohort of black women community activists across urban America, and her career reflects an underappreciated moment when agency and ideas interacted to shape American urban political development. Where other works on urban political development emphasize the role of elites, this chapter underscores how the ideas generated by black women and black communities can effectively reframe debates about renewal and change. This ability to reframe urban development using racialized and place-based metaphors demonstrates the power of grassroots activism to resist and beat back competing narratives and approaches to urban change and political economy. From New Jersey to Philadelphia to Chicago, black women developed ideational tool kits to form effective strategies of resistance against the powerful urban planners and elites around urban renewal. This chapter explores the life and political activism of Lipscomb in postwar Philadelphia to demonstrate how ideas and metaphors building on notions of the South, segregation, and Jim Crow coalesced into a powerful political platform against urban renewal.

The Birth of an Activist

Born in 1916, the seventh of eleven children, Lipscomb graduated from South Philadelphia High School and in 1943 married a longshoremen (John Lipscomb) with whom she had one daughter (Deloris). Lipscomb and her family lived in Hawthorne, a neighborhood immediately south of Center City, the two square miles between the Delaware and Schuylkill Rivers that had been the original city and encompassed the central business district and the city's oldest neighborhoods. Hawthorne also overlapped with the Seventh Ward—or, as it was known, the "Black Seventh Ward," since it at one point contained the highest concentration of black Philadelphians of any ward—which served as the subject for W. E. B. Du Bois's classic study *The Philadelphia Negro* (1899).

Lipscomb dated the beginning of her activism to the early 1950s, after she ran inside a burning Seventh Ward tenement building and discovered a young girl who, Lipscomb also quickly realized, was her niece. Both Lipscomb and her niece were rushed to the hospital, where her niece, upon being declared dead, opened her eyes, turned her head, and called out, "*Aunt Alice.*" "The doctor was amazed. To me it was an omen," Lipscomb told *Inquirer* reporters, adding, "There was something she wanted me to do, to make sure it doesn't happen to another child."

While for some Philadelphians the Black Seventh Ward was "the city's worst slum," Lipscomb held mostly fond memories and feelings about the neighborhood, and these feelings provided the motivation for her community activism:

> That's what got me so involved in the community. . . . I grew up poor but my mother taught us manners and respect. We were a good Christian family and we were raised in a good atmosphere. We sat down for breakfast, blessed our food, went to school together and did our chores. You don't see much of that anymore. It was just a loving family. Good buddies all of us. Girlfriends and boyfriends.[3]

Thus motivated and inspired, Lipscomb spearheaded and led an interracial interneighborhood coalition against urban renewal, using ideas of collectivity and metaphors emphasizing how Philadelphia was not unlike the Jim Crow South in its tendency to devalue and segregate black communities.

Lipscomb's narrative suggests what political scientist James Scott has called "infrapolitics," meaning actions that are not seen as formally political but ultimately have political ends. Infrapolitics is thus a type of politics-from-below, which in the case of Lipscomb is rooted in a belief in neighborhood preservation and the idea that residents should take ownership of their neighborhoods and city—an idea that later blossomed under the label of "community action" in President Lyndon Johnson's Great Society. Where many saw a deteriorating community, Lipscomb and residents like her saw an opportunity to empower a community-based program of redevelopment by identifying patterns of racial exclusion caused by urban renewal plans.

South Street is the South: Alice Lipscomb vs. the Crosstown Expressway

Although overcrowding and urban decay plagued many parts of Philadelphia, Center City and its surrounding neighborhoods became the local focus of postwar rebuilding. The Black Seventh Ward was an especially obvious site for urban renewal. Viewed for decades as a "slum" or "Hell's Acre," the neighborhood's gradual decline suggested that resistance from residents would perhaps be minimal or at the very least easier to manage than that of the larger black communities in North and West Philadelphia.

In 1940 a group of reform-oriented professionals ("bankers, businessmen, architects, lawyers, planners"), led largely by the patrician activist Walter Phillips, had formed the City Policy Committee, which lobbied for the creation of a planning commission, ultimately formed by the city council in 1942. With the planning commission's approval, Phillips transformed the City Policy Committee into the Citizen's Council on City Planning (CCCP). As its founder, he asserted that the purpose of the CCCP was "to criticize or praise from the citizen's standpoint, proposals of the City Planning Commission."[4] Sharing office space with the housing advocacy organization Housing Association of Delaware Valley (HADV), the Phillips-led CCCP began to put its redevelopment plans in motion. The proximal relationship between the offices of the CCCP and the HADV was no accident, indicative of the shared investment in the construction of new housing as key to redeveloping Philadelphia.

In 1945 the Pennsylvania General Assembly passed the Urban Redevelopment Law, allowing for the establishment of the Philadelphia RDA. Organized by Mayor Samuels in 1946, the RDA was headed by a board composed of five men: John P. Crisconi, Joseph McDonough, Kevy Kaiserman, Earl Barber, and Irwin Underhill—all realtors except for Underhill, a prominent black missionary and theologian and manager of the Richard Allen Homes (one of the city's earliest federally funded housing projects, completed in 1941).[5]

The new development law required the City Planning Commission to identify and then certify neighborhoods for redevelopment. Following certification the RDA would then work to relocate residents in targeted areas to new housing, usually outside the redevelopment zone. The CCCP, with Phillips at the helm, worked virtually in tandem with the newly created planning commission, specifically with community leaders, to increase the appeal of and involvement in redevelopment plans for Philadelphia. With a primary goal of reestablishing Philadelphia as a "bright" and "clean city," by 1947 the CCCP established a membership base that included more than one hundred community organizations.

Raising more than $400,000 from Philadelphia-based firms and corporations, the CCCP and the City Planning Commission in 1947 presented the Better Philadelphia Exhibition, a public event hosted by the Gimbels Department Store near City Hall to provide Philadelphians and interested parties an opportunity to look at a diorama of a redeveloped city. Alongside the windows and displays showcasing the latest fashions, city planners publicized the newest image of Philadelphia as a modern, clean, and desirable urban space. The exhibit proved extremely popular, and those willing to pay the $1 entrance fee were seemingly impressed with the redeveloped version of Philadelphia exemplified in the diorama.

Included in the plans for a new Philadelphia were a riverside promenade, a revitalized Independence Mall, and a series of highways and expressways, including one that ran through Lombard Street, one of the southernmost east-to-west streets of Center City, which was also in the Seventh Ward. Tentatively titled the "Lombard Expressway" and suggested by the executive director of the planning commission, Robert B. Mitchell, the proposed road was lauded as a key component of the proposed new highway network, since it would provide a high-speed connection between expressways running north-south planned for the western and eastern edges of Center City (the Schuylkill and Delaware expressways, respectively) and would be integral to the successful redevelopment and revitalization of Philadelphia. The Lombard Expressway was also the linchpin for redevelopment plans for the broader "South-Central" area.[6]

The City Planning Commission designated the Lombard/South Street area as a "combination highway and re-development project" and called for the RDA to begin relocating area residents and businesses. The passage of the Federal Highway Act in 1956 provided the city with the federal assistance necessary to build the expressway, with a projected cost of $60 million. After considering "six locations between Lombard and Bainbridge Street," which were two blocks apart, city officials and engineers recommended the predominantly black South Street–Bainbridge Street area for the site of the expressway, the name of which was thus changed to "Crosstown Expressway." With the preliminary report concluded and federal assistance assured, in 1960 the city formally adopted redevelopment plans for the area, highlighting the Crosstown Expressway as a top priority. With extensive construction and displacement looming, the Black Seventh Ward became a critical site upon which both reform and change in the city converged.[7]

The consequences of urban renewal for the Black Seventh Ward received little attention from established black organizations. From the late 1940s through the early 1950s, major black civil rights organizations in Philadelphia such as the NAACP and the Urban League were focusing their energies, activism, and resources on issues of education and economic inequality.

Although civil rights leadership had successfully protested against the Philadelphia Transit Company's practice of "refus[ing] to hire blacks to positions of 'motorman' or conductor on the company's trolleys and subway cars," by 1950 such leadership was fraught with conflict.[8] The NAACP in particular was just recovering from a protracted period of internal conflict around the issue of "whether civil rights activism would be helped or hurt by working in coalition with the Communist Party and its Popular Front allies."[9]

With hopes of shifting the city's prodemolition bias toward an approach that integrated community preservation, Lipscomb and fellow Seventh Ward community activist George Dukes became key critics of the administration and the larger growth coalition. Facing extensive highway construction and the disinterest the city seemed to have for the area's residents and businesses, Dukes and Lipscomb, like many of their black neighbors, believed it their responsibility to protect and save their neighborhood.

By 1956, Dukes and Lipscomb had channeled their concerns into community-based organizations, organizing and chairing the Rittenhouse and Hawthorne Community Councils, respectively. While both organizations focused on compelling the city to preserve the communities in the South-Central area while also providing financial assistance to support revitalization, the Lipscomb-led Hawthorne Community Council was especially interested in bringing attention to the ineffectiveness and inaction of city officials in providing adequate and affordable housing to the area's black residents.

Gathering several thousand signatures, coordinating rallies, and inundating the City Planning Commission and mayor's offices with letters, Dukes and Lipscomb's efforts helped to delay the city's plans to build the Crosstown Expressway throughout the mayoralty of Joseph Clark, from 1952 to 1956. Near the end of Clark's term in office, in 1955, plans to build the Crosstown Expressway were halted, and key leaders within the growth coalition sought to push harder to see the urban renewal plans for the area come to fruition. With promises that he would move urban renewal forward using federal funds, Richardson Dilworth—Democrat and founding member of the reform-oriented so-called Young Turks—was elected to replace Clark as mayor of Philadelphia, assuming the role in January of 1956.

Holding true to his commitment to the Crosstown Expressway, Dilworth held informational meetings and hearings throughout his first term in the South-Central area to address and possibly allay the rising antiurban renewal sentiment that had thus far thwarted the expressway's construction. These meetings also provided a venue to discuss the benefits of the soon-to-be built Hawthorne Square, a high-rise public housing complex located within the South-Central redevelopment area. Located between South and Christian Streets, Hawthorne Square, also referred to as Martin Luther King, Jr. Plaza, was intended as the primary location to which the area's black residents were to be relocated. Yet rather than reassuring black residents that they would be provided affordable housing, the proposed project instead intensified fears and anger.

Between 1956 and 1960, hundreds of residents voiced opposition to the Crosstown Expressway in various hearings and venues, convinced that city officials did not intend to rebuild the area for existing residents so much as they intended to demolish the Black Seventh Ward in order to expand Center City and redevelop South-Central as a primarily commercial and upper-middle class white district.[10] Hawthorne Square also angered many black residents. As historian John Bauman notes, black leaders "denounced the Housing Authority's practice of cramming public housing in or near ghetto sites."[11] In the years following the completion of the Richard Allen and James Weldon Johnson Homes in the early 1940s, public housing projects no longer registered with black residents as a completely positive prospect. Limited and provided under a well-known racial formula, public housing had proven mixed in its effectiveness and further illustrated the city's practice of Jim Crow South tactics that resulted in mutually exclusive black and white neighborhoods.

Despite the pushback of residents, the Crosstown Expressway was prominently featured as a part of the Philadelphia Comprehensive Plan adopted by city officials in 1960. Although a housing shortage hampered the RDA's relocation efforts and the efforts of Lipscomb delayed construction of the Crosstown Expressway, the growth coalition, with Dilworth at the helm, had success with the construction of the Schuylkill Expressway (completed by 1959) and the Delaware Expressway (construction of which began after completion of the Schuylkill). Framed as a necessary link between the Schuylkill and Delaware Expressways, the Crosstown Expressway was given an air of inevitability.[12]

While all of the city's attention and most of its police force focused on quelling the violence in North Philadelphia, most notably during the 1964 riot, plans for the Crosstown Expressway moved forward. Yet the salience of race, racism, and racial conflict reflected in the North Philadelphia riots provided Lipscomb with the idea to frame the Crosstown Expressway as environmentally and racially unjust, mirroring the repressive regimes typically associated with the Jim Crow South. She thus developed a series of critical arguments to frame the costs of the Crosstown Expressway.

First, Lipscomb contended that the Crosstown Expressway would effectively function as "Philadelphia's Mason Dixon Line," placing a physical barrier between the "white middle and upper class community" and the "poorer and greatly neglected Negro area." Conjuring this power metaphor for demarcating the American South proved effective, with the phrase findings it way into letters and protest signs. Given the climate of the civil rights movement, arguments drawing out metaphors for racism were effective because they were in line with a general sentiment among blacks broadly invested in changing racial policies across a range of social issues, including public housing and urban renewal.[13] Drawing on the geographic line for the American South, Lipscomb's framing emphasized the South as a set of ideas and practices that extended into the "North" and were best refracted by urban renewal plans of northern elites such as the Crosstown Expressway.

Second, Lipscomb framed the Crosstown Expressway as a "carbon monoxide curtain." Positing the environmental effects of highway construction appealed to residents across racial and class lines, as neither black nor white residents believed that urban renewal should take precedence over the health of residents. Finally, Lipscomb argued that urban renewal, as city officials envisioned it, precluded a more grassroots and community-based revitalization effort that engaged with and was built upon area stakeholders' desires for their community. Emphasizing the importance of the needs and ideas of residents, such an argument prefigured provisions such as Community Development Block Grants and the Model Cities programs offered under later federal programs. These three major frames resonated not just with the nearly 6,000 Black Seventh Ward residents but also with black and white residents throughout the South-Central redevelopment area.

Shifting away from rhetoric that relied heavily on race-based arguments against the Crosstown Expressway was perhaps fortuitous if not strategic, as between 1962 and 1964 Philadelphia's wards and legislative districts were reapportioned. With the relocation efforts of the RDA stalled, even members of the growth coalition began to break with previous redevelopment plans. Most notably, Cushing Dolbeare, housing advocate and managing director of the HADV, assailed city planners for aggressively pursuing the Crosstown Expressway without an effective relocation program: "Where will people go in the meantime? Our conviction is when a public agency takes property and displaces people it has a moral obligation to relocate them."[14]

In response to claims about air pollution and the decimation of the Black Seventh Ward, city planners changed the Crosstown Expressway from an aboveground to a depressed highway. However, even the plan for a depressed highway meant altering the residential character of South Street and displacing residents in order to dig beneath existing structures. Yet new plans also slated the Crosstown Expressway to change from a six-lane to an eight-lane highway running "between South and Bainbridge sts., from 2nd to 22nd sts., and from there south to an interchange with the Schuylkill and Cobbs Creek Expressways," with a new estimated cost of $320 million.[15] The new plan for the expressway now impacted the Grays Ferry area just to the southwest of Center City, as that would be where the interchange between the highways would be located.

When these plans became public in 1967, residents and proprietors were only more incensed by the continued unwillingness of the city planners to remove the Crosstown Expressway from city plans altogether. Stretching the Crosstown Expressway into the Grays Ferry area provided just the ammunition Lipscomb needed to strengthen grassroots efforts and establish a larger constituency against the expressway. That same year, two hundred residents in the area filed a legal injunction in common pleas court. Additionally, in April 1967 Lipscomb sponsored a heavily attended public meeting in conjunction with a predominantly white residential group, the Society Hill Association, at McCall Elementary School, located at Seventh and Delancey Streets, a decidedly white upper- and upper-middle-class neighborhood.[16]

Capitalizing on the growing anti–Crosstown Expressway sentiment, in that same month Lipscomb organized the Citizens Committee to Preserve and Develop the Crosstown Community (CCPDCC). Set up as an umbrella organization encompassing and working on behalf of the various community councils affected by the Crosstown Expressway, the CCPDCC was representative of the newly emergent interracial coalition opposing the city's plans for the South-Central and Grays Ferry areas. Groups included in this coalition were the Rittenhouse Community Council, the Society Hill Residents Association, the Hawthorne Community Council, the Queen Village Neighborhood Association, Areas I and H of the Philadelphia Anti-Poverty Action Council, the Armstrong Association (Urban League), Ministers of the Crosstown Expressway area, and the Schuylkill–Grays Ferry Residents Association. The coalition was unprecedented, including upper-middle-class and working-class whites from the Society Hill and Grays Ferry sections, along with black residents from throughout South Philadelphia.[17]

The summer of 1967 was a busy one for the newly formed CCPDCC, as members began an aggressive campaign to raise awareness and increase its membership. Lipscomb and Dukes set up headquarters for the CCPDCC at 2102 South Street, right where the Crosstown Expressway was to be built. From that row home on South Street, Lipscomb began an aggressive writing campaign. Her mass memos framed the organization's goals and functions in an effort to mobilize a broader network of concerned citizens. In a memo to area businesses, the CCPDCC made clear its objections, purpose, and proposals:

> The purpose of the CCPDCC is to foster the development of the Crosstown Community. Continued planning and the construction of the proposed Crosstown Expressway as an open, depressed highway through this community is destructive of this development and, therefore, unacceptable. The Committee specifically opposes: 1) the lack of any provision whatsoever to provide adequate reimbursement and rehousing for the estimated 6500 people who will be displaced by the Expressway. 2) The construction of an open, depressed highway through the center of this community, which, because of its coincidence with segregated housing patterns, will act as a barrier to interaction between people of diverse races. 3) The lack of any provision to ease the other harmful effects of the proposed Expressway, such as the dislocation of commercial centers. The Committee specifically proposes: 1) That the planning for the Expressway on the proposed route and other related activities, such as property assessment, be suspended. 2) That the involvement of the community is an overriding objective in any improvement effort in this area, and that residents, businessmen, civic groups, and agencies affected by this effort must participate actively and meaningfully in the review of the State's proposals and in the development of policies and plans submitted to City Council. The CCPDCC offers the following three alternatives to the construction of the Expressway: 1) Unless the need for any Expressway can be demonstrated the planning and construction of it shall be stopped. 2) The route for the proposed Expressway shall be relocated. 3) The Expressway shall be built on the proposed route, only if the following requirements are met: a) Demonstrate the need for an Expressway placed specifically between South and Bainbridge Streets b) Develop a comprehensive rehousing, business relocation, and community development plan.[18]

This memo, like many other notices and letters sent by members of the CCP-DCC, emphasized a community-based approach to city planning and urban renewal and assailed city officials for their lack of interest in the wants and needs of those who lived and worked in redevelopment areas. This memo also reveals the ways in which the growth coalition's targeting of the area gave rise to what the late scholar Benedict Anderson termed an "imagined community," meaning one whose boundaries are not physically determined but instead are culturally and/or sociopolitically constructed. Much like the nation-states that Anderson discusses to illustrate his concept, the CCPDCC invented the notion of a multicultural "Crosstown Community" to highlight the shared threat of urban renewal. Here, the idea of community was as important, if not more so, as the neighborhoods themselves helping to unify otherwise antagonistic communities.

On May 23, 1972, Alice Lipscomb and George Dukes were gathering residents and proprietors from the South-Central area once again to stage a protest against the Crosstown Expressway. However successful their efforts had been during the Dilworth and Tate administrations in the 1950s and 1960s, the CCPDCC again faced the threat of the expressway based on a proposal for the area developed by notorious former police commissioner Frank Rizzo following his 1971 mayoral election victory. Rizzo proposed a "Southbridge Plan" that included the Crosstown Expressway along with other provisions such as a parking garage and high-rise/low-rise apartment building construction alongside the roadway.

Still slated to run along South Street and to connect the Delaware and Schuylkill Expressways, the Southbridge Plan also called for the expressway to serve as a transfer road with the proposed Cobbs Creek Expressway, located in southwestern Philadelphia. Announcing such plans in late 1971, Rizzo used much of the same rhetoric of previous mayoral administrations, emphasizing the importance of the roadway for reducing congestion in Center City and connecting the Delaware and Schuylkill Expressways. Different, however, from previous iterations of the Crosstown Expressway was Rizzo's conception of expressway construction occurring at the same time as extensive residential construction. Dubbed the "megacity" plan, the Rizzo-led city-planning model proposed development of a mixed-income residential community alongside the expressway.

In response, the CCPDCC developed a different plan. Referring to the proposal as the "Hawthorne Plan," members proposed redevelopment in the area with a focus on rehabilitating and renovating existing residential structures. The proposition of renovation and rehabilitation was a significant difference from existing city planning models, as the Hawthorne Plan incorporated such measures to prevent and reduce displacement. Meeting at the Bellevue-Stratford Hotel, Lipscomb and Dukes finalized what they believed was a community-based proposal for redevelopment in the area. In addition to support from the area's residents and proprietors, the Hawthorne Plan had also received the approval of the City Planning Commission, the state government, and the Department of Housing and Urban Development following Tate's formal disavowal of the Crosstown Expressway plans. Following a final discussion of the Hawthorne Plan, the organizers headed to City Hall to confront Rizzo. When the group arrived, Lipscomb immediately confronted Rizzo: *stop this expressway and start the Hawthorne Plan.*

Taken aback by Lipscomb's sudden appearance at City Hall, Rizzo was reluctant to speak. Lipscomb, however, was not. She condemned the Southbridge Plan and challenged Rizzo to kill it on the spot. In turn, Rizzo suggested that such could only be done after he talked it over "with all of the people." While efforts to directly confront Rizzo were not immediately successful, they had brought attention to the issue once more and facilitated new alliances, most notably that with HADV affiliate and head of the Philadelphia Council for Community Advancement, future mayor and political rival W. Wilson Goode. Goode, over the previous fifteen years, had established himself as a force for affordable housing and an even-tempered progressive civic leader.

Due to the provision of mixed income housing alongside the expressway, there were those who began to believe that the Southbridge Plan was the best way to revive the area. Opponents of the plan highlighted the emergent revitalization of the lower end of South Street by private businesses and investors and the importance of a community-based approach to redevelopment in the area and across Philadelphia. Such differing positions led to violent outbursts at various public gatherings on the matter throughout much of 1972. Expressing his sentiments at one of Rizzo's public hearings on the matter, Goode exclaimed:

> So Southbridge, as it has been proposed, is absurd. What will we get if the Crosstown Expressway is accepted today? At best, a $200 million underground road, and an expansion of Society Hill with homes only the wealthy can afford. More likely, after displacing thousands of families, wreaking havoc with surrounding neighborhoods, destroying an irretrievable historic section, polluting the air,

> and congesting traffic, we will have expanses of vacant land slowly developed as capital and labor become available. What will be built will be determined by what is most profitable for developers, not the paper idea before us.[19]

Inundating Rizzo's office, in such letters residents reminded Rizzo and city planning officials of the cause of the area's decline, often writing that "a twenty-year threat of demolition is enough to cause any area to decay." By 1973, Goode's critique of the Southbridge Plan, along with the continued efforts of the CCPDCC, garnered the support of Pennsylvania governor Milton J. Shapp and Edward W. Furia, regional director of the US Environmental Protection Agency. However resistant Rizzo was to "burying" the Southbridge Plan, with the lack of state and federal support he was compelled to give into the demands of the CCPDCC.[20]

Subsequently, by 1974 the metropolitan planning organization for the Philadelphia region, the Delaware Valley Regional Planning Commission, dropped both the Crosstown Expressway and the Cobbs Creek Expressway from its capital schedule and dictated that the funds earmarked for the projects be used instead for mass transit. The funds were ultimately used by the Southeastern Pennsylvania Transportation Authority to pay for 120 subway cars on Philadelphia's Broad Street line, 100 regional rail cars, 110 trolleys, and 190 buses. Thus ended the nearly quarter-century debate over the Crosstown Expressway.

By defeating the Crosstown Expressway, black and white residents in the South-Central area altered plans for revitalizing Philadelphia. While managing to protect those residents who were predominantly poor and working-class blacks from the displacement prompted by expressway construction, such activism also had unanticipated consequences. Black-led activism forced city planners to acknowledge the voices and desires of residents who were otherwise disenfranchised from the local political structure. On the other hand, the long battle over the Crosstown Expressway prompted those with means to withdraw and withhold their investments in the area until the city finalized a decision on the highway.

Some federal and state funds were lost once local officials and planners laid the Crosstown Expressway to rest. Saving the neighborhoods of black and white residents in the South-Central area was coupled with the loss of funds that could have been used to address some of the serious housing issues in the area. The failed urban project left an indelible mark on the city, forcing city planners to rethink and rework city highway plans, cancel the construction of complementary roads in other areas of the city (for instance, the Cobbs Creek Expressway), and redirect slated funds for the roadway to support public transportation while also fostering lasting friction among proponents of the growth coalition.

How Black Women's Ideas Changed Urban American

Lipscomb's life and impact would go on to include more than just the defeat of the Crosstown Expressway; this chapter's opening scene suggests the important work she did on the RDA under the leadership of the city's first black mayor, W. Wilson Goode. The power of her ideas and narratives of resistance were part of a larger movement of black women community activists in the postwar and post–civil rights era. Drawing on the Mason-Dixon Line as both a metaphor and an idea about the Jim Crow South, Lipscomb extended the boundaries of the American South to illustrate the racial and environmental contours of the city's postwar urban renewal plans.

Alongside conjuring the American South to fight against the plans, Lipscomb also incorporated a grand idea of community to broaden the appeal of the antiexpressway coalition. Much like her better-known contemporary, scholar-activist Jane Jacobs, Lipscomb championed a progressive community-driven vision of city growth and change. Expanding beyond Jacobs's approach, however, Lipscomb's intersectional politics successfully framed the Crosstown Community as a metaphor for the lack of care and concern that civic leaders and urban planners had for poor and working-class black families and communities.

Lipscomb's strategy reflects the urban and local politics emergent from the ideas and perspectives of black women. Sensitized to issues of displacement, poor housing, underserved communities, and race, Lipscomb developed an antiurban renewal campaign that made necessary connections between the North and the South and between racial practices under Jim Crow and racial division. The interpretation of urban renewal as establishing the Mason-Dixon Line in the city had a powerful impact on the ideas that white and black residents had about the expressway, illustrating that the city's plans would geographically and culturally marginalize the residents in the working-class communities that comprised the band of working-class neighborhood planners strategically coined the "Crosstown Community." Joining ideas about the urban growth, race, and the South, Lipscomb generated an effective resistance and future template for redeveloping urban America; thus, her efforts demonstrate the landscape of idea competition whereby the grass roots and elites attempt to ensure that their vision of the city wins out over competing claims. While true for this terrain, Dilworth and Weaver in Chapter 1 of this book show that urban America and its residents become both case studies and testing grounds for competing ideas and visions for the city.

CHAPTER 5

Manufacturing Decline

The Conservative Construction of Urban Crisis in Detroit

Jason Hackworth

"Detroit is a model of tax-and-spend liberalism," writes Cato Institute senior fellow ideologue Michael Tanner. "The city's own choices," he continues, "not free markets and limited government, are really responsible for Detroit's failure."[1] This facile diagnosis for urban decline is common from conservative think tanks, and Detroit is the frequent object lesson of this sermon because of its high visibility.[2] That this vision emerges from institutions such as Cato is not terribly surprising, but the fact that it so closely aligns with actual policy made by public officials in Detroit and many other Rust Belt cities is much more so. This chapter examines the alignment between conservative ideas[3] and actualized policy forged by nonconservative city officials in the Rust Belt.

The alignment between conservative ideas and city policies is part of a broader long-standing question: How and why does *any* idea (or set of ideas) get converted into actual urban policy?[4] One particularly compelling answer involves the intersection of ideas and institutions. In a historical study of the rise and fall of Keynesianism in the United States and Sweden, Mark Blyth argues that the two essential elements for broad paradigmatic change are crisis and the presence of an alternative ideational framework.[5] For one policy paradigm to dissolve there must be a crisis that challenges its veracity, which for laissez-faire economics was the Great Depression of the 1930s and for Keynesianism was the stagflation of the 1970s.[6] Both events caused the prevailing paradigm to lose credibility, as the policy tools that flowed from its logic no longer seemed capable of mitigating the economic crisis. In addition to external crises, Blyth points to the importance of idea makers, who in both the

United States and Sweden in the 1930s and 1970s were relatively unknown economists arguing for an alternative to the prevailing paradigm of that era.[7]

The relationship between economic crises and the introduction of new ideas and paradigms, as conceived by Blyth and echoed by others,[8] aptly describes national-level change but at least on the surface does not seem to describe the relationships between ideas and policies at the city level. By almost everyone's definition Detroit is in crisis, and there is sufficient organization—via left-wing think tanks, sympathetic scholars, and parts of the Democratic Party[9]—to offer a counternarrative to the conservative argument that the cause of the city's problems is profligacy and moral decay. Yet the existence of left-leaning organizational and intellectual resources is *insufficient* for a set of policies built around a counternarrative to emerge. The actualized policy universe in cities such as Detroit is much closer to the conservative conception of decline, with an emphasis on penality for existing residents and concessions to nonresident investors.

I would like to suggest that the reason for the different relationship between crisis and policy change at the city level is a result of different conceptions of crisis—and thus different understandings of how those crises are to be resolved—that do not have to be universally accepted to gain policy traction. The conservative conception of decline in Detroit is generally rejected by the residents and political figures of that city. Yet most of the important policies designed to mitigate decline in places such as Detroit, Cleveland, and Buffalo are set by state legislatures, which are often hostile to their interests and, conversely, very receptive to the facile diagnoses of "the problem" that emerge from conservative think tanks. Moreover, the rhetorical strategies used by the Right and the Left are very different. The conservative conception of decline is uncompromising, rigid, and focused on vilifying a broad undifferentiated Left as the problem. The Left, by contrast, is open to compromise, is consumed with "balance," and does not frame the conservative institutions as a problem. Within this frame, actualized policy details more often get pulled rightward than leftward. This chapter focuses on how the narrative of one city, Detroit, is used to reinforce the values of austerity, penality, and market fundamentalism despite the presence of an alternative conception of crisis.

The Manufactured Decline of Detroit

No American city embodies economic crises and decline more or has drawn as much attention from both the public and conservative think tanks as

Detroit. Despite being the eighteenth-largest city in the United States, only five cities are discussed more in the popular press and only seven in academic sources (Table 5.1). Within the world of conservative think tanks, the city is similarly overrepresented as a subject of inquiry (Table 5.2). While the issues facing the city are not unique, Detroit is uniquely visible.

The simple and long-standing conservative narrative in which much of Detroit's failure can be blamed on liberal social policy consists of three main elements.[10] First, Detroit's leaders were profligate and bankrupted the city with poor decisions. Second, the city became too dependent on large institutions—large firms, unions, and government in particular—and as a consequence lost its entrepreneurial edge. And third, the concentration of black municipal empowerment alienated white people, who then moved to the suburbs.

The putative crisis of profligacy is the most common theme in this narrative. To the manufacturers of decline, the recent bankruptcy and fiscal crisis are less a consequence than a cause of Detroit's problems.[11] The message and style of this argument is tied to the classic argument made by Charles Tiebout sixty years ago: Residents will migrate from places with high taxes and bad services to places with low taxes and great services. This will in turn discipline even the most entrenched governments from overspending.[12] According to this line of thought, we are simply witnessing the long-overdue disciplining of Detroit's reckless profligacy right now. For Cato's Dean Stansel, the path forward is simple: "If high-tax, low-growth metro areas like Detroit, Milwaukee, Buffalo, and Syracuse want to be more like high-growth areas such as Dallas, Tampa, San Antonio, and Austin, they should lower their onerous burden of taxation and bring spending under control."[13] The framing of Detroit as a tax-and-spend wasteland whose wounds were self-inflicted is not confined to the aerie halls at Cato. Various efforts by the state to exact control over its resources have been tried repeatedly in the past and guided by the same essential logic. Despite the miserable track record of these efforts, the profligacy canard gets confidently reapplied while more moderate government-oriented efforts with a mixed track record get dismissed because they have "obviously failed in the past."

The second dimension to the explanation of Detroit has been deemed "the entrepreneurial deficit."[14] The basic argument is that early twentieth-century Detroit was host to a large number of inventive entrepreneurs such as the Dodge Brothers, Henry Ford, and David Buick who fought for market share by refining their product, opening new markets, and keeping costs down. There was a flowering of industry and invention during this period.

Table 5.1. Ranking of the eighteen-largest American cities on population and prevalence in academic and popular articles (Sources: US Census, Scopus Academic Article Search, Proquest Media Search)

City	2010 Population[1]	Population Rank	Scholarly Citations[2]	Scholarly Rank	Popular Media References[3]	Popular Media Rank
New York City[4]	8,175,133	1	3,474	2	1,726,907	1
Los Angeles	3,792,621	2	2,455	3	765,543	3
Chicago	2,695,598	3	4,578	1	1,039,537	2
Houston	2,100,263	4	449	9	237,773	6
Philadelphia	1,526,006	5	1,086	5	194,354	8
Phoenix	1,445,632	6	527	6	153,105	11
San Antonio	1,327,407	7	199	11	218,175	7
San Diego	1,307,402	8	523	7	178,902	9
Dallas	1,197,816	9	264	10	176,800	10
San Jose	945,942	10	144	15	63,839	14
Jacksonville	821,784	11	47	18	67,723	13
Indianapolis	820,445	12	159	13	88,043	12
San Francisco	805,235	13	1,442	4	320,241	4
Austin	790,390	14	195	12	51,923	15
Columbus	787,033	15	145	14	50,326	16
Fort Worth	741,206	16	76	17	20,106	17
Charlotte	731,424	17	105	16	10,229	18
Detroit	**713,777**	**18**	**516**	**8**	**254,192**	**5**

1. Population figures and rank were derived from the US Census, http://www.census.gov/popest/data/cities/totals/2012/index.html

2. Scopus Academic Article Search was used here. Citations were limited to English-language, social science and humanities, journal articles published between 1993 and 2013. These counts refer to the number of academic articles where the city's name appeared in the title, abstract, or keywords.

3. Proquest Newstand, a search engine that indexes thousands of newspaper and magazine archives was used. The search was limited to English-language references that occurred between 1993 and 2013.

4. Because "New York" can refer to both a state and a city, the search (Scopus and Proquest) for this city included mutually exclusive references to "New York City," "Brooklyn," "Staten Island," "Bronx," and "Manhattan." "Queens" was not added to this list because of the possibility of false hits for other invocations of that word.

Table 5.2. Frequency of mention on conservative think tank websites (Sources: Website search engines for the Cato Institute, the Heritage Foundation, the American Enterprise Institute, and the Manhattan Institute)

	Population	Cato Institute		Heritage Foundation		American Enterprise Inst.		Manhattan Institute	
City	Rank[1]	Citations	Rank	Citations	Rank	Citations	Rank	Citations	Rank
New York City	1	1,733	2	2,385	1	2,429	1	5,261	1
Los Angeles	2	1,052	3	1,456	3	1,339	3	1,304	2
Chicago	3	1,774	1	1,875	2	2,367	2	1,149	3
Houston	4	308	8	448	8	438	8	318	8
Philadelphia	5	573	5	890	5	618	6	456	6
Phoenix	6	188	11	243	10	57	16	35	14
San Antonio	7	99	15	163	14	123	13	102	12
San Diego	8	309	7	361	9	426	9	296	9
Dallas	9	300	9	513	7	470	7	244	10
San Jose	10	127	13	175	13	129	11	353	7
Jacksonville	11	34	17	46	18	61	15	14	18
Indianapolis	12	195	10	228	12	125	12	122	11
San Francisco	13	613	4	932	4	897	5	594	4
Austin	14	171	12	236	11	191	10	90	13
Columbus	15	61	16	126	15	76	14	31	16
Fort Worth	16	5	18	56	17	36	18	25	17
Charlotte	17	115	14	78	16	39	17	35	15
Detroit	**18**	**422**	**6**	**789**	**6**	**938**	**4**	**488**	**5**

1. Population ranks are for 2010. See Table 5.1 for more details and sourcing.

By 1930 the city was the fourth largest in the United States, and workers from the South migrated by the millions to seek employment there. The early twentieth-century period is an intriguing one to be sure, and there was certainly a significant component related to the flowering of creative engineering that took place there, but the manufacturers of decline have utopianized the period as part of their explanation for the city's fall.[15] For example, economist Edward Glaeser in his popular *Triumph of the City* laments that the chief problem for Detroit was turning its back on this idea-making period:

> The irony and ultimately the tragedy of Detroit is that its small, dynamic firms and independent suppliers gave rise to gigantic, wholly integrated car companies, which then became synonymous with stagnation. . . . Ford figured out how to make assembly lines that could use the talents of poorly educated Americans, but making Detroit less skilled hurt it economically in the long run.[16]

"If Detroit and places like it are ever going to come back," Glaeser continues, "they will do so by embracing the virtues of the great pre- and postindustrial cities: competition, connection, and human capital."[17]

Of course, corporations are not the only big institutions responsible for this trajectory. Within this worldview, labor unions are even more at fault for killing innovation, wealth, and the cities that depend on them.[18] Detroit's labor history is complicated and multifaceted to be sure, but neoliberal economists are unequivocal in their view that unions killed Detroit because they were able to attract public sympathy, which translated into labor protections that drove up costs.[19] In 1937, Walter Reuther and his fellow United Auto Workers protesters attempted to cross a bridge to the then-largest auto factory in the world, Henry Ford's River Rouge Ford Plant, to organize its workers. They were mercilessly beaten by Ford's thug security forces, and the attack was captured by a *Detroit News* photographer who eventually won the Pulitzer Prize.[20] The subsequent publicity turned the tide toward unionization in the United States. To the manufacturers of decline, this event was unfortunate for precisely that reason, namely because it made the public more sympathetic to unions, which served to steal wealth, stifle creativity, and initiate the decline of Detroit. "It was a public relations disaster for Ford and it made heroes out of the union men," laments Glaeser.[21] It helped hasten the end of the "golden period" for Detroit and ushered in a deskilling idea-killing machine that eventually destroyed the city itself. Eventually firms decided that the cost of production was too high in Detroit and decamped for the Sunbelt, where right-to-work laws had been passed and the pathway to innovation was paved.[22]

This general notion has been embraced by the city's policy-making elite. "The goal," says current Detroit mayor Mike Duggan, "is to create a city where we're a center of invention and entrepreneurialism, like we were in the early nineteen-hundreds."[23] This time, though, the city is not looking to boat manufacturers and machine shops for innovation. It is looking to the arts, finance, and technology sectors. Investment is being focused around the places that this activity was already somewhat present: Midtown (and Wayne State University), Downtown, and Corktown.

The final and most dubious element of the manufactured decline argument is that black people, led by Coleman Young and his "unhelpful" and "angry" social justice ambitions, conspired to scare away whites to ensure political power.[24] Glaeser scolds black Detroiters for being so "foolish" as to start a riot, largely because it scared off wealthy whites. When the riot started, police forces were not quick or violent enough to put it down.[25] "Cities with more cops actually had smaller riots," he muses. "Unfortunately, draconian enforcement seems to be the only effective way to stop a riot once it starts."[26]

When black people finally did get into office, they alienated whites by not funding the services they valued and spent too much on "black services." Glaeser and Shleifer argue that the experience of former Boston mayor James Curley is instructive in understanding the arc that occurred in Detroit and thus deems it "the Curley Effect."[27] Curley was Irish Catholic, and his politics were singularly focused on getting Anglo-Saxon Protestants to vacate the city so he could more easily win elections.[28] To Glaeser and Shleifer, this is exactly what happened in Detroit—the city's first African American mayor, Coleman Young, embarked on a similar project (replace Irish with African Americans and anti-Protestantism with antiwhite animus) and in so doing destroyed the city. "In his 24 years as mayor, Detroit's Coleman Young drove White residents and businesses out of the city," similar to how "Zimbabwe's Robert Mugabe abused White farmers after his country's independence."[29]

To the manufacturers of decline, Young did not inherit a dying city against which corporations, state government, and federal officials had systematically stacked the deck. Young *created* it by engaging in a form of racial patronage designed to scare off whites. Building on the apparent logic that only white people enjoy good police, fire, and garbage removal service and that only black people live in subsidized housing, he writes:

> Young initiated large building projects that put his supporters on the payroll. He lobbied for federally supported public housing . . . to keep his supporters, as opposed to Whites, as city residents. At the same time, Young cut back on the basic services that White Detroiters valued, such as police and fire. In 1976, he cut the police force by 20 percent, which along with his other attacks on the police department, perpetrated lawlessness in Detroit. Trash collection declined by 50 percent during Young's early years.[30]

But perhaps most damaging of all was Coleman Young's desire to subvert the law of Tiebout. When corporations continued to locate their businesses downtown but residents moved to outlying suburbs, thus denying Detroit the ability to fund services for said businesses, Young and the city council attempted to institute a wage tax. This exercise in taking "money from the rich to fund services that helped the poor" generated a crisis that other "more reasonable" cities that elected centrist mayors avoided. As Glaeser comments, "The indirect effect of a local income tax is to encourage richer citizens and businesses to leave. . . . In a declining place like Detroit, well-meaning attempts at local redistribution can easily backfire by speeding the exodus of wealthier businesses and people, which only further isolates the poor.[31]

In short, the conservative construction of decline suggests that black Detroiters overreacted to discrimination, were coddled by police forces when they rioted, and then elected a social justice warrior who engaged in a systematic campaign to purge white people from the city.

The Functions of Manufactured Decline

As an academic matter, the conservative narrative of Detroit is not particularly compelling. It is easily countered by thousands of academic articles emphasizing, among other forces, racism, exploitation by the suburbs, an emaciated welfare state, and overly aggressive policing.[32] Nor is the narrative particularly surprising. It fits with simple conservative talking points and is written by committed ideologues who believe that virtually every form of the social economy is unnecessary. And yet despite the vulnerability to serious scrutiny, this narrative has several influential functions within the actualized world of policy making.

The most obvious function is that the conservative narrative frames policy outcomes in places such as Detroit and beyond. By framing Detroit as a bête noire parable of what happens when governments spend too much or overregulate, it acts as a foil for policies beyond such places. Austerity becomes not only normal but also *necessary* to ensure future growth and stability. Conservatives began to more aggressively use highly visible cases of urban malaise in the 1970s after almost a century of progressives successfully mobilizing such spectacles into interventionist policies.[33] The Triangle Shirtwaist Fire in 1911, for example, was such an outrage to all those who saw and read about it that politicians were able to invoke it to create labor regulations, first in New York City, then in New York state, and eventually as part of the New Deal in the 1930s.[34] Decades later when Cleveland's polluted Cuyahoga River caught fire, the widely broadcast event was used by activists to agitate for the creation of the Environmental Protection Agency.[35]

By selectively revising the story of Detroit, conservative manufacturers of decline have been able to frame future policy approaches. It is not poverty, wealth, or racism—it is intervention itself that caused Detroit to decline. Policy approaches that flow from this logic emphasize austerity. Within declining cities, the impact of this narrative is particularly severe. Urban policy in heavily abandoned cities such as Detroit consists of a mix of intensified penality (everything from code violations to law enforcement to restrictions on publicly subsidized housing), demolition, and austerity, paralleled by incentives to get investors to return (everything from tax breaks to public subsidy for development to title-clearing capacity).[36]

A second important function that the conservative manufacturing of decline serves is to fuse various elements of the Right together. As many have written, the American Right is composed of various factions that do not always align perfectly with one another.[37] Prointerventionist military conservatives, anti-interventionist libertarians, family values evangelicals, secular corporatists, anti-immigration Reagan Democrats, and proimmigration corporate bosses all sit within the proverbial tent of the Republican Party. Formal efforts to fuse the Right together date back at least to the efforts of William F. Buckley's *National Review* in the 1950s but were arguably most perfected during the Reagan years. Fusing has taken on a variety of forms but typically foregrounds a rhetorical object, common cause, or common enemy.[38] During the Cold War that was the Soviet Union, but since then the foils have been smaller in scale; "welfare queens," "Islamic terrorists," inner-city drug dealers, and immigrants (of color) have all taken turns in this role. The manufacturers of decline have used Detroit in a similar capacity.[39] As one *Washington Post* columnist recently described the "Republican obsession with Detroit,"[40] every four years the Republican presidential candidate visits the city, surrounds himself with white corporate employees from the suburbs, and rails against how the city is what happens if you vote Democrat. The city is a potent political symbol for the Right, used in part to fuse together its varied constituencies. Despite all of the putative differences between the think tanks of the Right, there is remarkably little difference when it comes to the diagnosis and prognosis for Detroit and places like it.

A third function that the manufacturing of decline serves is to sanitize, deny, or elide the racism that led to Detroit's current predicament. Scholars have long noted that rural African Americans who made the trek north as part of the Great Migration were met with a very different set of realities than what their white migrant counterparts experienced. African Americans were forced to live in dilapidated ghettos and were denied access to good jobs and homeownership.[41] When some middle-class black people were able to move into white neighborhoods, they faced a steady array of opposition from racist realtors, residents, city officials, and police officers. When white reformers tried to help by "renovating" the ghetto, instead they simply demolished and displaced black neighborhoods with vacant lots and expressways that made it safer for whites to go to work downtown without stopping in the city. When whites moved en masse to avoid having their children attend schools or be neighbors with black people, they took middle-class property values and incomes with them. State legislators made it increasingly difficult for cities to annex satellite communities.[42] Black municipal empowerment emerged only after whites had left en masse. A crop of new black mayors were left with the ashes of white flight, fiscal chaos, and an increasingly hostile state legislature.[43] Conservative manufacturers of decline have converted this set of inconvenient truths into a political opportunity by replacing them with "commonsense" economics. Detroit failed because of poor decisions, not impossible circumstances. White people did not flee black people; black people scared them away. By inverting causality, the narrative sanitizes more openly racist sentiments and policy actions. This approach has been common in various circles and is necessary at a time when the vast majority of white people deny that racism exists and do not want to be associated with the cases where it does—"racism without racists," as one sociologist deems it.[44] The conservative manufacturing of decline supports this narrative by sanitizing, denying, or distracting from the racialized reasons that led to the demise of cities such as Detroit.

The final function worthy of mention is that the conservative manufacture of decline frames as deeply socialistic what was ultimately a puny Keynesian moment in American history. Serious scholars have long noted that the United States (along with Canada and the United Kingdom) adopted a very mild form of Keynesianism in the mid-twentieth century.[45] Scandinavian countries more fully immersed themselves in the logic of Keynesianism, building more robust safety nets, centralized regulation, and income supports.[46] Conservatives, by contrast, have long framed the period of the mid-twentieth century as an incredible overreach and overregulation of the state. The paranoia that an overbearing state was an automatic "road to serfdom"[47] motivated the rise of conservative think tanks and the conservative movement more generally.[48] A variety of scare tactics have been used over the years—ginning up fears of taxation and government involvement in schooling, for instance—to reinforce this paranoia. The manufacturing of decline in Detroit serves a similar purpose, providing a dystopian stage on which to assert that this is what big government brought you—never mind that it was never "big" by Global North standards. Even more subtly, the decline allows conservative lawmakers to agitate for "small government" while continuing to push for the most obvious (domestic) exception to this—the carceral state.[49] Detroit simultaneously offers conservatives a "scary" example of what happens when you spend too much (e.g., on social services) and too little (e.g., on incarceration). This is completely without context (or factual basis), but it is effective propaganda.

The Efficacy of Manufactured Decline

That a small group of ideologues affiliated with the Cato Institute or the Heritage Foundation feel that Detroit's decline was created by profligate liberalism[50] is not terribly surprising. Nor is the notion that this group would be trying to promote this narrative to influence public policy. That is, after all, the point of being a think tank ideologue. Far more surprising is how closely this vision aligns with actualized policies in the American Rust Belt. Urban policy, to the extent that it exists, is dominated by intensified austerity: increased attempts to incentivize land investment, on the one hand, and growing penality—through code enforcement, welfare restrictions, and the criminal justice system—for remaining residents, on the other. Such alignment would not be so surprising if the Heritage Foundation was in charge of appointing the mayor of Detroit or Cleveland, but the foundation of course is not.

Every major city in the American Rust Belt is dominated by left-leaning Democrats.[51] Major cities such as Detroit, Cleveland and Chicago have been important locales for black municipal empowerment. Some of the most liberal-leaning federal congressional districts in the United States are located in the region's inner-core areas. So why would urban policy in these locations align so closely with the vision of a small group of ideologues who are openly hostile to the politics of the region's elected leadership? There are multiple ways to think about this question, but this chapter will conclude by focusing on two: the political geography of urban policy making and the lack of an ideational counterweight to conservative think tanks.

Much of what is commonly thought of as urban policy is in fact forged at the state level in the United States. A wide range of land-use, taxation, housing, and educational policies are created or bounded at the state level. Even states where local control is more complete reserve the right to circumscribe the policy actions of cities. When, for example, the city of Charlotte, North Carolina, openly mused about enacting a citywide minimum wage that was higher than the rest of the state, the state legislature preemptively prohibited it.[52] Cities are the legal creatures of states. The political and racial geography of the Midwest therefore almost predetermines that this relationship will be a rocky if not openly hostile one. Though the region contains several cities with majority black populations, the states themselves are heavily white, suburban, and rural on balance. Most Republican state legislators not only represent white rural districts whose interests are different from those of the inner-city areas of their states but are also often politically hostile to the latter.[53] Running for election as a white Republican or even an outstate white Democrat in Michigan consists of promising to restrict the perceived abuses of Detroit when you are elected. In Ohio, Cleveland is the bête noire; in Pennsylvania, Philadelphia and Pittsburgh share this role.

When these closely divided (by Republican and Democratic seats) state legislatures take office, much of this myth-derived animus about the state's most prominent city infects the policy-making apparatus.[54] At a minimum, the assumptions of Republicans and centrist Democrats about places such as Detroit are very similar to the aforementioned manufacturers of decline—profligacy, black militancy, and a lack of entrepreneurship are "the problem" that needs to be solved. Even more extreme and direct is the influence of the think tanks themselves in policy making. As Akers has chronicled, for example, the Hudson Institute (a member of the conservative think tank network American Legislative Exchange Council) actually wrote Michigan's land bank legislation over a decade ago.[55] Like the others that followed, that legislation emphasized the virtues of the market. Land banks had to be self-funded, had to work to lower barriers to investors, and had to build their purpose around being market-centered.[56] Such laws are not built on careful consultation with Detroit's (or Cleveland's or Buffalo's) local left-leaning city councilors. They are deeply influenced, if not actually written, by the very think tanks that manufacture decline ideationally. Many of these laws or assumptions prove not to work,[57] but the legislators who promote them only gain politically because the impacts are not felt by their constituencies. Rural politicians not only ignore the needs of the main city; they also rejoice in punishing it.[58] The sanitized language of the manufacturers of decline allows them to do with fewer accusations of racism and lack of empathy. The fact that the failures of such approaches never reach their constituents allow such legislators to do so without electoral consequences.

An additional factor has to do with the dissonance between the rhetorical strategies of Right and Left think tanks in the United States. As Stahl has argued, the conservative think tank movement began in earnest in the 1960s.[59] Conservative benefactors wanted to create a counterweight to the perceived abuses and power of Keynesian-liberalism that dominated in the day. Many felt that the Brookings Institution was the ideational heart of the Keynesian movement in the United States and sought to create institutions that would favor a counterideology. A "marketplace of ideas" emerged to replace the perceived ideational oligarchy of Brookings, but the sides that emerged were far from identical or equal. Conservative think tanks, then and now, enjoy greater funding and a closer alignment with the most extreme fringes of the conservative movement.[60] By contrast, left-leaning think tanks are dominated by an obsession with "balance" or "marketplace" of ideas and are heavily influenced by corporate money.[61] Unlike their conservative counterparts, liberal think tanks have actually fought the left wing of the Democratic Party for influence—most recently when they led the charge to marginalize Jesse Jackson and the movement he built with his presidential run in 1988.[62] Even more than the financial imbalance, the rhetorical strategies of modern-day conservative and liberal think tanks are strikingly different. Center-left think tank conversations about places such as Detroit foreground social problems and rarely situate conservatives as one of them. Brookings, for example, has published many pieces on Detroit in recent years. The institute isolates factors such as racism, economic opportunity, and poverty but rarely the conservative movement or legislators fighting reform or intervention. Conservative think tank voices on Detroit and urban decline are by contrast defiant, unequivocal, and uncompromising in tone. They situate liberalism itself—or its institutions such as unions and the Democratic Party—as the problem. The policy framing that has emerged from this is an Overton window that is pulled to the right by committed ideologues, while the potentially countervailing tug is performed by compromise-obsessed centrists. Within this framework, policy ideas get pulled to the right more frequently than they get pulled to the left.

Ideas, as has been posited, only begin to move the machinery of policy when two conditions are met: a crisis of invalidating magnitude and a sufficiently organized alternative idea around which to build policy. As this case illustrates, however, the idea of crisis is not fixed, nor is it a natural by-product of the experienced crisis. Moreover, just because an alternative is present and organized does not mean that its leaders have the institutional power to implement it. To the Right, Detroit is simple. It is in decline because its black leaders were too militant, too profligate, and not respectful enough of (white) entrepreneurs who built the city. Extreme, facile, and racist as this narrative might be, it is deeply influential owing in large part to the political geography of city-state relations and institutional structure of think tanks in the United States.

PART II

Ideas in National Urban Policy

CHAPTER 6

The Neoliberal City and the Racial Idea

Lester K. Spence

Neoliberalization takes on particular but variable forms in different cities and in metropolitan areas. In this chapter I suggest that ideas about race and racial difference and the political decisions that can emanate from these ideas play an important and underrecognized role in the neoliberal turn and in explaining variations in neoliberalization.

The Neoliberal Turn

The term "neoliberalism" describes a set of large-scale institutional transformations,[1] a class project promoting upward wealth redistribution,[2] and a unique rationality.[3] Scholars generally agree that neoliberalism comprises a number of ideas about how the economy (and the governments, institutions, populations, and individuals that constitute it) should function. These ideas became a new common sense in the 1970s when high inflation and unemployment—"stagflation"—helped destabilize the Keynesian consensus.

Some scholars have suggested that ideas work primarily at a cognitive and normative level, in either the "foreground" or the "background,"[4] but this does not quite explain why ideas matter more than interests or institutions. Mark Blyth,[5] thinking through how ideas function during moments of uncertainty, posits that ideas reduce uncertainty, make collective action and coalition building possible, serve to delegitimize prior institutions, and act as blueprints for new institutions.

The scholarship examining the neoliberal turn as either ideological or a set of macrolevel institutional transformations operates at such a high scale that it does not tend to tackle intrastate geographic variation well, if at all. Critical geographers[6] have long recognized that key aspects of neoliberalization can be found in the attempt to problem-solve major urban centers. Here a range of processes—including the turn away from manufacturing, increasing financialization and privatization of a range of public goods, and the growth of the carceral state in policing poorer urban populations—are all understood to be crucial components of neoliberalization, something that more recent work from political scientists also draw attention to.[7] Politically and institutionally constrained from raising taxes on residents and businesses as well as going to the federal or state government for resources, cities now routinely float bonds as a way to pay for infrastructure and other developmental projects, engage in public-private partnerships or full privatization for both basic service delivery and urban redevelopment, and focus on downtowns to the relative exclusion of neighborhoods.

We know that neoliberalization increases inequality, reduces the ability of governments to collect revenue (particularly for the purpose of redistribution), reduces the ability of labor to organize, and increases the size and scope of the carceral state. We also know that popular consent was required to make neoliberal policies the new common sense. Given the effects of neoliberalization, what made people support it? One of the signal gaps in both the literature that examines the neoliberal turn from the national and international levels and in that which examines the urban aspects of the turn is that they largely ignore racial politics. I suggest in this chapter that racial politics plays a crucial role, both broadly and in specific metropolitan regions. A "core identity"[8] that people turned to in the middle of the 1970s-era crises was race. Elites used ideas about race in order to build support for neoliberal policy.

Racial Ideas and the Neoliberal Turn

While acknowledged for much of the nation's history as a biological "fact," race is now recognized as being socially constructed through discourse.[9] As an idea, race organizes individuals and populations into categories based on a combination of phenotype and genetic inheritance for the purpose of generating ascriptive hierarchies.[10] Black populations are deemed to be lazy, unintelligent, prone to criminality, culturally dysfunctional, sexually irresponsible, and dangerous.[11] While scholars such as Adolph Reed Jr.[12] argue that racial categories are primarily created for distributing civic resources, this approach misses the numerous ways that racial ideas have also shaped labor and capital and access to civil society. Blacks did not simply constitute "unpaid labor" in their status as slaves; they constituted perhaps the original form of "human capital" as well as some of the first examples of depreciated capital and monetized securities.[13] Racial ideas shaped civic identities (the citizen was by definition white), material interests (whites had a vested interest in hoarding resources from blacks and other nonwhites), and institutions (although institutions such as the census were not created for the purpose of maintaining racial hierarchies by counting racial populations, they helped to reproduce these hierarchies).[14] Though they evolve over time, shaping and being shaped by interests and institutions, racial categories have real material and ideational consequences. Black and nonblack populations differ systematically in political attitudes and behaviors, and in that way they are treated by the state and civil society.[15] These differences are reflected in the fact that black lives tend to be shorter and poorer.[16] Although there are also important class distinctions within black populations that render some black populations better off than others,[17] ignoring the reality of interracial inequality has particularly important political and intellectual consequences when it comes to the neoliberal turn, as many of the regressive policies associated with the turn come to pass through racial politics.

Take, for instance, one of the signature changes to state tax policy in the early neoliberal era, California's Proposition 13, passed in 1978, which placed a cap on real estate taxes and created a supermajority requirement for tax increases, thereby significantly hampering governments' ability to raise revenue and significantly reducing the quality of California's public education system. The results were horrific for public schools but a boon for homeowners, particularly wealthy ones. Scholars such as Mark Blyth suggest an interest-based account generated by elites—California homeowners voted for Proposition 13 in part because they were upset with their tax burden, that animus elites took advantage of in proposing Proposition 13 in the first place. The resulting success of the proposition at the ballot box in turn fueled the national tax revolt.[18] And there is some support for the interest-based account. However, white racial attitudes rather than income, ideology, or even partisanship best predicted support for the measure.[19] In this specific instance, elites promoted ideas about the unworthiness of populations believed to be the prime beneficiary of taxes (black and increasingly brown populations). These ideas in turn shaped (white) California voters' preferences for taxes.

Racially heterogeneous cities and especially cities with high percentages of black residents find support for most forms of public spending diminished compared to cities that are more racially homogenous, especially those that have higher percentages of whites.[20]

Over the course of the neoliberal turn, proponents of the turn levied a range of attacks on welfare-state policies that supposedly make people less self-reliant and responsible and more dependent on government, thus hampering free markets. As black women became overrepresented among single mothers who received aid from the state (and even more overrepresented in images associated with the program), support for the program itself dropped.[21] Racial attitudes predict animus toward taxes generally but represent one of the strongest predictors of welfare animus specifically.[22] Before welfare neoliberalization, localities with higher percentages of black recipients were far more likely to exert oversight of recipient behavior than those with lower percentages and were far more likely to dampen benefits.[23] After welfare neoliberalization, this trend increased. The racial population of a given state predicts both devolution and how punitive the devolution is.[24] Neoliberal and neoconservative policy makers and politicians drew on racial ideas in radically neoliberalizing welfare, and in doing so they also constrained the target population themselves. Poor single black mothers found themselves facing a form of affect (disgust) that they did not have the political capacity to effectively contest.[25]

Neoliberalization has also transformed and in some ways created the carceral state.[26] Incarceration rates in the United States have increased significantly over the past few decades,[27] as have attitudes supporting punitive approaches to crime. The carceral state does not grow without a shift in policing such as the shift inspired by the idea of "broken windows," which suggests that police need to maintain order by expressing no tolerance for a range of minor infractions.[28] As with tax policy and welfare, research shows that white racial attitudes predict support for punitive approaches to crime and that race played a powerful role in structuring criminal justice and policing policy.[29]

In the instances of Proposition 13, welfare reform, and the carceral state, racial classifications produced and reproduced explicit and implicit ideas about labor capacity, civic value, and how the economy (and polity) should work. These ideas structured the broad attack against Keynesianism by ginning up racial resentment against "undeserving beneficiaries," which determined the policies that were more likely to be repealed, the policies that will replace those that were repealed, and the calculations that politicians and other officials made in deciding to support or oppose those policies. Ideas about race act as constraints, working in the same way paradigms do in policy shifts,[30] making some ideas and some policies far more likely to prevail than others. Ideas about black populations helped generate support for the neoliberalization of those policies. Furthermore, though it is possible to sync neoliberal ideas with antiracist sentiment—indeed, many if not most black elites who support the neoliberal turn also evince antiracist sentiment[31]—such ideas allow what Desmond King and Rogers Smith refer to at the "white supremacist order" to gain political currency.[32]

The Neoliberal Urban Landscape

Neoliberalization involves destabilizing ideas associated with the previous ideational regime, including ideas about reducing inequality, providing a social safety net and a robust suite of public goods, restricting capital mobility, and facilitating labor organization, among other things. Those ideas are then replaced with ones about incentivizing market-like behavior, devolving responsibility to lower rungs of government, and starving those governments of the resources required to handle those responsibilities. Racial classification makes destabilization of the Keynesian regime more likely and then bolsters support for neoliberal policies among those at the top of racial hierarchies least likely to personally benefit from them. But this process is varied and contingent. It does not occur in all spaces at the same time. The transformations in both welfare and crime policy did not come solely because of a set of assumptions made about the populations associated with them or because these populations are represented as being concentrated in certain types of spaces. This brings us to the urban landscape.

Over forty years ago, states and the federal government provided significant amounts of revenue to cities, and cities were in many ways hubs of democracy. It is difficult to imagine, for instance, the gains of the labor movement and the civil rights movement without urban protest and political action. Today, cities are increasingly forced to rely on municipal bonds rated by international agencies and in some instances have had their abilities to practice democracy taken from them, as in the cases of state financial takeovers and legal preemptions. What determines the extent to which this "rolling back" of Keynesianism and its neoliberal replacement occurs and when it occurs in a given city?

Racial minorities in general and black ones in particular are stereotyped as being lazier, less intelligent, less rational, and more crime prone than their white counterparts. Under the process of neoliberalization, a significant percentage of these populations are either disciplined (to incentivize them to develop their human capital) or punished (to sanction their inability to develop their human capital and to prevent them from contaminating others). They are simultaneously used symbolically to generate disdain and disgust for the welfare state and affection and approval for the neoliberal regime. Racial ideas do not just classify, organize, and order populations; they also classify, order, and organize the spaces (neighborhoods, cities) those populations inhabit.

When the government got into the real estate business during the Great Depression, it created the Home Owners Loan Corporation (HOLC) to provide mortgages to struggling homeowners. The HOLC developed a neighborhood-level means of assessing lending risk and thus the likelihood of getting a mortgage.[33] One of the most important risk indicators was the racial profile of the neighborhood. Realtors in Chicago and elsewhere were legally prevented from "block busting" or disrupting neighborhoods' racial demographics.[34] For decades the National Real Estate Board's code of ethics expressly forbade realtors from "introducing into a neighborhood a character of property or occupancy, members of any race or nationality, or any individual whose presence will clearly be detrimental to property values in the neighborhood."[35] These ideas themselves helped determine what specific aspects of the Keynesian regime are removed, what specific forms of neoliberal policy are articulated, and when and where those forms were articulated and proposed.

There have been a few attempts to examine the process of urban neoliberalization. Jamie Peck has examined the speed with which neoliberal policies move from place to place and how neoliberal ideas are translated into policies on the ground.[36] Timothy Weaver has examined the way the neoliberal rollout process occurs and specifically whether it occurs with intent or simply through happenstance.[37] Jason Hackworth has shown that national-level patterns exist even as local forces shape bond ratings, public housing provision, public-private partnerships, real estate values, and gentrification.[38] Yet these and other authors rarely address the role of race, in part because they wish to focus more attention on class. I understand this urge but would caution against this move.

The neoliberal Hope VI program, begun in 1992 under President Bill Clinton, funded the demolition of many large housing projects and their replacement with combinations of private homes and housing vouchers, physically redesigned public housing to emphasize personal responsibility, imposed strict behavioral requirements on recipients, and further devolved decision making to local officials.[39] But this process varied by locale, as local public housing authorities and other housing market actors were primarily responsible for its implementation. For instance, Seattle saw a significant number of public housing units demolished as well as a significant number of new units developed; Chicago saw most of its public housing units demolished with little to no replacement; and New York City saw little to no change. Why did Seattle transition to Hope VI in a way that provided a similar quality of service to public housing residents while Chicago did not? Hackworth argues that demographic variation does little to no work in predicting the Hope VI rollout and that local institutional variation explains more of the difference. I suggest that race works in part as a set of ideas that are also embedded in those institutional frameworks.

Chicago, the city with the highest disregard for public housing, is also highly racially segregated, and its poor black population is arguably the most isolated and concentrated in the country. In writing about Chicago, Hackworth notes that "though it is the second-largest housing authority in the United States, overseeing 34,669 physical units and 33,852 Section 8 vouchers, the Chicago Housing Authority. . . does not have the wider political support enjoyed in New York or Seattle. Chicago's history as a cauldron for land use disputes associated with the siting of public housing is an important reason for this."[40]

Between 1940 and 1960 Chicago's black population nearly tripled, from 278,000 to 813,000. As the result of a combination of labor market dynamics and federal law, approximately 75 percent of that black population was cordoned off to the city's South Side. The battle for public housing became not just a battle for the right to housing but also a battle against segregation. Robert Taylor, the black chairman of the Chicago Housing Authority, wanted to locate public housing in white neighborhoods. White political officials and residents (and, for different reasons, black middle-class citizens and organizations as well) consistently mobilized against the threat of (limited) public housing integration using a combination of electoral politics (voting) and protest politics (riots and threats of riots).[41] Racial classifications shaped ideas about populations and spaces. These then shaped attitudes (interests) about public housing as an idea as well as the institutional framework designed to regulate housing.

The "spatial fix"—that is, the role of geography in the crisis of overaccumulation[42]—shapes urban and suburban developmental trajectories and has at least three important consequences. The first is inner-city gentrification, attracting middle- and upper-income residents while ejecting lower-income residents and increasing land values in doing so. Second is inner-ring suburban devaluation, and third is outer-ring and exurban sprawl. There is an overall national order to gentrification, devaluation, and sprawl that belies the argument that these phenomena are primarily the result of local forces.

Examining real estate values in major American cities in the early 2000s, Hackworth found evidence for all three trends associated with the neoliberal spatial fix with the exception of Philadelphia, Los Angeles, and Detroit, where he found no increases in inner-city property values. Hackworth is primarily interested in the spatial fix itself and less in charting the role of other factors. And while he does not present any demographic information about the census tracts he analyzed, two of the three cities for which he found no inner-city property value increases (Philadelphia and Detroit) experienced the lowest increases, or the highest decreases, in the areas that have the proportionately largest black population.

The few Detroit census tracts that appear to have had any positive property value growth are racially integrated ones such as Rosedale Park, Sherwood Forest, and Indian Village. And predominantly black tracts in South Philadelphia also saw property values drop precipitously. In the case of public housing, racial ideas help shape the institutions that then shape public housing as well as ideas about public housing itself. In the case of land value, the relationship between racial ideas, racial populations, and racialized property appears to be more straightforward, although again it is important to note the role that institutions and interests continue to play in generating the value of "white exclusivity."[43]

Understanding the role of racial ideas in shaping the metropolitan real estate markets helps to explain why the fight for public housing was a losing battle in Chicago while taking a very different shape in Seattle and why real estate in some places is consistently undervalued, while in other places it consistently increases in value. "Racing" communities, neighborhoods, and populations render them problem spaces that require repopulation and restructuring.

Interest in the carceral state and in policing has grown over the past several years, particularly with the rise of antipolice activism in the wake of the spectacular deaths of Michael Brown, Eric Garner, and Freddie Gray. As cities are increasingly disciplined by bond rating agencies, we see policing take on two overlapping functions. In cities such as Baltimore and New York, we see police used as agents of social control. On the one hand, in cities such as Ferguson, police are increasingly used as agents of social control and revenue generation (until the US Justice Department stepped in, more than 20 percent of city revenues came from police activities, notably fines). This is not a matter of Jim Crow–style racism only imported over into the present. On the other hand, this is not simply a class issue, with race being the scapegoat.

In Baltimore, the two police districts that receive the most resources are those that contain the city's downtown corridor and Sandtown-Winchester, where Freddy Gray lived most of his life and died after an encounter with Baltimore police officers.[44] More money has also been spent incarcerating the residents of Sandtown-Winchester than in any other Maryland neighborhood.[45] Under New York City's stop-and-frisk policy, blacks (and after that Latinos) were far more likely to be stopped than whites and were often far more likely to be stopped in majority white neighborhoods. Research also suggests that most of the stops in places where blacks were the minority also occurred in gentrifying neighborhoods (and do not appear to be driven by citizen demand for policing).[46]

The idea of order maintenance policing articulated by James Q. Wilson and George Kelling in the pages of *The Atlantic* is at base an idea that argues forcefully that there are populations and spaces that are unruly and disordered and require disciplining.[47] Crime is the function of disorder. Besides the fact that the idea—much like the other ideas connected to neoliberalism—does not in fact *work* the way it purports to,[48] it requires a set of preexisting (racial) beliefs about populations and spaces in order to become the equivalent of "fast policy."[49]

Over the past decade we have seen three stark examples of urban crisis, in New Orleans, Detroit, and, most recently, Flint, Michigan. In each instance, crises beset these cities in ways that "naturally" called for drastic interventions that significantly reduced their ability to provide public services, the nature of the public services they did provide, and more generally their ability to govern.

In 2005 the largest hurricane ever to hit the United States, Katrina, devastated New Orleans, among other places. Approximately 1,800 people in the Gulf region died, more than 700 were declared missing, 3 million residents lost electricity, and over 1 million people were displaced. New Orleans alone sustained almost $23 billion in property damage.[50] Much of this devastation was arguably a result of government failure, specifically of inadequately funded, constructed, and maintained levees.[51] In the aftermath of Hurricane Katrina, federal, state, and local officials gutted the public school system, replacing it with a charter system; demolished most of the city's public housing stock; and then outsourced many disaster recovery services to private entities (significantly reducing the ability of residents—displaced or otherwise—to fully recover from the disaster).[52]

In 2011 the State of Michigan enacted Public Act 4 (PA 4), which gave the state the ability to place financially troubled municipalities, townships, and school districts under receivership, or "emergency financial management." The largest example and thus something of a special case was, of course, Detroit, which experienced the largest municipal bankruptcy in US history. The effect on local democracy was stark; elected officials had little to no authority to pass or sign legislation and little to no authority over the budget, and voters had little to no authority over the emergency financial manager. And the emergency financial manager had almost complete authority over the budget, including retirement pensions, and all municipal contracts, including union contracts.

As of March 2015, every major city and almost every major school district in Michigan with a majority black population, which includes nearly half the state's black population, had been placed under emergency financial management.[53] Flint represents perhaps the most egregious example. As part of a cost-cutting move, the city's emergency financial manager decided to stop buying water from Detroit and instead rely on its own water. Doing so without making the requisite infrastructure modifications resulted in over 100,000 people being exposed to dangerous levels of lead.[54]

In the cases of New Orleans, Detroit, and Flint, political actors used "crisis" as an opportunity to both roll back Keynesian-era policies (public housing, public schools, and public services in general) and to roll out neoliberal policies (charter schools, low-income private housing, and fiscal austerity more broadly). In each case, class was more prominent than race in predicting what populations were more likely to suffer. In New Orleans, for example, age and class were better predictors of suffering than race.[55] In all three cases black political elites also promoted neoliberal policies.[56] Yet racial discourse heavily shaped the narrative of urban dysfunction that made the neoliberal rollout far more likely. In the case of New Orleans, political officials, policy makers, and media journalists, black and white alike,[57] trafficked in racial stereotypes in describing black behavior during the hurricane, arguably helping to produce attitudinal differences between blacks and whites about the causes and consequences of the disaster.[58] In the cases of Flint and Detroit, a long history of racial discourse helped to establish the conditions whereby both cities were placed under emergency financial management.[59]

The neoliberal turn represents a radical state remaking project that ends up significantly increasing wealth inequality and significantly decreasing the ability of citizens to fight for and receive public goods. Although some would argue that race represents an extra economic factor that may exacerbate the consequences of the turn, I would argue instead that the idea of race and racial difference is required for the turn to take hold. The inner city represents the knife's edge of neoliberalism in part because of the specific function the city plays in modern-day capitalism. However, the inner city also serves as this edge because more than any other space, the racial character of the inner city best represents the space used to call the Keynesian welfare state into question.

Conclusion

At base, neoliberalism represents a set of ideas that radically harnesses the power of the state to impose market values and logics on individuals, populations, and institutions. Neoliberalism has the effect of significantly increasing inequality, significantly reducing the ability of workers to organize the scope and size of public goods and the welfare state, among other things. The idea of race classifies populations and spaces and orders them. "Black" populations are deemed to be lazy, less intelligent, prone to criminality, sexually libidinous, and uniquely ungovernable and hence less civilized than their "white" counterparts. Ideas about racial populations help to delegitimize progressive uses of public goods and to destabilize ideas about the public in general. Racial ideas generate cross-class support for racial projects that reproduce the neoliberal turn and make it difficult to generate cross-racial, class-based support for projects that contest it.

In moments of crisis, when interests are unclear and institutions are not stable, racial ideas help to generate collective action, articulate new institutional arrangements, and create new institutional blueprints. We can understand why the neoliberal turn uses racial ideas, and we can understand further why and how the neoliberal turn takes hold more so in some cities than in others. Given the role that black elites play in the neoliberal turn, focusing on race can end up ignoring intraracial class distinctions on the one hand and also foreclosing more radical political possibilities in favor of ending "racial disparities." Yet it is also clear that focusing on race and the racial idea can empirically help us understand the process of neoliberalization as well as politically give us what we need to more effectively contest it.

CHAPTER 7

Contested Conceptions of Pluralism Between Cities and Congress over National Civil Rights Legislation

Thomas Ogorzalek

> [Lynch mobs] protected life and property, at least in a way, and made those sections of the country, where there was no organized government, very safe sections in which to live.
>
> —Rep. Hatton Sumners (D-TX), 1934

> The frontier days are gone, and few of us familiar with the rigors of living in that era are likely to bewail its departure.
>
> —Rep. John Rooney (D-NY), 1949

In December 1963 the new US president, Lyndon Johnson, and House Speaker John McCormack were hitting the phones to wrangle votes for a cotton subsidy bill. southerners were in strong support, but the urban wing of the party was restive—for decades southerners had supported only pieces of the urbanites' agenda while accepting a lion's share of federal largesse. Johnson and McCormack called perhaps the most influential big-city power broker in the party, Mayor Richard J. Daley of Chicago, who sat at the helm of the Cook County Democratic Party as well as the nation's second-largest city. McCormack and Johnson tried to bring Daley (and thereby the Chicago delegation) on board. Daley's response was to suggest a logroll: "[We'll] be alright if they support any part of our civil rights program or the tax bill, but [we] won't support anything and then not get a commitment back from them.... We've been doing too much of that." Knowing that southerners would never support civil rights (they had done everything to oppose big-city efforts at racial liberalism for a generation), Daley went further to suggest the most aggressive legislative strategy: using a discharge petition to push the landmark civil rights bill into the congressional agenda, raising the issue even against urgings of his national party leaders.[1]

Of course, the prevailing reputation of Daley and the Chicago machine on race is less rosy. During the same time that he and his lieutenants in Washington had supported (vain) attempts to pass civil rights legislation, they had opposed racial integration and equality in Chicago nearly as consistently. No account of Daley gets very far without addressing his fraught relationship with black Chicagoans.[2] As a young man Daley developed his political chops in the Hamburgs street gang, who were largely responsible for an infamous 1919 race riot.[3] His Bridgeport neighborhood, still the beating heart of the Irish-led local Democratic organization, was famous for its racial turf defense, including both intense use of restrictive covenants and mob actions against would-be integrators. As mayor, Daley distanced himself from these positions, but throughout the machine's heyday racial segregation of the city increased, driven in large part by the racist implementation of local housing policies. Most notoriously, Daley encouraged officials responding to unrest in the wake of the assassination of Martin Luther King Jr. to open fire on looters, an order that resonated with hundreds of racially conservative whites near and far; one Bridgeport resident wrote the mayor a note with the informal estimate that the area was "all pro, no con" in agreement with this decision.[4] After Daley's death, the machine's latent tensions led to a decade of open racial rancor in Chicago politics.

However, local Democrats also worked for racial progress, supporting national civil rights both publicly and privately. The city had a fair employment law long before 1964 and advocated for national fair employment practices (FEP) for decades. At a 1961 hearing on employment discrimination, Daley argued that "Chicago is a melting pot city, as you know. Chicago was built by the people of many lands, of every race, creed, color, and ethnic origin.... Negroes are not the only segment of our population that has benefited from the city's [fair employment] policy, for nationality and religious groups benefit when the employer adopts fair employment practices."[5]

Daley's "melting pot" metaphor is inapt, because organizations such as his recognized and supported ethnic, racial, and national origin identities rather than melting them away. Even the largely assimilated native-born white ethnics of Chicago's outlying working-class districts maintained their group identities (as well as their newly inclusive construction of a white racial identity) in both daily and political life. Such group consciousness is still never far from the surface in Chicago and other racially and ethnically heterogeneous cities. Still, Daley's conception of urban intergroup dynamics reveals an important theme in twentieth-century race relations, namely that they were tough to manage and that the goal wasn't color-blindness. Rather, *consciousness* of difference and ethnicity was always on the tongues of urbanites and their leaders as they sought to navigate the diverse terrain of the midcentury city. They thought of the city when they thought about race, and they thought of city-specific solutions to racial challenges. This political thinking led to a paradox of city politics and race that Daley exemplifies: The traditional party organizations that controlled politics in so many cities were simultaneously ethnically exclusive hierarchical organizations *and* forces for civil rights liberalism—conservative at home in the streets, liberal in the halls of Congress. What explains this divergence, often by the same people or organizations?

In this chapter, I bring together two strands of research on American politics to attempt to better understand one important puzzle of our racial politics: how our cities are simultaneously well-known sites of deep, persistent racial inequalities of many types and the source of our best ideas (and staunchest political support) for ameliorating those same inequalities. In American politics, there is probably no area in which ideas have been as important and in flux so much as in race. A leading account of American political development contends that many of the most important and recurrent conflicts in American history are best understood as contests between opposed "racial institutional orders"—shifting, rival coalitions seeking, in the simplest form, either to advance racial egalitarianism or to strengthen white supremacy.[6] In the case of city politicians, however, the reality was (and is) often more complicated. The same political coalition, whose members both ruled the city and represented it nationally, simultaneously acted as both a progressive and regressive force in American racial politics. To help explain how and why, I will focus on the idea of cultural pluralism as informed by the conditions of city life and deployed by members of locally rooted traditional party organizations at different levels of government. Locally, they were institutions that upheld conservative visions of the city based on segregation and hierarchy. Nationally, however, they were the most consistent defenders of a vision of civil rights liberalism that was rooted only in cities during the Long

New Deal, in the run-up to the midcentury racial realignment. Before considering how these ideas can fit together, I will contrast the city leaders' local and national attitudes toward race.

Race and Local Stratification

The first side of the contrast has to do with cities' well-known history of racial conflict and hierarchy. In short, before the era of white flight, local officials of all stripes—Democratic or Republican, machine boss or reformer—were notable for their nonresponsiveness to African Americans and other racial minorities.[7] The close cohabitation of so many new arrivals amplified the governance challenges faced by the burgeoning metropolis, often spurring group rivalries. Local government was often biased toward in-groups as well in ways consistent with the racial ideologies of the day.[8] Across a wide range of policy areas—private and public-sector hiring, service provision, schooling, public safety, and others—African Americans were especially deprived.[9] Discrimination and reinforced hierarchy were strongest in housing policy in which a separatist ideology informed a mix of local and national institutions, which in turn reinforced and strengthened existing individual attitudes about neighborhood-level diversity and members of other groups. This coalescence of institutional and personal practice created the starkly delineated racial demography of all twentieth-century American cities.[10] Geographic separation strengthened political marginalization: The group territoriality of representation led local politics everywhere to take on an ethnoracial basis (with less emphasis on class), and nonwhites, who were more segregated than other groups (such as different ethnic whites) suffered the most because underprovision of services could take on the same geographic basis as membership in the dominant organization.[11]

Where African Americans *were* incorporated into political organizations, it was typically as junior partners due in part to the timing of their arrival in northern cities and their political alliances but also to prevailing prejudices. Typically, co-opted peripheral-bloc leaders served as loyal organization members, delivering particularistic goods rather than seeking systemic change.[12] This peripheral position in local organizations meant less access to the most valuable benefits (both personal and policy-related) available to core members and constituencies, and when electoral wins were comfortable enough, this marginal constituency was held captive with policy leftovers.[13]

While there is still debate over which kinds of city leaders were *less* responsive to African American communities' interests and preferences, the importance of local governance in both political marginalization and social inequality for minority groups (especially African Americans) is clear.

Cities and National Racial Liberalism, 1920–1963

Local politics in large cities was rooted in hierarchical ethnic and racial identities, and nonwhites were forced to the bottom of this hierarchy at the beginning of the twentieth century. Despite the resilience of local hierarchy, however, this era also saw a new idea regarding racial liberalism emerge from the group dynamics of city life. Over the course of the Long New Deal, race became associated with cities in political discourse. Racial issues were not particularly urban before the 1920s, because until then the typical referent groups for national race relations (African Americans and indigenous groups) lived mainly in rural areas. With the Great Migration of the twentieth century, however, black Americans became a significant (though initially still fairly small) presence in urban places, and arguments made in defense of racial liberalism took on an urban character that was not present in earlier discussions.

To illustrate how the urban liberal position on race developed, we can examine statements made by members of Congress during committee hearings, which provide context for the ideas underlying more discrete actions such as roll call votes. Because participation in hearings requires extra effort, the record reveals members' priorities and does away with the ambiguity sustained by silence. The give-and-take structure of these meetings reveals attitudes by members of Congress toward others' views and affords opportunities for spontaneous exchange. Unlike floor debate, hearings also include participants from civil society, adding further information about allies and foes.

In hearings on racial issues and policy proposals during the early and middle decades of the twentieth century, members of Congress from urban areas articulated support for the racially liberal position rooted in urban experience. Participation in these hearings during the New Deal was largely the domain of conservative southern and city Democrats. The liberal position was disproportionately urban and over time became disproportionately urban Democrats, with the Republicans remaining largely silent.[14] The hearings naturally also included many more witnesses who were not members of

Congress; the overwhelming majority of these witnesses were liberal urbanites, especially on fair employment proposals.

Urban New Dealers consistently and assertively engaged with southerners on civil rights. National race and civil rights legislation began with antilynching legislation that was considered repeatedly but never passed into law over the ensuing decades. The original bill was introduced by Leonidas Dyer, a St. Louis Republican whose district included many African Americans and was the site of a major race riot in 1919.[15] Support for antilynching legislation at this point was articulated as a universalist understanding of rights and African Americans' worthiness of full rights and citizenship. In a typical argument in favor of the antilynching law, Senator William B. McKinley (R-IL) argued in 1926 that

> Although he [the African American] has been in possession of (political and civil rights) for relatively so short a time he has shown himself to be worthy of them. As a free man he has always been amenable to reason and persuasion; as a citizen he has uniformly been a patriot, and as a voter he has consistently aligned himself with the intelligence, the efficiency, the administrative ability, and the forces that stand for order and property. What can be said of any other group of our fellow citizens?[16]

McKinley's argument appeals to abstract principles of citizenship in defense of rights and full protection by the state and does not make reference to a lived environment or social context in which rights or citizenship may be exercised. Similarly, at a 1921 hearing about the Ku Klux Klan (KKK), Bostonian Peter Tague argued (after a trip through the South) that "the rights of citizens throughout that section of the country . . . had been violated, and they had not been protected in those rights which are allowed and given to them under the Constitution of the United States."[17]

At the same time, however, urban members of Congress were developing a new position on race relations that was distinctively urban: civil rights liberalism was the best way to handle this issue in a big-city context, and other legislators should defer to that city position on this potentially divisive issue.[18] While the residents of these cities were divided over race at home in the streets, this division was not represented in congressional debate. These representatives articulated a set of three distinctively *urban* justifications for racial liberalism: a recognition of pluralism, the usefulness of legislated social regulation, and the danger of racial conflict to social peace.

Most relevant to the focus of this volume is the articulation by members of Congress of group pluralism and the importance of group identity as opposed to a strictly liberal individualism. This new argument relied on analogies to groups with experiences similar to those of African Americans but that were typically not the primary subjects of the legislation under consideration. Thus, attacks on lynching and the southern racial order included references to religious minorities such as Jews and Catholics, who were generally less exposed to lynching but who might become allies because they faced prejudice from the white Protestant mainstream. For instance, as early as 1921, Thomas Ryan (R-NY) argued against the KKK that "any organization that is anti-Catholic, anti-Negro, anti-Jew, and against the foreign element in this country, which comprises over 25 per cent of the voting strength of the country, is really a menace to the community."[19]

Ryan included Catholics and Jews in the same list as African Americans, even though at this point these groups shared little besides their relatively marginal social status within American society. While Tague's argument above might resonate with a conservative or a liberal because of its reverence for the Constitution and individual rights, Ryan's would have been more controversial outside of the polyglot cities both because it understands groups as a basis for political and social inclusion and because of the actual groups he names as promising analogues. After all, for those who successfully sought to restrict immigration from Southern and Eastern Europe (and elsewhere) during this era, including the KKK itself, the transformation of American demography was itself a "menace to the community."

Reference to other marginalized groups would later become a theme in the urban argument for FEP legislation in the 1940s. Arguing for FEP, Adolph Sabath (D-IL, Chicago) noted that "Jews, colored, and . . . minority groups in wide variety throughout the country . . . are the victims of unjustified local prejudice (and) actual discrimination."[20] Thomas Scanlon (D-PA, Pittsburgh), a career union official, declared that "bad as it is, discrimination against a man because he belongs to a union is not nearly as evil as discrimination because a man is a Negro, a Jew, a Catholic, or because his ancestors came from another country."[21] Victor Anfuso (D-Brooklyn) also emphasized pluralism (as opposed to straightforward racial justice for individual citizenship) as Americanism when defending broad civil rights legislation. "Our country is comprised of people who come from all races, religious beliefs, and national origins. All of them have made important contributions toward the development of the US as a great Nation and toward shaping its destiny. . . . I do not believe in the superiority of one race or one nationality group over another."[22]

Each of these city representatives, coming from a local traditional party organization and each having local black allies (though very few black constituents themselves), articulated a view of racial liberalism that was multicultural and tied to the experiences of nonblack marginalized groups concentrated in cities. Such arguments could be persuasive to listeners who were ambivalent about racial equality but might identify themselves as the object of similar discrimination. Roman Pucinski (D-IL, Chicago) added that in Chicago "8 out of 10 workers suffer some form of discrimination . . . [and] therefore this committee is trying to look (beyond) racial discrimination, tragic and lamentable as racial discrimination may be."[23] In this articulation, controversial antidiscrimination legislation primarily targeting African Americans was presented as also benefiting religious and national-origin minorities. This urban understanding of difference in which almost everyone is importantly "different" in addition to cities' historical experiences in dealing with new groups made racial liberalism the city position on these issues and softened the potential downside for taking what might have been riskier positions if articulated as strictly black-white racial issues.

Two other arguments with urban sensibilities were articulated in support of federal civil rights. First, urban members of Congress framed federal intervention as desirable and effective when local officials were unable or unwilling to act in general. Against rural representatives and southerners who typically (and fairly cynically) argued that the horrors of lynching and racial inequality could only be overcome by a generations-long process of education and norm changing, city representatives often made analogies to other areas of regulatory intervention and the power of legislation to shape behavior and change minds. For them, federal lynching laws could establish new norms regarding the acceptability of racial violence, a logic later extended to employment discrimination. Again, city representatives, coming from traditional party organizations, representing cities (but not districts) with sizable black populations, voiced faith in the power of state interventions to alter norms in favor of pluralism.

Second, the urban perspective on the relationship between racial liberalism (or at least nondiscrimination) and the basic public order was different from that voiced by southerners and rural representatives. Southerners and their allies emphasized the importance of segregation for maintaining social peace, as Charles Bennett (D-FL) argued in 1949 when he acknowledged that "they are not perfect, but I personally feel that race relationships are better in the South than they are anywhere else in the country. . . . You will find a lesser percentage of race riots, less hard feeling, and less misunderstanding in the section of the country where I live than anywhere else in the country."[24]

Even when we see through claims of black satisfaction with the existing state of affairs, this statement reveals Bennett's basic belief that public order was *more* compatible with the prevailing arrangements of racial domination. In the large urban spaces of the North, with their continual upheaval and dense populations, this was unpersuasive. There, deep discontent was understood as a time bomb, and when riots did occur, they were far costlier than in less developed areas. Accordingly, enforcement of nondiscrimination was seen as necessary for *keeping* social peace, not for upending it. Representatives from cities' own local FEP boards (several cities and states had implemented their own permanent boards by 1949) advocated on behalf of a national law, adding to the previous arguments the idea that FEP was an important measure to keep the "powder keg" of race from exploding in their cities. This urban perspective was clear and also clearly urban: state regulations against discrimination and institutions to oversee their enforcement help resolve intergroup conflicts. Such resolution is much more important in urban areas, where violence is more costly, can involve more people, and cannot be quelled as easily as a rural uprising.[25] Coming up with ways to avert such violence and actively manage group relations in the context of an inexorably changing status quo, rather than trying to reinforce a more static one, was the urban approach to race.

Together, the consciousness of group difference as something to be managed rather than dreaded, faith in legislation to reorder social practices, and support for some amelioration rather than outright oppression (or simply lower confidence that oppression could be effectively applied) combined to form the urban position on civil rights. The place basis of the main positions taken on race are reflected in the quotes that lead off this chapter. When Hatton Sumners defended lynching as a kind of traditional frontier democracy, he made an argument that would not have been accepted in a city. In cities, such spontaneous popular violence sometimes did erupt, often in defense of the established racial order. But under urban conditions, such acts were seen from above as a *threat* to the community's well-being, not a defense of it. John Rooney, then a young congressman from the Brooklyn Democratic organization, said seemingly in reply (though fifteen years later) that few would bewail the passing of the frontier days. In an America obsessed with the mythologies of the rugged frontiersman, such a statement entails at least a little controversy.

Rooney was arguing on behalf of fair employment legislation, which (like city Democrats' efforts at antilynching measures) would fail before southern obstruction. He argued that the interdependence of modern urban life made the institutions and practices of the frontier obsolete and that it was time to embrace the city perspective, including the pluralism and rules it entailed. In this respect, Rooney voiced a city position, on a city issue, in support of allies in his city delegation.

Rooney and his colleagues from similar local traditional organizations were the heart of the era's Democratic Party. They brought a new style and idea of community to national politics, one of group accommodation and bargaining that was expansive enough to (imperfectly) include African Americans as well. Their local ties and organization made their commitment to group pluralism strong enough to withstand the racist pushback within their national party (and within their cities).

Along with the speech acts above, one very important "nonobservation" should be noted. In Congress during this time, urban racial conservatism was absent. The record of hearings about civil rights during this era reveals no city representative from outside the South opposing the liberal position on the issue in question. This is crucial because of the racial division that was continually manifest in the streets and sometimes quite central to these cities' politics. Although they lacked the elaborate legal architecture of white supremacy constructed in the southern states and despite their sometimes self-righteous pride at not being as racist as southerners, many northern urbanites actively resisted integration, and many more harbored serious doubts about the prospect of close. But this division or ambivalence about the important changes afoot in national race relations was not reflected in the record of *how urban places represented themselves in the nation*. Urban representatives and their local allies articulated a position that would manage racial conflict by likening African Americans, at least rhetorically, to other newcomer groups and would seek to establish and sustain institutions to manage potentially explosive social conflict. They also redefined racial issues in ways that were directly relevant to urban life—focusing on the plurality of groups, on the usefulness of new rules for changing social norms, and on the grave danger of not finding ways to manage inevitable change (as opposed to trying to resist it or relying strictly on privately or individually evolving attitudes to deal with it).

This liberalism became the core of the city position on racial issues during this era, which would be reflected in the voting records of urban representatives on controversial issues, and in the later "Blue" alignment dominated by city representatives.

What to make of this double position by urbanites, of sustaining racial hierarchy at home while pushing for civil rights in the halls of Congress? It is possible that these national positions were cheap talk, delivered to a Congress they knew would be obstructed by southern recalcitrants. But they also knew that the talk *wasn't* cheap—racial conservatives were angry about these civil rights pushes, and the use of hearings and the discharge position meant that urban representatives were bringing these issues to the agenda and risking the cohesiveness of their national coalition. City representatives were working this very question out when they spoke about race in a new way during this era. We can get a glimpse of the answer by considering the divergent approaches as the political extensions of variant species of the idea of cultural pluralism that had emerged in the preceding decades.

Cultural Pluralisms and City Governance

To see the ideas behind city representatives' positions on civil rights, we should visit the long era of urban growth before the Long New Deal. American cities at the turn of the twentieth century presented all kinds of new governance problems, such as rampant corruption, unprecedented population size and density, toxic pollution, rapid technological change, and on and on. It is these unprecedented challenges, all intersecting and right on top of each other, that make cities such fascinating objects of inquiry. What made the American cities of the mid-twentieth century particularly difficult to govern—relative even to their European counterparts, who were also rapidly growing and industrializing—is that American cities were made of persons arriving from all over the country and the world, creating polyglot centers in which not only interests but also entire worldviews contended. In the framework articulated in Chapter 1 of this volume, this nineteenth-century mass in-migration disrupted the urban status quo, and the idea of cultural pluralism provided a new ideological framework for city government. Decades later when civil rights questions reappeared on the national agenda and civil rights took on greater importance outside the South, this urban idea for managing group difference was used to argue for national civil rights—though the interpretation of cultural pluralism had a different policy valence on the Hill than it did in the streets.

The twinned political insights of this era were, first, that rapid social change meant that maintaining order was very difficult and, second, that the diversity of the modern polis meant that the age-old "vision of a politics that was both inclusive and consensual" was bound to fail.[26] Political order has always been fundamental to authoritative action, especially for local governments during an era of dynamic city growth. Leaders of the era tried to project an image of stability and progressive development in order to attract investment as cities competed with each other for regional and national primacy.[27] The second insight, however, undermined the very basis on which order had traditionally been achieved—an articulation of a common good based on significant shared interests and experience. This had historically been achieved by exclusion of various classes (including women, newcomers, and workers) from political decision making and through a basic common worldview shared by those who could participate.[28] This was no longer democratically practicable in cities such as New York, where "cultural differences combined with class resentments made common ground unimaginable."[29] In such a context, political entrepreneurs took on the challenge of developing a new practice of politics rooted in interest groups, material exchange, and organizations to coordinate elites who acted as power brokers for geographically based constituencies.[30] Thus, machine politics was rooted not (or at least not only) in venal self-interest but also in a realistic recognition of cultural pluralism, which was reflected in a specifically political pluralist vision of how to provide order and make policy decisions.

The cultural and ethnic differences of urbanites would have been obvious to anyone walking the streets of American cities and were a primary concern for many of those attempting to govern them. Indeed, racially diverse and divided cities became a primary concern for many of those attempting even to simply understand America itself, as the assumption of a heritage shared with the founders no longer held for those who now clamored for full membership in American democracy.

Social and political theorists of the era did not always agree on what the underlying nature of diversity was or on the proper way to address it. These theorists elaborated understandings of cultural pluralism that were not all egalitarian, and these divergent ideas about intranational difference can help us understand the seeming paradoxes of cities' representatives over time. Pluralism was an alternative to both melting pot assimilation and authoritarian

Anglo-Saxonism in that its proponents sought to "acknowledge ethnic difference as a fact of twentieth-century American life, and to recognize it as a virtue,"[31] but the role of groups and their relative positions varied significantly across conceptions. For philosopher Horace Kallen, the fundamental assumptions of now-debunked race science led to a vision of enduring, stratified ethnic hierarchy. In his famous essay "Democracy vs. the Melting Pot," Kallen articulated a vision of ethnicity in which group hierarchies are resilient because group differences are biologically heritable, each generation has to be re-Americanized, and the subaltern can never really catch the dominant groups.[32]

Alternatively, John Dewey espoused a cultural pluralism more consonant with a contemporary liberal position: each group and tradition had something important and distinctive to contribute, and together the various strains of tradition are "transmuted into authentic Americanism."[33] In this vision, groups contributed to the broader society (as instruments do to an orchestra); personhood was thus more malleable for Dewey than for a biological essentialist such as Kallen.

Each of these pluralisms described different aspects of life in American cities. However urbanites conceived it, pluralism was a useful concept for understanding and managing city life and provided a commonsense language through which urban leaders could acknowledge group claims. In local politics, group consciousness became associated with group politics in which segregation and enclave life heightened group rivalries.[34] In national politics, the city fought on a different plane—against southern repression and for a citywide position of managing intergroup conflict, which required at least basic elements of the civil rights agenda.

Ideas and Organizations

The different valences of cultural pluralist politics—local hierarchy and national egalitarianism—deployed by the "new stock" of traditional organization urban politicos of the midcentury do not sit nicely within a framework emphasizing competing racial policy alliances.[35] The machines and their adherents were simultaneously fighting and supporting segregation and white supremacy. Political scientists Desmond King and Rogers Smith allow that although racial policy alliances or political orders may not be consciously constructed, members of these orders tend to be united by "agreements on the basic way to resolve the fundamental racial questions of their eras."

But if we consider the basic "ways" to be egalitarian transformation or the retrenchment of white supremacy, it is not clear which order to put the urban machines in—they seem to *dis*agree with themselves and everyone else. Did the machines and their adherents want separation of the races or didn't they? Did they want black political empowerment? More practically, were they with the NAACP and other civil rights activists (the anchor organizations of the transformative egalitarian order) or against them? It depends where you look—urbanists would probably say against, but scholars of national politics would see them on the same side in every civil rights issue.

King and Smith's racial orders framework has helped scholars map the place of racial ideologies in American politics. Crucially, it emphasizes the separability and opposition of actors, ideas, and institutional orders in American politics.[36] As usual, the story is more complicated. One of the most insightful amendments to the racial orders approach is provided by Skowronek, who argues that the deployment of an idea should not be considered separately from the precise policy goal being pursued—this allows us to better understand seemingly paradoxical positions taken on either side of a racial issue that is ostensibly about groups. The sides are not always clear, the ideas deployed in pursuit of goals are malleable, and specific policy context matters.

Something similar happens in our cities. Pluralism was an inescapable fact of modern city life, but this does not mean that the practitioners of pluralist politics saw cosmopolitan transcendence of group identities as the end goal or that they believed that all groups would contribute equally to the new Americanism. The hierarchical organizations described repeatedly by scholars of urban politics were not managed by John Dewey; rather, they were the creations of the same kinds of men who would riot, race-bait, and show group favoritism in their governance—men such as Richard J. Daley and his machine. In the cities, their idea of pluralism was closer to Horace Kallen's, recognizing the legitimacy of democratic participation by marginal groups (itself a major advance for the time) but simultaneously operating from a seat of power to sustain group stratification. In Congress, these organizations supported positions that were inclusive and supported civil rights. But in both places they were pluralists, putting groups alongside the individual as the fundamental unit of politics.

Reconsidering how these actors sat at a kind of hinge in American racial politics—connected to transformative egalitarians nationally but hierarchical racists locally as civil rights worked its way into the center of American political life—can help us understand the nature of antiracist coalitions. Racial politics is messier than the racial orders perspective might lead us to believe; actors and institutions can uphold white supremacy even as they work toward transformative egalitarianism. This can happen across policy issues or across levels of the federal system. Local party bedfellows were just as strange as the national Democratic coalition—but they did not become estranged. They maintained organizational cohesion despite apparent ideological incoherence, embracing different versions of pluralism depending on the setting.

Organizations that were not dedicated to racial egalitarianism and were often in direct conflict with the black newcomers in their cities muddy the water of racial orders in American politics, particularly the notion of a Manichean ideological antiracism pitted against white supremacy. As landmark accounts such as that by Eric Schickler have demonstrated, ideological interest groups such as the NAACP, ADA, and the CIO focused elite attention on these issues and brought support for civil rights into the very meaning of liberalism during this time. The national urban cohesion on civil rights was not dependent on shared antiracist ideology; however, civil rights groups frequently campaigned locally against the same mayors who were on their side in national politics. Pluralisms rooted in city life were developed decades before their more inclusive versions were incorporated into national liberalism. These ideas laid the groundwork for inclusive national politics but also for local hierarchies and organizations based on the idea and practice of such pluralisms linked city representatives to other parts of their city and made them more likely to agree with their local allies' positions, a pattern that was especially important on potentially divisive issues like race.

Further, pluralism played a slightly different role in the urban position on civil rights than in the ideological liberal position. For cultural pluralists, recognition of difference and fluency in group-identity appeals often served to uphold the political-economic status quo, sometimes even directly undermining more revolutionary appeals. For at least some of the ideological liberals (especially the CIO's core), embrace of racial egalitarianism was a way to build class solidarity across racial groups. In the end, the project worked halfway. As Lizabeth Cohen's classic account shows, white ethnic identities became less salient over time, but African Americans still not been fully welcomed into this group despite the best efforts of ideological activists. Only in national representation by city leaders were local divisions transformed into cohesive positioning on racial issues.

The coalition voicing support for racial liberalism was less a coherent institutional order than an uneasy alliance that deployed new arguments about city life to justify civil rights policy, not because they were all selflessly committed to helping defend minority rights or obliterate whiteness as a governing principle but instead because African Americans were better allies than the Dixiecrats and because their idea of the pluralist city guided their thinking. This is encouraging for those who would promote the rights of vulnerable or unpopular minorities, for such political-institutional links may help provide support for such changes without reliance on saints or altruists. Programmatic antiracists played a key role and set the liberal agenda in many instances, but they worked through institutions that were not themselves programmatically antiracist, merely politically pragmatic and cognizant that group difference was part of city (and national) politics. And crucially, it was the powerful political organizations at the hinge—of local and national politics, of social transformation and traditional community—that helped drive national change.

CHAPTER 8

Ideas in US Education Policy

Reform, Localism, and Immigrant Youths

Douglas S. Reed

In the spring of 2011 in Alexandria, Virginia, a federal bureaucrat who was visiting the local high school to hear about the progress of federally mandated reforms reflected on his impressions after presentations from school officials, teachers, and students. "A year and a half ago," he said, "we started out this process of writing regulations around the school improvement grant, and we've always wondered how it was going to play out."[1]

The lack of federal foresight and knowledge about the means of implementing a federal mandate is not surprising. The federal government's reliance on local communities and school districts to deliver federal educational objectives is an inherent element of US education policy, but it is one that is not well understood. This blind spot often limits our analysis of education politics and policy making, particularly when the federal appetite for aggressive education reform grows.[2]

My chapter considers how ideas about schools and education connect to the political and institutional contexts in which schools are immersed. The inherent localism of the US educational system constrains higher-level reform objectives because the daily administrative imperatives of running schools give local officials broad discretion as they respond to both state and federal policy initiatives.[3] In addition, local policy initiatives may emerge as activists and officials develop their own ideas about educational best practices or in response to local political needs. Whatever the impetus, locally launched policy innovations are key drivers of the political development of education in the United States.

The task, then, is to first sort out the flow of ideas and the institutional constraints that federalism imposes and then connect those ideas and constraints to the multiple constituencies that are involved in public education. To do this, we must understand how locally developed policy ideas both challenge and sustain local political patterns that support the coalitions needed to deliver education. These issues are further obscured when the policy initiatives of state and federal governments introduce other political variables.

Thinking about localities as sources of ideas regarding education requires recasting the long-standing tension between "cosmopolitans" and "provincials" that has characterized both the goals and techniques of education reform for over a century. This depiction has been used to describe a variety of political contests, such as rural residents resisting state-led efforts to consolidate school districts in the early twentieth century, southerners resisting federal court-ordered desegregation in the 1950s and 1960s, and Tea Party activists' claims that the Common Core State Standards represented the death knell of public education. The "provincials versus cosmopolitans" narrative views local activists as seeking to protect an inegalitarian status quo wherein local policy making and governance buffer schools from disruptive outside forces. This frame, while accurate for much of US educational history, nonetheless discounts the ways that locals use policy innovations to solve political problems and promote egalitarian ends rather than simply defending the prerogatives of local elites.

This chapter examines the interplay between local educational officials and federal actors in order to highlight the ways that local ideas about schooling generate an educational politics that federal and state officials are sometimes slow to grasp. I first provide a theoretical frame for thinking about the origins of ideas in education, paying attention to the sequencing of institutional innovation in US educational history and the emergence of ideas about schooling. Then the chapter turns to two episodes in contemporary education reform and activism, focusing on different ideas at play in addressing the needs of immigrant students and English learners within two specific contexts: the International Academy in Alexandria, Virginia, and the Mexican American studies program in Tucson, Arizona. This section situates the ideas about culturally relevant pedagogies for English-language learners (ELL) and immigrant students within a national context and looks to the tensions that these particular policy responses both created and resolved at the local level.

The Contours of Educational Ideas

Few ideas loom as large in US public education as the idea of local control. As Chief Justice Warren Burger wrote in *Milliken v. Bradley* (1974), "No single tradition in public education is more deeply rooted than local control over the operation of schools; local autonomy has long been thought essential both to the maintenance of community concern and support for public schools and to quality of the educational process."[4] Despite *Milliken*'s endorsement of localism, the federal role in education policy has grown over the past forty years. The assumption of local legitimacy still exists, but the policy objectives of the federal government are often deemed equally legitimate. In many ways, localities have internalized the federal equality demands. Despite this normative shift, however, there are frequent conflicts over who ought to be responsible for achieving more widely accepted egalitarian goals.

In the United States, the public educational system is marked by the weakness of centralized educational policy makers, the role of courts as promulgators of education policy, and the initial creation of public schooling by states and localities. Taken together, this "loosely coupled" system of public education fits Karen Orren and Stephen Skowronek's notion of political development as intercurrence, in which "the institutions of a polity are not created or recreated all at once, in accordance with a single ordering principle; they are created instead at different times, in the light of different experiences, and often for quite contrary purposes."[5]

Emerging as a religiously inspired, national social movement yet one deeply rooted in the aspirations and commitments of local communities,[6] public education has always carried multiple organizational and ideological tasks. Educational crusaders initially urged public schools on rural communities as a means to fuse an ideology of egalitarian opportunity with the necessity of civic education in a democratic republic. In large cities they simultaneously emphasized its "civilizing" function on urban youths, dislocated and unmoored by the centrifugal forces of the industrial revolution. At the turn of the twentieth century, public education was an important vehicle through which a coalition of urban Progressives and business leaders gained an upper hand over urban political machines and recently arrived immigrants. In New York City, the consolidation in 1898 of the five borough school systems under one superintendent, William Maxwell, allowed "administrative progressives" and reformers to marginalize a highly decentralized ward-based school board system (which often connected immigrant youths and immigrant teachers) and implement a centralized decision-making structure for New York City schools. This structure was made permanent in 1917 when the citywide school board of forty-seven members was replaced by a seven-member board that echoed the management of corporate America.[7]

Other institutional transformations within public education highlight its organizational complexity and wide-ranging ideological terrain. The district consolidation movement in rural America, a classic battle between "cosmopolitans" and locals,[8] pitted "efficiency" of greater economies of scale against localist democratic autonomy of small communities. In the mid-twentieth century the emergence of a federal role in education—first through judicial rulings and later through congressional regulation—not only directly challenged the racialist order of southern Jim Crow but also promoted "compensatory education" as a weapon in the war on poverty.[9] Today the standards, choice, and accountability wings of the educational reform movement elicit sharp ideological battles over the virtues of state and national supervision of schools and the role that market mechanisms ought to play as levers of organizational change within schools.

In short, the political and institutional contexts of US public education—particularly its organizational complexity, the variegated nature of the political fights, and the multiple ideological commitments and duties among its proponents and the institutions responsible for public education—deeply complicate efforts to provide a nationally coherent account of how ideas about schooling (or political ideas more generally) shape the political development of education. Yet if we accept that intercurrence is both rife within the American public educational system and is "a foundational concept on which other historical-institutional constructions of politics" rest,[10] then public education offers an ideal vantage point from which to study American political development. The key is to focus on the highly localized contexts in which these ideas emerge.

The Importance of Local Primacy in US Education

The decentralized but coordinated common school movement, inspired by religious ideas and by the notion that civic education nurtured republican democracy, transformed the institutional educational landscape of the mid-nineteenth century. Given its meager support from the federal government (generally in the form of land grants), the common school movement must be regarded as one of the most successful social movements in American history. As described by David Tyack and Elisabeth Hansot, "By 1880, attending a public school had become a standard part of the life cycle of all but a small proportion of American children. . . . There was no federal ministry of education to structure schooling by fiat. The tiny state departments of education could do little to police compliance at the local level. The creation of common schools and everyday decision making rested with hundreds of thousands of local people, but the result of their actions was what could be regarded as a 'national system.'"[11]

The lack of an initial federal role in public education has traditionally been explained through the "Three Rs" of "reds, race, and religion." That is, ideological concerns that an overweening federal government was tantamount to socialism, southern opposition to the disruption of Jim Crow schooling and opposition to funding Catholic schools yielded a stalemate that prevented federal aid to public schooling. Aside from a federal vocational aid bill enacted in 1918 and a 1950 "impact aid" bill for districts with a large federal presence, no federal general aid bill providing money for elementary or secondary education passed out of Congress between 1870 and 1957.[12] It was not until *Brown v. Board of Education* (1954) fractured the solid South and the Soviet Union stoked fears of US technological backwardness that federal money began to flow to US classrooms under the 1958 National Defense Education Act.[13] This eighty-seven-year federal stalemate channeled ongoing innovations within education through the institutions and organizations actually focused on creating and administering schools—states, localities, and school districts—leading them to become creative innovators of new models of schooling. It was through state and local adoption (sometimes prompted by national social reformers and business groups) that reforms such as compulsory schooling, the graded school, the comprehensive high school, and even standardized assessments came into being. These reforms were not invariably good for education or all local constituents. Indeed, southern states and some northern, midwestern, and western localities adopted Jim Crow schooling as part of a white supremacist domination of educational resources and opportunities.

Because the sequence by which public education was constructed gave primacy to local institutions, however, any federal innovation within education had to solve not only the policy problem of how to make schools better but also the political problem of how a national governing coalition was strengthened by aiding schools while at the same time not undermining key commitments of the local educational coalition. In other words, all those earlier localized reform efforts during the era of federal stalemate came about through local-level political organizing and coalitional alliances. The federal push at reform thus had to advance an argument about why reforms boosted a national political coalition without undermining these localized educational coalitions, which could vary substantially across time and place.

While federal efforts to improve education often addressed inequalities, until the 1970s the singular aim of local public schooling organizations, particularly in the Jim Crow South, was to entrench educational inequalities. The competing logics of local and federal political ideas for education, combined with the early arrival of local actors into the political space, meant that federal efforts to organize a constituency for educational improvement failed repeatedly and for a long time. As a result, there was no political space in which policy entrepreneurs in the federal government could effectively solve the political problem of why the federal government should become involved in public education.

All of that changed after *Brown v. Board of Education*, the 1964 Civil Rights Act, and the 1965 Elementary and Secondary Education Act. Through judicial compulsion, federal pressure, and the enticement of federal desegregation dollars, segregated school districts slowly rebuilt their highly inegalitarian school systems. It was only a partial success; through tracking, unequal school financing, and a reliance on special education as a form of "minority containment," many school districts often reinstated inequalities that the federal government sought to undo. But the civil rights moment also changed views in many places, and a number of educators and public officials also internalized the norms and rhetoric of equality that prompted federal pressure in the first place. The idea of equality in schooling—initially a federal idea—came in many places to be a local idea was well, particularly within liberal communities.

For the remainder of this chapter, I explore the organization and features of two policies that advanced egalitarian ends and have emerged primarily from local actors: the International Academy model of instruction for English learners and the creation of Mexican American studies in Tucson, Arizona. These two bottom-up efforts sought to promote greater educational equality for students who in many ways are seen as outside the conventional white middle-class norm. They also prompted two very different reactions by local and state elites, illustrating the complexity of local innovations within US education.

The International Academy in Alexandria, Virginia

Alexandria, a small city in Virginia with a population of approximately 150,000, lies across the Potomac River from Washington, D.C.; the Capitol Dome is visible from Alexandria's waterfront. Despite its proximity to the nation's capital, Alexandria is in many ways a typical school district: it enrolls roughly the same number of students as the average US school district (15,000). Unlike many suburban cities in the D.C. metropolitan region, Alexandria has a coherent downtown core that is the social and cultural center of the city. Alexandria also is home to a long-standing African American community, many of whom experience central city poverty more typical of larger cities than suburbs. On Alexandria's western flank, the city more closely resembles the freeway-based suburbanization of its larger neighbor, Fairfax County. Alexandria also has an older, more affluent, predominantly white residential section. Finally, there are large Latino (primarily Central American) and East African communities in the northern and western regions of the city.

Although Alexandria experienced court-ordered desegregation from the late 1950s to the 1980s, there is still a strong racial cast to the distribution of students within the city's public schools. In addition, there are high concentrations of students in poverty and ELLs in particular schools. Most recently, Alexandria's single flagship high school, T. C. Williams High, was declared in 2010 to be a "persistently lowest-achieving" school because it scored in the bottom 5 percent of all Title I schools in Virginia.

The "lowest-achieving" designation made T. C. Williams eligible for $6 million in federal School Improvement Grant funds but also challenged the community's perception of the school as essentially well functioning, albeit with its share of underperforming students. Local headlines announced "T. C. in Crisis" and deemed the federal designation a "wake-up slap" for the school, which highlighted clear racial cleavages in test score performance and in graduation and college attendance rates.

In response to this federal challenge, T. C. Williams focused its energies on two correctives: an "individual academic plan" for each student and the creation of an "international academy" for recently arrived international students. Most of these students spoke little or no English and often had seen their formal education interrupted by violence, civil wars, or migration; more than a few lacked basic literacy in their first language. Compounding these academic challenges were social ones: Many newcomer students were undocumented or unaccompanied minors and had arrived in northern Virginia looking for work, not a diploma. Given their academic frustrations and the lure of work, many of these students are at much greater risk of dropping out or not meeting Virginia's graduation standards. The International Academy plan aimed to address these issues by creating a "school-within-a-school." Although not a bilingual program, the academy would provide greater academic and social support to ease the transition of these students into a large suburban high school and enhance the chances of academic success.

Alexandria's track record with immigrant and English-learning students was poor at best. In the early 1980s as the number of Central American immigrants spiked, the school district ignored and then largely marginalized Latino students. In the early 1990s Latino students and their families routinely faced racial resentment from whites who viewed them as "problems" that would hopefully soon "disappear." Indeed, despite over a decade of growing numbers of Central American students, raising the share of Latino students to 20 percent, T. C. Williams did not have a bilingual high school counselor until 1993. Evelin Urrutia, an activist who graduated from T. C. Williams in 1990, recalled the marginalization of Latino students who were set apart from the rest of the school and given busywork in sheltered immersion courses that were aimed for early childhood English learners. High school students were given no information about post–high school options, such as college or even course selection options that would lead to a high school diploma.

A breakthrough occurred in 2009 when a new school superintendent, Mort Sherman, signed a memorandum of understanding with the Alexandria-based low-income community activist group Tenants and Workers United to adopt a number of measures designed to improve the educational outcomes of Latinos and students of color. One of the proposed measures was the International Academy, a program designed to offer additional services to Alexandria's high school English learners in order to improve their chances of success. The idea of the International Academy, however, raised concerns about perceptions in the community over the segregation of English learners. After being briefed by the ELL Planning Committee, Superintendent Sherman instructed T. C. Williams principal Suzanne Maxey to "revisit this whole plan." In Maxey's words, Sherman was worried about the perception of segregation: "The criticism is, or the concern is, that we are isolating those kids into a certain part of the building and that will have negative consequences."[14]

The high school teaching staff pushed back on resistance to the International Academy and indicated the dire situation of many of these students and that this program would better serve their needs. In response, Maxey urged the International Academy planners to include key members of the community in their planning, stressing that the meeting should not be just an update: "I wouldn't make it informal, I'd make it formal. I'd have a formal meeting inviting them and so that they are part of this. . . . I think they'll be pleased, if we sell it the right way, they'll be pleased that their children are no longer invisible, and that's the word that I keep using, I think our kids are invisible."[15]

Previous controversies in Alexandria's schools spilled over into the school district's plans to address the academic needs of English learners. The history of Jim Crow segregation and the persistent black-white achievement gap—in part sustained by continued tracking of students after integration—became a central political consideration as the school system developed the International Academy. During one of the planning sessions Amy Yamashiro, a school district accountability analyst, cautioned that other groups beyond the Latino or immigrant communities might object to the perceived segregation of the International Academy, saying "I think you'll get backlash from . . . well, like you know, the NAACP. . . . It could be any group that says, why are you isolating these kids who are mainly kids of color?"[16] Peter Balas, executive associate principal at T. C. Williams, warned the steering committee that "this concept has been tried before, and [it] became very explosive and controversial."[17]

Eventually, the outreach efforts and the federal pressure to do something in light of continuing underperformance of English learners enabled the International Academy to get off the ground, launching in the fall of 2012. While the segregation of newly arrived students in one wing of a comprehensive high school still raises concerns, the academy's staff is a talented, dedicated, and focused group of educators who are aware of both the challenges confronting their students and the trade-offs and limitations of the current model. The school district's ability to avoid conflict over the creation of the International Academy is due in no small part to the efforts of the faculty to meaningfully address the educational challenges of newly arrived high school–age English learners.

At the same time, however, the political invisibility of these students—and their families—stems in large part from the continuing inability of the federal government to enact comprehensive immigration reform, which would regularize the immigration status of many of T. C. Williams's students. This invisibility still diminishes their likelihood of making persistent and demanding claims on local governmental officials, as their capacity to vote or to speak out is highly attenuated for fear of deportation. Instead, these students rely on local activist groups and a liberally minded bureaucratic school administration to advocate on their behalf. The policy compromise that the International Academy represents stems in part from a broader political compromise in Alexandria: Segregation is tolerable as long as additional educational resources are delivered to racial minorities and students in poverty. In many ways, despite appearing as a new policy innovation, the International Academy is an extension of old patterns of educational provision and politics.

Mexican American Studies in Tucson, Arizona

In contrast to the recent arrivals in Alexandria, the Mexican American students in Tucson did not migrate to the United States and then enroll in school. Instead, the school district migrated to them. Founded in 1775, Tucson was until 1854 a northern garrison of the Mexican Army. At the conclusion of the Mexican-American War and with the Gadsen Purchase, Tucson became US territory. In 1867 settlers created the first school system in Tucson—with classes taught only in Spanish.[18] Over the years, however, Anglo population growth combined with racial and linguistic discrimination meant that the educational needs of Mexican American students were systematically marginalized.

By the 1970s two desegregation lawsuits—one filed by African American plaintiffs and another by Mexican American plaintiffs—contended that the Tucson Unified School District (TUSD) segregated students and did not provide equal educational opportunities. Eventually merged into a single suit, *Fisher-Mendoza v. Tucson Unified School District* (1978), the lawsuits led to a settlement in which the TUSD began racial integration of the school system and provided additional programs to improve the educational outcomes of black and Mexican American students.[19] In 1981, the TUSD created a black studies program, offering courses in black history and culture.[20]

Additional litigation was necessary to prompt greater attention to the needs of Mexican American students. One case filed in 1987 contended that the TUSD's services for ELL students were inadequate. After the US Department of Education's Office of Civil Rights joined the fray, the parties brokered an agreement dubbed the Alvarez-Jasso Consent Decree in 1994 that provided better identification, placement, and exit criteria for ELL students and more money for ELL programs. In 1996, a group of activists and teachers sought the creation of a Hispanic studies program, aimed at engaging Mexican American students at risk of dropping out.

A number of teachers had somewhat informally been offering courses that engaged the literature, history, and culture of both indigenous and immigrant peoples in the American Southwest, drawing on both critiques of colonization and settlement as well as analyses of existing power and economic inequalities for Mexican Americans. The goal for the Hispanic studies program was to build on this base and develop a series of courses across subject areas and at multiple schools that would represent a coherent plan for serving more holistically the educational needs of Mexican American students.

In response to new lawsuit threats and continuing pressure from activists, the TUSD in 1997 created the Bilingual Education/Hispanic Studies and Second Language Acquisition Review Committee. Composed of parents, community leaders, teachers, administrators, union leaders, University of Arizona professors, and a student representative, the thirty-four-member committee reviewed the existing research on pedagogical approaches to both ELL and Mexican American students and held multiple community engagement meetings. According to some estimates, at least five hundred community members turned out for the meetings. The resulting committee report called for the creation of a Mexican American studies department tasked with creating a K–12 curriculum designed for Mexican American students.

These developments were in part the result of Tucson superintendent George F. Garcia's commitment to multicultural education. Garcia had previously implemented nondiscriminatory multicultural curricula and, during his time as superintendent in Kansas City, Missouri, had administered the expansive desegregation remedy that was at issue in the landmark *Missouri v. Jenkins* litigation.[21] Strategically building political support through the community-based committee, Garcia and the school board were able to adopt a program that responded to activist demands for a culturally responsive education and to ongoing federal litigation that demanded greater attention to the needs of Latino youths.

The creation in 1998 of the Hispanic Studies program—later renamed Mexican American Studies (MAS)—relied on an existing foundation of courses as it constructed a systematic approach toward educating at-risk students. MAS was eventually folded into the TUSD's response to the federal desegregation court consent decree as a means of improving educational opportunity for Latino students. The program primarily focused on the last two years of high school, and its adoption coincided with declining high school dropout rates, particularly among Mexican American students.

In 2003 through the efforts of a new MAS director, Augustine Romero, and a number of talented and committed teachers, the school district found itself at the national forefront of blending culturally relevant pedagogy with progressive educational models that challenged students to analyze their own educational contexts and the distribution of power that produced educational inequity. MAS administrators and faculty saw themselves as emancipatory and even revolutionary educators who would engage students to think critically about their own contexts and undertake actions to transform those inequities. At the center of this exploration were the racial, class, and gender inequalities that structured the educational contexts of these students. Both the US conquest of the Mexican Southwest and the historic discrimination against indigenous, Latino, and immigrant communities in Arizona informed the social and historical contexts in which students learned to analyze their own educational opportunities and the avenues available to transform those opportunities.

One analysis termed the development of this program "the best of times in TUSD and its Mexican American student population" and "an idea that had strong roots in the tolerant and caring Tucson community."[22] Yet the politically charged understanding of how to engage at-risk students did not go without criticism. By 2008 MAS was still small—reaching roughly five hundred students across several high schools—but was drawing increasing fire from conservative state officials who contended that the program's attention to racial and economic inequalities was "radicalizing" students.

In 2007 Tom Horne, state superintendent of public instruction, published a document titled "Open Letter to the Citizens of Tucson" in which he asserted that "the evidence is overwhelming that ethnic studies in the Tucson Unified School District teaches a kind of destructive ethnic chauvinism that the citizens of Tucson should no longer tolerate."[23] Insisting that the program's emphasis on racial and economic inequality was providing students with an illusory sense that they were "oppressed," Horne argued that "students should be taught that this is the land of opportunity, and that if they work hard they can achieve their goals." He concluded the four-page letter with a call for the "citizens" of Tucson to demand the elimination of ethnic studies programs within the school district, insisting that the "TUSD can intimidate its employees. But it cannot intimidate you, the citizens. You are in a comfortable position. You can speak out. . . . The school board represents you. I can use my pulpit to bring out the facts, but only you can bring about change."

Whether Horne's call for "citizens" to demand action was a racially charged use of a code word or simply an effort to rally precisely the power differentials that MAS sought to illustrate is unclear. Either way, Tucson residents did not clamor for the program's repeal—and the federal court overseeing the desegregation suit explicitly called on the TUSD to expand the program.[24]

Arizona Republicans, however, did not allow Tucsonians to set their own course for MAS. As anti-immigrant fervor grew—in significant part because of the efforts of politicians such as Tom Horne, Russell Pearce, and Horne's successor John Huppenthal—the legislature backed a series of bills aimed at the state's immigrant community. After several failed attempts, the legislature eventually passed HB 2281, which barred a school district from offering in its program of instruction any courses or classes that include any of the following:

1. Promote the overthrow of the United States government.
2. Promote resentment toward a race or class of people.
3. Are designed primarily for pupils of a particular ethnic group.
4. Advocate ethnic solidarity instead of the treatment of pupils as individuals.[25]

Although technically the law applied to programs throughout the state, Horne made it clear that it was aimed solely at Tucson's MAS program.

Governor Jan Brewer signed HB 2281 into law two weeks after she approved SB 1070, the notorious anti-immigration law eventually declared unconstitutional in federal courts. SB 1070 and HB 2281 were part of a larger mobilization of public opinion and policy against immigrants (documented and undocumented) in Arizona. The heated rhetoric and persistent language demonizing Mexican Americans in Arizona tapped into long-standing practices of prejudice in the Grand Canyon State. The attack on MAS, however, was particularly focused on Tucson and its long tradition of liberal activism on behalf of migrants. HB 2281 only affected the TUSD, and the subsequent enforcement of the law only sought the termination of MAS, leaving African American and Asian American studies programs unaffected.

In 2010 Save Ethnic Studies, a teachers' group, filed a lawsuit against Horne and the Arizona Department of Education to block the implementation of HB 2281, claiming that singling out MAS was a violation of both Fourteenth Amendment equal protection and First Amendment freedom of expression rights of students and teachers. Tucson's school board declined to join the legal effort against HB 2281, and the litigation did little initially to blunt the state's campaign against MAS. Ultimately, the state's targeted enforcement tested the local policy consensus that MAS was central to the TUSD's efforts to ensure greater educational opportunity, and this sowed growing distrust among the groups previously party to that consensus.

Tucson's long-standing traditions of activism and liberalism stem from the work of religious, community, immigrant, and indigenous groups as well as the role that the University of Arizona plays within the city. These traditions are not without their own racial and class tensions. The push by Arizona's Republican political establishment to eliminate MAS exacerbated tensions, as it radicalized some members of the Tucson community and led others to withdraw from the effort to defend the program. Simultaneously, the Republican action gave legitimacy to anti-immigrant political activists within Tucson who supported the statewide effort to diminish the influence of Mexican Americans, whether recent arrivals or long-standing citizens. Importantly, the focused effort to eliminate one program ultimately fragmented Tucson's liberal consensus that MAS and its activist pedagogy was in the best interests of the TUSD.

As HB 2281 went into effect in January 2011, students, unions, and community groups mobilized. Some members of the school board sought to defuse the situation by altering or reconstituting MAS; others sided outright with state officials who wanted to end the program. School board chair Mark Stegeman sought to make MAS simply a series of elective courses. Doing so, however, meant that these courses would not satisfy Arizona's social studies requirements for high school graduation, forcing students to take traditional history and civics classes in order to graduate (and driving down MAS enrollments).[26] Stegeman's effort, however, was met with resistance from a group of TUSD students who had formed the group United Non-Discriminatory Individuals Demanding Our Studies (UNIDOS) to fight the elimination of MAS. UNIDOS mobilized members to stage a direct action against Stegeman's resolution during the school board meeting at which a vote was scheduled on his plan.[27] The ensuing disruption caused the school board to suspend its vote and cancel the meeting, prompting scorn from conservative media. At the following meeting community members rallied to support UNIDOS and, through demonstration and vociferous opposition, forced the board to table the motion relegating MAS to elective status.

While local politics seethed over whether to suspend the MAS curriculum, the Arizona Department of Education had hired Cambium Learning, Inc., to conduct a "curriculum audit" of MAS. Ultimately, this audit found that MAS as a whole did not in fact violate HB 2281.[28] Despite this finding, Superintendent of Public Instruction Huppenthal (Horne's successor) ordered an additional investigation to be conducted by the Arizona Department of Education. Although the investigation did not visit any classrooms and proceeded without the cooperation of any MAS teachers (who were pursuing their own legal action against HB 2281), state officials concluded that the MAS curriculum violated HB 2281,[29] and in 2011 Huppenthal issued a finding to that effect.

The school board then pursued an appeal through an administrative law judge, who ruled in favor of Huppenthal. The administrative law ruling in hand, Huppenthal reasserted his finding that the TUSD was in violation and withheld 10 percent of its state revenues, as authorized by HB 2281, retroactively assessing the penalty based on his original June 2011 finding.[30] Faced with this financial crisis, the TUSD School Board voted to end the MAS program in January 2012. In dramatic fashion, it also ordered all textbooks that Huppenthal found in violation of HB 2281 to be removed from all MAS classrooms.

Despite the closure of MAS and the departure of many of its teachers and administrators, the lawsuit against the State of Arizona continued. In 2013, the federal district court in Tucson largely found in favor of the state defendants, but the Ninth Circuit Court of Appeals reversed much of that decision in the summer of 2015 and ordered the case to proceed to trial to determine whether the students' and teachers' Fourteenth and First Amendment rights had been violated. The trial, held in the summer of 2017, enabled the plaintiffs to critically cross-examine the claims of Horne, Huppenthal, and others about the nature of MAS teaching and curriculum and to introduce expert witness testimony about the effectiveness of culturally relevant instruction. More sensationally, the plaintiffs were allowed to introduce racist anonymous blog posts written by Superintendent John Huppenthal at the time of HB 2281's enactment and enforcement, posts that had come to light after the elimination of MAS. In short, the trial put on display the racial bias of the law as enacted and enforced in Tucson. As Judge Wallace Tashima stated in his August 2017 ruling, the plaintiffs had introduced "important and direct evidence that racial animus had infected the decision to enact" HB 2281.[31] In December 2017, Tashima placed a permanent injunction against the implementation of HB 2281.

Conclusion

In many ways, the contrast between Alexandria and Tucson is stark: one school system developed a modest school-based program for newcomer students, aware of concerns about political perceptions of "Juan Crow"–style education; another school system developed an innovative and transformative educational program that achieved dramatic results but was shut down within a few years. Yet the two school systems share similarities. They both confront rising white flight and increasing numbers of brown and black students. They both are liberal bastions within relatively conservative states, and both have been under federal supervision as they developed strategies to improve educational outcomes for English learners and immigrant youths. Additionally, both systems confronted historical legacies of discrimination and exclusion and sought to develop liberal, pedagogically responsive policies to engage students who are at high risk of not completing high school. In both contexts, the federal government encouraged, even demanded, significant innovation that required these new policies to be developed.

In the course of that innovative policy making, however, the two school systems played their political cards very differently, yielding diverse outcomes. The local contexts of Tucson meant that challenging state authorities and existing power dynamics in the state would create opportunities for conservatives to undermine a liberal consensus within the city. Despite the court victory, the state's suppression of MAS effectively achieved its objective of destroying the program, fragmenting its talent and making TUSD much more cautious to this day about adopting innovative, culturally relevant pedagogy. In Alexandria, meanwhile, school officials were less transformative (maybe even timid) but may have created an educational reform model that is more sustainable in the local and state contexts, even if it is less effective as a policy response to the needs of students.

The lessons learned in Alexandria and Tucson, however, reveal the depth of local educational innovation in US educational systems and also highlight the influential role that historical patterns play in the creative effort to generate and deploy new ideas. The development of new ideas and new policies for education must confront a past distribution of local power that often systematically suppressed these ideas and policies. Even as preferences (and demographics) of community members shift, producing more egalitarian policies, the political structures and expectations that kept transformative claims at bay in prior eras continue to extend a long hand. The idea of the new order must always confront the legacy of the old—and it does not always win.

CHAPTER 9

Ideas, Institutions, Intercurrence, and the Community Reinvestment Act

Amy Widestrom

In this chapter I examine the role of ideas in the creation and evolution of the Community Reinvestment Act (CRA), originally passed by Congress in 1977 to combat redlining practices by banks and other lending institutions. Policy makers continue to confront considerable obstacles to the successful implementation of the CRA and have engaged in several disjointed efforts to change the law over time.[1] Contemporary liberal lawmakers and activists argue that the CRA is ineffective in part because what passes for compliance is often corporate charity. At the same time, conservative lawmakers and activists say that the CRA creates compliance costs, promotes an anticompetitive environment, and introduces inefficiencies in the market and, more recently, created the foreclosure crisis that began in 2008.[2] While there has been and is little agreement about how best to design and implement the law, there does seem to be agreement that it is not working very well.[3]

After discussing how we can think broadly about ideas and institutions in political analysis, I review the history of the CRA and examine the evolution of the law in terms of ideational and institutional orders. I conceive of ideas in the policy process as singular propositions, and with regard to the CRA I focus on ideas related to government regulation, federalism, and the separation of powers. The expression of these ideas over time forms ideational orders, or "configurations that serve to organize some reasonably broad aspect of political life over some span of time."[4] This is the concept of "order" I apply in this analysis.

Ideational Orders, Institutional Orders, and Intercurrence

In the study of American political development, a "political order" has been defined as "a regular, predictable, and interconnected pattern of institutional and ideological arrangements that structures political life in a given place at a given time" with "multiple institutional and ideological components, which shape and constrain political action by providing incentives, opportunities, and grounds for legitimation to political actors."[5] At the same time, however, "political arrangements are rarely, if ever, the products of a coherent, total vision of politics that informs institutions and ideas and knits them together into a unified whole . . . they are inevitably the products of compromise, partial and circumscribed, incoherent and jury-rigged . . . they will collide and chafe, creating an ungainly configuration of political circumstances that has no clear resolution, presenting actors with contradictory and multidirectional imperatives and opportunities."[6] Orren and Skowronek have attempted to capture the contingency and complexity of political orders as "intercurrence," in which "the normal condition of the polity will be that of multiple, incongruous authorities operating simultaneously."[7]

Research in this vein forces scholars to understand the historical construction of politics. Specifically, old and new systems of governance can operate simultaneously, complex institutional relationships produce multiple mechanisms of ordering and control that are just as likely to produce conflict as they are coordination, and this conflict, or "friction," not only can be problematic but can also drive or affect political development.[8] Federal urban policy is an ideal test case for examining intercurrent orders because it almost always involves complex local-state-federal relationships. This can be further complicated by policies relying on third-party actors, such as special-purpose governments (e.g., housing authorities) and private industries (e.g., banking).

In the case of the CRA the ideational order—that is, the nature and structure of ideas—defined specific ideational commitments that structured debate and thus limited the range of policy options.[9] More specifically, three distinct ideational and institutional orders emerged in the evolution of the CRA. First, lawmakers were motivated by a commitment to the idea that banks were free-market actors that should be relatively unencumbered by government regulations. Second, lawmakers had an ideological commitment to federalism that ultimately favored devolution. Finally, lawmakers had specific ideas about the constitutional principle of separation of powers, made manifest in the distinct institutional relationship between the executive and legislative branches of the federal government.

Institutional and Ideational Orders, Intercurrence, and the Community Reinvestment Act

The origins of the CRA are often traced to the efforts of community activists, especially those organized under the group National Peoples' Action (NPA), founded in 1972 to combat urban disinvestment and redlining, a practice used by banks to deny loans to minorities as well as residents of low-income neighborhoods.[10] The NPA is also often given a good deal of credit for passage of the Housing and Community Development Acts (HCDA) of 1974 and 1977, and the CRA was established as Title VIII of the 1977 HCDA.[11] At the same time, the CRA also fit into a larger pattern of community development laws passed in the 1970s, including the Community Development Block Grant (CDBG) and Urban Development Action Grant (UDAG) programs. The CRA, the UDAG, and the CDBG all relied on local institutions (both political and financial) to implement policies while requiring only minimal federal oversight.

The CRA encourages banks to lend in low- and moderate-income areas in their community but, importantly, does not require it. Over time, however, lawmakers have implemented regulations that do require evaluation of banks' lending activities by the Board of Governors of the Federal Reserve System, the Federal Deposit Insurance Corporation, the Office of the Comptroller of the Currency, and the Office of Thrift Supervision.[12] Today, the CRA requires that federally insured depository institutions undergo examination by federal agencies to check compliance with the law, and that compliance, or lack thereof, is "taken into account in considering an institution's application for deposit facilities, including mergers and acquisitions."[13]

In early 1977 prior to passage of the CRA, the US House Committee on Banking, Currency and Housing embarked on a series of hearings on the rebirth of the American city and the progress (or lack thereof) that had been made under the 1974 HDCA. The Senate pursued its own hearings on community credit needs in March 1977. These hearings set the stage for the debates surrounding passage of the CRA, in October 1977, and reflect the ideational and institutional commitments embedded in the law.

Witnesses in these early hearings called for an amendment to the 1974 HCDA that would increase regulatory oversight of lending institutions to ensure that they would lend money in low- and moderate-income communities, especially those that were minority communities. Yet lawmakers also had clear ideas about the virtues of banks as market actors that should not be overburdened by regulations through, for instance, a system of mandatory credit reallocation. As William Proxmire, chairman of the Senate Committee on Banking, Housing, and Urban Affairs, said of the CRA, "Whatever we can do to prevent it from being a credit allocation bill I want to do. What this bill would do would be to try to make the banks more sensitive than they have been in the past."[14] Thus, the CRA sought to regulate the banking industry, though with very little federal oversight. The initial law only stated that "each appropriate Federal financial supervisory agency shall include in its annual report to the Congress a section outlining the actions it has taken to carry out its responsibilities under this title"[15] and that "regulations to carry out the purposes of this title shall be published by each appropriate Federal financial supervisory agency."[16] The law did not specify criteria for assessing compliance, and more importantly, there were no punishments for noncompliance. It is not unusual for lawmakers to leave rule making for policy implementation up to regulators. However, the brevity of the CRA and the lack of any consequences for noncompliance suggest a real hesitance on the part of lawmakers to hamstring private financial institutions by dictating their lending practices.

Critics of the CRA started calling for amendments almost as soon as the bill had been passed into law. Hearings were held in 1978 during which three major amendments were ultimately proposed that focused on increasing federal oversight (such as increased visits by agency auditors and increased auditor tracking of lending practices), providing clearer guidelines for how to increase equality in lending practices, and establishing specific guidelines for regulators to better assess whether or not banks were in compliance with CRA suggestions.

All of these amendments sought to strengthen the regulation of lending institutions, which of course required that lawmakers revisit their ideational commitment to maintaining a free lending market. The debate over these issues reached a fever pitch in 1981 and 1982, when Congress launched specific investigations into CRA compliance of several banks in New York City. At one committee hearing Representative Benjamin S. Rosenthal (D-NY) demanded of Thomas Murray, vice president of Chase Manhattan Bank, "Does it offend you like it offends me that you loaned more money for mortgages in

Bethesda than you did in Brooklyn?"[17] When Murray attempted to evade the question, Rosenthal said, "I think we are going to have to pursue this matter with a little more vigor than we have so far. We will have to hold a hearing in New York City, either in executive session in which you may want to be more forthcoming, or by way of a subpoena."[18] Members of Congress made good on that threat with a hearing in New York City of the Subcommittee of the Committee on Government Operations in March 1982. Yet stricter mechanisms were not added to the law, due in part to the fact that bank executives were neither more forthcoming nor more supportive of greater government intervention and in part because of a general trend toward deregulation and devolution during President Ronald Reagan's administration.[19]

This brief attempt to amend and expand the regulatory authority of the CRA suggests at least two things. First, lawmakers were not afraid of challenging large powerful interests in their own districts to pursue remedies addressing the shortcomings of the CRA. Second, the banks' ability to thwart new regulations under the CRA was due in part to their own influence and actions but also to the larger deregulatory and devolutionary trends that characterized the early Reagan administration. These hearings also highlight the extent to which the nature of government oversight of lending institutions with regard to the CRA had been left unresolved in the law. This established the parameters for debate among future lawmakers and the contours of the ideational order regarding the role of the federal government in ensuring community access to credit.

The first major amendment to the CRA came twelve years after its creation in the form of the 1989 Financial Institutions Reform, Recovery and Enforcement (FIRRE) Act, the formulation and passage of which was facilitated by the savings and loan crisis of the late 1980s, which practically required new government interventions into at least one portion of the banking industry. This also followed the Democratic capture of the Senate in 1986, which unified party control of Congress. Among other things, FIRRE stipulated that "upon the conclusion of each examination of an insured depository institution . . . the appropriate Federal financial supervisory agency shall prepare a written evaluation of the institution's record of meeting the credit needs of its entire community, including low- and moderate-income neighborhoods."[20] While there were still no repercussions for noncompliance, regulators became obligated to submit a written evaluation of each lending institution insured by the Federal Deposit Insurance Corporation. More importantly, meeting the credit needs of low- and moderate-income neighborhoods was established through FIRRE as the explicit goal of the CRA, which placed greater responsibility on regulators to assess specific outcomes, cementing the complex relationship between Congress, executive agencies, private institutions, and the communities in which these private institutions operated.

Yet the ideational order that underwrote the CRA—and in which weak regulatory tools were an inherent part—allowed little space for anything other than incremental changes. This ultimately made it difficult for lawmakers to move much beyond the enforcement of lending practices codified in 1977. In other words, while individual actors are motivated to act by specific ideas, they operate within an ideational context that may or may not be defined by ideas that they share. Thus, as Senator Alan Dixon (D-IL) noted during his questioning of Housing and Urban Development (HUD) assistant secretary Austin Fitts at a 1989 hearing, "The law does not direct you now to look at lending practices," only at whether or not the institution was meeting community needs. Fitts responded that "there has been a preference to use testers in the areas where we are receiving the most complaints" rather than direct regulation of lending practices, indicating executive branch reluctance toward more stringent guidelines from Congress.[21]

The debate among lawmakers continued over the proper stringency of regulation and how best to achieve the stated goals of the CRA. In 1991 the law was strengthened to require relevant federal agencies to include data regarding CRA compliance with their examination of financial institutions. And in 1992, the Federal Housing Enterprises Financial Safety and Soundness Act (FHEFSSA) indirectly affected the CRA by stipulating that HUD could (but importantly, not should) establish quantitative goals for supporting affordable housing that government-sponsored enterprises (for instance, Fannie Mae and Freddie Mac) had to meet, thereby affecting a segment of the housing market—low-income housing specifically—that should benefit from the CRA. In effect, these changes sought to change lending practices by strengthening regulatory rules that HUD could exercise over government-sponsored enterprises rather than dictating specific actions required by banks to comply with the CRA.

These changes ultimately did little to radically improve oversight and regulation. A more substantial change came in 1994 with the Riegle-Neal Interstate Banking and Branching Efficiency Act, passed in part to repeal restrictions on interstate banking that had been established in 1956.[22] The 1994 act allowed CRA ratings to be considered when states were determining whether to allow a national bank to establish branches within its state.

Thus, an act that removed regulations paradoxically strengthened the CRA by incorporating a greater role for state-level evaluation, which was itself a reflection of the devolutionary pattern of the "new federalism" reflected in much of the Reagan-era policies and in the contemporaneous changes to federal welfare policy that led to Temporary Assistance to Needy Families.

Thus, between 1977 and 1995 historical events such as the savings and loan crisis and the political trend toward policy deregulation and devolution, along with the institutional characteristics of the branches of the federal government, affected the ways in which lawmakers thought about, codified, and changed the relationship between the public and private sectors with regard to the CRA. Both the idea of the free market and the institutional relationship between these two sectors embedded within the law changed over time and at certain critical junctures—1989 and 1994 specifically—that were themselves the result of historical trends, legislative attributes, and timing. Yet the change was incremental, ultimately reflecting the original ideas captured in the CRA that had created the initial ideational and institutional orders. In this way, the idea of limiting the free enterprise of banks became only slightly more acceptable over time, with the regulatory force of the CRA primarily strengthened through rule making, while the institutional relationships responsible for implementation and oversight became more complex.

Federalism as an Ideational and Institutional Order

Witnesses in the 1976 and 1977 House and Senate hearings on urban disinvestment argued for more funding from the federal government to cities. Yet witnesses also contended that money by itself "cannot fundamentally change or correct the problem we are faced with. . . . At the national level, clearly one ground rule change that is called for is for the Federal government to take responsibility for welfare and health."[23] This was joined by calls for "the Federal government [to] provide the primary source of funding for education, health and welfare."[24] Local activists also argued that lawmakers needed to increase their commitment to local control over funding allocation and redevelopment goals. As one witness, Robert Merriam, chairman of the Advisory Commission on Intergovernmental Relations, stated, "The Federal government's role in establishing better balance in the American federal system is already well established . . . [and] to this end ACIR recommends that the Federal government . . . place more emphasis upon enhancing the capability of State and local governments to solve their own urban problems with their own decisions about how best to apply Federal aid in their own communities."[25]

In general, witnesses were adamant that a strong federal hand in urban policy was needed but also voiced a simultaneous commitment to the idea of local control and locally defined solutions to urban problems. At the same time, there was a notable distrust among lawmakers toward local policy actors. For instance, in questioning a witness, Paul Tsongas (D-MA) repeatedly implied that the problem with urban policy was in fact with federal involvement, which might obviate the need for local control and administration. In one hearing he asked, "Given the amount of money that the Federal Government has put into the cities, however we may come out on whether we think it is enough or too much or whatever, what difference would it make in terms of the competence of the administrators?"[26] This simultaneously sounds like a critique of federal involvement in urban policy and a weak statement of support for, or at least apathy about, increased local control because the local authority does not really matter. The tension between federal and local authority displayed here may be driven in part by the fact that Tsongas represented Massachusetts's Fifth District, which included the city of Lowell and had only elected three Democrats in its entire history. Tsongas might have felt electoral pressure to question federal intrusion in local affairs and to support increased local control, but as a Democrat he may not have been wholly committed to this position. This friction between local actors wanting control but strong federal guidance and federal elected officials expressing skepticism about local competence also became a key aspect of the institutional ordering mechanism embedded within the CRA.

The CRA originally only encouraged lending practices and did not establish any rules or regulations to test compliance, nor did it identify an agency to oversee compliance, demonstrating reluctance on the part of lawmakers to meddle in local (and private) affairs. The 1989 reform of the CRA required additional reporting on banks' CRA compliance, specifically documenting lending activities in low- and moderate-income communities, even if it did not provide for any sanctions for noncompliance (or rewards for compliance). This suggests a shift in thinking whereby lawmakers now recognized banks as being partially culpable in creating urban disinvestment while still acknowledging that government had a role in mitigating it, though importantly not shifting responsibility or authority down to local units.

Just prior to passage of the FHEFSSA in 1992, Senator Alan Cranston (D-CA) noted that the "CRA has been in force for 15 years. Presumably more than enough time to work out any procedural or process problems. Regrettably, that does not appear to have been the case. It seems that we are still struggling with the basics of implementing this law."[27] Indeed, a year later lawmakers were asking about the government's role in regulating the policy: "As lawmakers, I think we tend to like to make laws. My question to you is, do we need any more laws under this [Clinton] administration to achieve our goals stated here?"[28] These statements suggest ongoing tension between federal government intervention to ensure the provision of adequate resources within communities to address community needs and sufficient empowerment of state and local governments in implementing the CRA. Interestingly, the entire point of lax federal involvement was initially to empower state and local governments, and yet at the inception and subsequent revisions of the CRA, federal lawmakers demonstrated reticence about relinquishing control.

It is, however, important to note that these hearings do reveal the role that local officials and activists played in the policy-making process. Local practitioners and activists ranging from Michael Bodaken, community investment coordinator under Mayor Tom Bradley in Los Angeles in 1992, to Gilda Haas, head of a coalition of local grassroots organizations called Accountable Investment, testified in front of the Senate Subcommittee on Housing and Urban Affairs.[29] Congress's obligation to oversee the executive branch required that it hear testimony from those within the communities that the CRA was designed to help, which allowed local politicians, practitioners, and activists to pressure policy makers. Local actors conveyed to Congress local needs, redevelopment goals, and the resources necessary to achieve these goals,[30] input that further complicated the ordering mechanisms that structured the CRA. In fact, congressional oversight reinforced and reproduced previously established local-federal relationships and complicated them by layering new relationships on top of old, a key aspect of intercurrence. Indeed, the reform of 1994, which allowed states to use CRA compliance when determining if a national bank could establish interstate branches within their borders, added some heft to the law but also added another layer of governmental authority—state government—reinforcing the congressional commitment to federalism.

President Bill Clinton's administration complicated the layers of actors, activists, and authorities with its homeownership initiative, under which HUD secretary Henry Cisneros planned "to work with leaders of the housing industry, with nonprofit organizations, and with leaders at every level of government to develop a plan to boost homeownership in America to an all-time high by the end of this century."[31] This alternative push to achieve goals similar to those in the CRA, but outside of the CRA, included many of the same actors involved in promoting compliance with the CRA, such as local activists and lending institutions. As a result, the Clinton homeownership initiative complicated the efforts of local, state, and private actors to comply with the CRA by introducing a new programmatic vehicle and policy venue to achieve similar ends. Thus, an ideational order emerged that was committed to federalism—a policy forged by the combined efforts of local, state, and federal authorities—followed by an institutional ordering committed to this federalist arrangement, and devolution more specifically, that shaped the development of the CRA over time.

Separation of Powers as an Ideational and Institutional Order

The final ideational and institutional orders shaping the CRA are ideas about the relationship between the legislative and executive branches of the federal government. There is a clear need for experts to regulate compliance with the CRA, as they can provide objective assessment of financial institutions. Yet the "apolitical" nature of executive agencies may harm their ability to accurately assess banks' responses to community needs, such as elections or town meetings, because there is no clear feedback process from the community to an executive agency.[32] Therefore, Congress has the responsibility of encouraging expert assessment, opinion, and advice regarding CRA compliance, which requires some knowledge of political context, while simultaneously preventing agencies from becoming too politicized. These contradictions manifested themselves in congressional reluctance to provide guidance on how to enforce the CRA or provide tools for experts embedded within federal agencies to do so.

Hearings documenting the development of the CRA include repeated references to the role of federal regulators in enforcing the law. From the beginning, community groups lobbied for additional training so regulators could properly identify and assess discriminatory practices, increased enforcement power so regulators could punish those not in compliance, and increased guidelines so regulators knew exactly what was expected of them. Conversely, the agencies responsible for enforcing compliance consistently claimed that they were appropriately enforcing the CRA and resisted congressional oversight. So, while some lawmakers were wary of too much federal regulation of the private lending market, some in the executive branch were wary of too much legislative interference.

The debate over legislative oversight and executive agency autonomy was evident in the hearings that immediately followed passage of the CRA. The third substantial amendment proposed during the 1978 hearings provided more explicit language regarding training agency auditors and ensuring compliance with and enforcement of the CRA. This was proposed because, as Andrew Biemiller, director of the Department of Legislation at the AFL-CIO, testified,

> The agencies provide only suggestions as to broad options on how a lending institution should go about determining the geographic community it intends to serve. In effect, each institution is left to establish its own criteria to delineate the area that will comprise its entire community. . . . The proposed regulations provide only an outline of the factors to be considered during the evaluation of an institution's responsiveness to community credit needs. . . . Is the evaluation to be on an ad hoc basis with each institution in a position to argue that it did not fail to meet any stipulated criteria?[33]

In 1981 when, upon repeated proposed amendments to enforce procedures that would require banks to serve specific geographic areas, Richard T. Pratt, chairman of the Federal Home Loan Bank Board, testified that increased enforcement guidelines would be equivalent to improper "bootstrapping" of federal agencies, which typically refers to an internally managed or self-starting process without external influence or control. For example, in business "when you decide to bootstrap, you commit to fund primary development and growth through internal cash-flow from real life customers."[34] Thus, while local officials, policy practitioners, and activists wanted increased governmental regulations and agency enforcement, agencies wanted to maintain the status quo or become more independent from congressional "bootstrapping," believing that it increased their legitimacy and autonomy and was better for the market.

Daniel Carpenter's work highlights the long-running conflict over the need for executive branch agencies that are overseen by and cooperative with Congress while remaining independently legitimate.[35] My discussion here highlights the role of this conflict in the development of the CRA and shows that the conflict created an ideational order that pervaded policy decisions because policy makers had yet to come to terms with the amount of regulatory oversight required to strike a balance between agency responsiveness and autonomy. This tension, then, was crucial not only to the development of the American state, as Carpenter argues, but also to subsequent policy development and effectiveness. Indeed, one reason Congress may have allowed CRA compliance as a factor for determining whether a national bank could establish interstate branches within its borders in the 1994 reform may have been to provide an institutional mechanism to enforce compliance—strengthening the institutional ordering of local, state, and federal governments in the absence of strengthening the institutional ordering of the executive and legislative branches—because they could not bring the proper executive agencies in line otherwise. This power sharing between federal and state regulators formalized a federalist structure in the CRA and made this institutional ordering mechanism more complex while weakening the ordering mechanism and highlighting the tensions between the executive and legislative branches.

Conclusion

Passage of the CRA established elaborate and complex ideational and institutional orders that evolved over time and at critical moments in history when small but important changes were made to the law. In other words, actors in federal, state, and local institutions as well as the public and private sectors have their own ideas, and they intersect in particular ways and at distinct moments in history, which generates ordering mechanisms that evolve over time. Ignoring this has hurt our understanding of urban politics and policy. I have suggested intercurrence as a way to understand the relationships between ideas and institutions that shape urban politics and policy. This is a framework that requires the examination of the ideational orders, or the arrangement of specific ideas employed in specific political arenas motivated by specific types of actors, and institutional orders, or the historical and organizational arrangements of institutions within a political arena.[36]

I selected the CRA to test and to begin building a theory of urban political development using intercurrence as a framework. To be sure, there are important limitations of this study that must be acknowledged. First, intercurrence is a broad and messy analytical framework, so determining more specific methodological tools would be useful. For example, scholars could develop a more precise conceptual map that layers ideational and institutional orders in specific policy arenas, allowing for a clearer articulation of when and where these orders overlap and/or intersect. Second, my argument that intercurrence is a useful analytical tool for examining the political development of urban politics and policy will be strengthened by future studies that use it to investigate other urban political phenomena and different urban policies. It is possible that the ideational and institutional orders I have uncovered define other urban political and policy changes as well and could rise to the level of a comprehensive theory of urban political development. But it is just as likely that other studies would uncover other ideational and institutional orders, making this study one step in building that larger theory. In any case, this is an important contribution to this effort, and this examination of the CRA has revealed that important ideational and institutional orders drive political policy changes related to the CRA.

PART III

Ideas and Urban Political Development in Comparative Context

CHAPTER 10

Immigrant Identities and Integration in the United States and Canada

Mara Sidney

Research has long identified public policies as containers and carriers of specific ideas about problems and their causes.[1] Policy formulation and implementation create and carry forward ideas about groups of people affected by those policies.[2] These ideas shape the political identities of group members and thus the actions that they undertake.[3] This volume's authors argue that such theoretical perspectives can productively highlight underexplored aspects of urban political development. In this chapter I examine how national immigration policies shape immigrant identities at the local level. More specifically, I examine Canadian and US immigration and integration policies and the ideas they advance about immigrants. I then compare local immigrant-serving organizations and their work in Newark, New Jersey, and Ottawa, Ontario, to examine how these policies translate into local political behavior and programs. Nonprofit organizations now are widely recognized as key political and policy actors locally;[4] thus, tracing how they respond and act in relation to policy ideas established nationally makes visible an important dimension of urban politics. While this chapter focuses on a particular moment in time in two countries and two cities, it lays the groundwork for comparing historical and subsequent evolution of these key urban actors with a focus on the frictions and consistencies between ideas emanating from different levels.

Canadian national and local policies define immigrants as prospective workers and as clients with distinctive challenges that policy should address.

In the United States, the overall thrust of national policy is to define immigrants as criminals, although local organizations (in Newark at least) adopt and communicate alternative ideas, namely that immigrants are legitimate local participants in social, economic, and political life and members of the city's racial and ethnic groups who compete for political influence and government responsiveness.

My analysis focuses on avenues through which integration processes intersect with government, linking these to particular ideas about who immigrants are politically. I explore two types of immigrant identities rooted in the types of claims that they make on the state: as clients knowledgeable about how service agencies can meet their needs and as rights holders equally deserving of a place in the city as native-born residents. I trace how local institutions, nongovernmental organizations (NGOs), and practices in my case cities intersect with national policies to embed and perpetuate these identities. While there is a consistent set of ideas about immigrants and integration across national and local levels in my Canadian case, that is not true in the United States case, where national policy ideas diverge from locally produced ideas about immigrants and integration.

Studying the link between national and local policies is not new. Urban scholars have analyzed how national urban and housing policies shape local policy decisions and local development and have also analyzed the impact of national policy on local political behavior and the impact of federalism, national transportation policies and, more recently, criminal justice policies and mass incarceration on prospects for regional collaboration, local policy making, and individual political participation.[5] This chapter argues for examining the linkage between national immigration policies and urban immigrant identities and the local political processes that unfold.

Comparing the United States and Canada is particularly fruitful for demonstrating these effects, because the two countries can be seen as "close cousins" but with very different immigration policies.[6] The United States and Canada share commonalities as settler societies with high rates of immigration, historical ties to Britain, ethnic and racial hierarchies and oppression, and advanced economies with traditions of civic nationalism. These commonalities exist concurrently with differences in national founding histories and core racial and ethnic conflicts and settlements, differences in emphasis of immigration policies, levels of public support for immigration, and some integration outcomes.

National Policies: Workers, Clients, Criminals

Canadian immigration policy emphasizes immigrants' contributions to the economy, defining them as important and necessary ingredients in the workforce. Canadian integration policies make propositions about new immigrants' needs for integration into society. By contrast, US immigration policy, with its sharper focus on enforcement against unauthorized entry, defines immigrants as criminals, and its lack of a national integration policy suggests the idea that meeting immigrant needs is not a public concern. The Canadian national government has long maintained—and arguably increased—its control over all aspects of immigration policy, including selection, enforcement, settlement, and citizenship. Even as other actors including provinces, employers, cities, and nonprofit organizations are invited to take part in the implementation of policy, its design and oversight remain primarily centralized. Shifts to executive authority for alterations in policy have taken it largely out of the legislative sphere and into the ministerial and agency sphere, also increasing centralization.[7] In the United States, by contrast, the national government controls selection, enforcement, and citizenship, with the window for unilateral executive action smaller; the courts and legislature are substantially involved in policy making. Another important contrast is that settlement is not a sphere of national policy in the United States.[8]

Canada

Canadian officials assess applicants for immigrant visas primarily in terms of how immigrants will contribute to the workforce. The country offers three years of assistance to new arrivals, with the primary aim of labor force integration. The national government also supports academic research on immigrant integration, and its programs advance the idea that collaboration and knowledge sharing across stakeholders can improve integration outcomes. As such, Canadian policy frames immigrants as workers, as clients of assistance programs, and as holders of knowledge about their needs that could be shared with officials and staff members of immigrant-assistance programs.

With Canada's low fertility rates and an aging population, Canadian officials recognize that labor force growth increasingly relies on immigrants.[9] The country's "point system," adopted in 1967, quantified the economic contributions of immigrants by assigning points needed for admission into the country on the basis of fluency in either English or French, educational attainment, and age (younger favored over older). Changes to the system in 2002 awarded more points than previously to educational attainment, language fluency, and managerial, professional, and technical work experience. Since the 1990s immigrants admitted under economic categories, as opposed to refugees or for family reunification, eclipsed those in other classes. Policy makers have focused on the need to attract highly skilled workers so that Canada can be globally competitive in knowledge-based industries.[10]

Recent changes reflect efforts to fine-tune Canada's immigrant flow to the country's economic needs, to create a "fast and flexible system of economic immigration" and a "tailored immigration flow."[11] For example, in early 2014 the citizenship and immigration minister announced a fast-track system based on matching prospective immigrants' skills and training to available jobs. Provinces and employers would have access to a database and could select applicants whose visas could be processed within six months rather than the more typical two years.[12]

National policy shapes both immigrant selection and integration. Since 1974 the Immigration Settlement and Adaptation Program has funded NGOs to provide services such as "reception, orientation, translation, interpretation and employment-related services" to newcomers.[13] NGOs receiving grants came to be known individually as "settlement organizations" and collectively as "the settlement sector." In 1990 funding for integration programs increased substantially with the introduction of the national Immigrant Integration Strategy, which conceived of integration as a two-way process through which both immigrants and Canadians would adapt to one another and introduced a series of new programs for which immigrants were eligible during their first three years of residence (prior to their eligibility for citizenship). In 2008 the national government emphasized cross-sectoral partnerships at the local level, with a pilot program in Ontario in 2008, in which federal grants funded strategic visioning and planning for immigrant integration that would connect stakeholders in local government, settlement organizations, other NGOs, and the private sector.

United States

Security and border enforcement objectives dominate the US immigration agenda. This means that national policy largely advances the idea that immigrants are criminals. Immigrant visa allocations prioritize family reunification, with a smaller set of visas issued to workers who have already secured jobs. In conjunction with the lack of national integration programs, one might say that US immigration policy advances the idea that immigrants do not deserve public assistance because they are criminals or do not need it because, if not criminals, they are members of families or are already plugged into the labor force and can thus be "on their own" to use these networks to settle into their new home.

"E pluribus unum" (out of many, one) appears on the US national seal and on many of its coins, and the phrase "a nation of immigrants" is part of the national narrative. Yet the country has been at worst exclusionary and at best ambivalent toward immigration. Certainly since the 1990s and especially after the terrorist attacks of September 11, 2001 (9/11), immigration policy has focused primarily on removing immigrants without visas and/or with criminal records and preventing such migrants from coming to the United States in the first place. As Meissner et al. found in 2012, "the US government spends more on its immigration enforcement agencies than on all its other principal criminal federal law enforcement agencies combined."[14]

The implementation of the "enforcement first" US immigration policy occurs primarily within the Department of Homeland Security's divisions of Immigration, Customs and Enforcement; Customs and Border Protection; and Citizenship and Immigration Services. Since 9/11, there has been an increased use of two 1996 laws to engage the manpower of local law enforcement in the immigration enforcement effort, expedite deportation proceedings, and limit the rights of detainees. In addition, President Barack Obama's administration developed the Secure Communities program, which requires state and local police to send the fingerprints of arrested people to federal officials, who will check for past criminal records and prior deportation orders. Called "deporter in chief" by immigrant rights advocates, Obama had deported a record 2 million people as of the spring of 2014, a number that President Bush (the previous record holder) had only reached after eight years of office.[15]

Finally, Donald Trump campaigned with the slogan "Build the Wall" and signed a series of executive orders restricting travel that came to be known as the "Muslim Ban," indicating a continuing depiction of immigrants as threats to security. The Supreme Court upheld a version in May 2018 that prohibits US entry for nationals of seven countries, six of which are predominantly Muslim. Trump ramped up enforcement across the country against undocumented immigrants, eliminating the priority on those with criminal records that Obama had put into place. In addition, border agents now turn away many people requesting asylum at the southern border because of a stated lack of capacity to process them, and agents have separated children from parents found to be entering the country without papers, this latter practice sparking widespread protests and a legal injunction in June 2018. President Trump's rhetoric continues to criminalize migrants: "You wouldn't believe how bad these people are. These aren't people, these are animals, and we're taking them out of the country at a level and at a rate that's never happened before."[16]

With a few exceptions, the most frequent topic of discussion on immigration policy by elected officials and candidates is the problem of illegal immigration and the need for border enforcement. The dominance of the discourse of illegality places limits on the sorts of policy changes that are possible; even if some political actors would like to extend benefits or take a different approach, they are working within a political environment colored by security concerns.[17] While many members of Congress support comprehensive reform that would create a path to legalization for unauthorized immigrants as well as other changes, such as expanding the number of high-skilled visas and continuing to fine-tune immigration enforcement, any such bill has for many years running eventually met opposition in either the House or the Senate strong enough to thwart passage. Obama used executive actions to address problems with the detention and deportation system, attempt to tailor deportation to serious criminals by granting greater discretion to immigration personnel, and create a stay of deportation for eligible youths. He unsuccessfully requested funds from Congress to cope with a surge of unauthorized youths coming from Central America.

In contrast to the ideas embedded in Canadian integration policy, the ideas suggested by the lack of US integration policy are that socioeconomic integration is a matter of private concern rather than for public policy. Thus, immigrants themselves should figure out and finance their settlement in the United States.[18] A scattershot set of quite small programs exists to help immigrants with the naturalization process, including with language learning. Some scholars view the protection of minority rights as part of the US integration framework, but these are not geared to immigrants in particular. One exception is a 1982 Supreme Court case that established the right of undocumented immigrant children to a free public education. The Obama administration also provided limited funding through a competitive grant program to five "Networks for Integrating New Americans," which in a way advanced the idea that NGOs were appropriate providers of help to immigrants, as most of these programs funded NGOs to provide services. On the other hand, since the mid-1990s several policy changes can be understood as damaging to immigrant integration. The federal government has withdrawn support for native-language instruction in the public schools and has placed limits on immigrants' eligibility for public health care and social welfare programs.

Linking National Policy to Local Action

My summaries of Canadian and US immigration policies highlight the underlying ideas that define either countries' general policy thrusts. Canada, of course, also engages in immigration enforcement, just as the United States also admits immigrants based on work-related criteria. Yet seen on the whole, the policies of either country propose different ideas about immigrants, and these ideas can be seen in the work of immigrant-serving NGOs and immigrant advocates in the Canadian and US cities that I examine here. NGOs mediate between immigrants and public policies and public institutions, often introduce immigrants to social and political life in cities, and play a role in advocating for immigrant-friendly policies. How they do their work conveys messages about how they see their members.[19] In both Ottawa and Newark, many NGO staff members are immigrants themselves.

In Ottawa, NGOs provide services to immigrants intended to help them find work, learn English or French, find housing, enroll their children in school, and enroll in the national health care system. NGOs also work collaboratively with prospective employers, institutions of higher education, and city agencies to determine how Ottawa can better meet immigrants' needs. In Newark, without funding to implement a federal menu of integration-related services, NGOs create their own menus and messages, and some organizations spend time addressing the precarious position of unauthorized immigrants in the city, partly by contesting the enforcement policy message of criminalization and partly by advocating for local policies to reduce vulnerability and to promote integration. They assert themselves as rightful claimants to power in the city and to responsiveness from elected officials. Thus, in Ottawa immigrants are cast as clients of settlement services who hold knowledge about how to meet their needs, while in Newark they are cast as claimants to an electorally based and rights-based political space in the city and in the country.

Newark and Ottawa make for a somewhat unusual comparison. The two cities differ in population size, population composition, economic base and economic health, and the socioeconomic status of city residents. That said, their immigrant population share is comparable, and each city has characteristics that provide an interesting context in which to examine the politics of immigrant integration. Newark is a poor and predominantly African American city with a history of ethnic and racial political competition and conflict; the city would thus seem to be a hard case in terms of welcoming a new immigrant constituency with new claims. Ottawa's immigrant population is well educated, as is its general population, and as the seat of national government Ottawa has long been a bilingual city, unusual for the province of Ontario; with a strong safety net and welfare state in Canada and the high education of many immigrants, Ottawa would seem to be a best-case scenario for immigrant integration.

My aim is not to argue for strict causality of ideas across cases using quasi-scientific logic that aims to hold other factors constant. Indeed, I am not sure from a theoretical standpoint whether ideas can be singly determinative of outcomes. I instead aim to trace national ideas within local political processes to generate insights about differences and convergences in these settings. This can be a point of departure for further comparison and understanding of the ways that integration policies unfold—a strategy of "launching distinctive analyses from specific urban contexts . . . into wider conversations."[20]

Newark, New Jersey

In raw numbers, New Jersey has the sixth-largest immigrant population in the United States, but in terms of population share, the state has the third-largest percent of immigrants after California and New York. Brookings Institution researchers call the New York City–northern New Jersey area a continuous immigrant gateway.[21] Newark is the state's largest city, with a population of about 275,000. At 26 percent, its share of immigrants is higher than that of the state as a whole. Adjoining cities have even higher proportions of immigrants. Newark's immigrant groups come from Latin America, Europe, and Africa. The top ten countries of origin are Brazil, Ecuador, Portugal, the Dominican Republic, El Salvador, Ghana, Haiti, Jamaica, Nigeria, and Mexico.[22]

Newark is a quintessential American industrial city that thrived more or less through World War II and then entered a period of economic and population decline stemming primarily from suburbanization, economic restructuring, and racial discrimination. It is known for riots in 1967 that brought the National Guard into the city in tanks and resulted in injury, loss of life, and property destruction. Newark leaders and residents have struggled with high poverty rates, high crime rates, and attendant social problems, along with economic disinvestment. Signs of revitalization starting in the 1990s have persisted, albeit slowed by the most recent economic downturn.

Since 1970 Newark has been a majority-black city. The city's first black mayor was elected in the early 1970s. The city experienced population declines for forty years until around 2000, just at the time when immigration rates increased. The Latino population is now 33 percent. In a city racially segregated and organized politically by wards, this demographic change has had political consequences. Of the city's nine council members in 2017, three were Puerto Rican, one was Portuguese, and five were African American. As a result of immigration, the ethnic backgrounds of the city's Latinos are shifting, reflecting a declining dominance of Puerto Ricans and a growth in Central and South Americans.

Until recently, Newark city leaders had been somewhat passive in terms of explicit immigrant policy. The previous mayor, Cory Booker, emphasized early in his first term that Newark was a "sanctuary city," meaning that city agencies were prohibited from asking about legal status or sharing that information with federal agencies. On the other hand, advocates said during Booker's tenure that few people knew about this ordinance. Booker was sympathetic but ultimately did not change policies in response to advocacy efforts on behalf of undocumented workers regarding license requirements for street vendors and efforts to create a hiring hall where NGOs could link workers with employers and provide a check on employers' exploitation of undocumented immigrant workers. Lack of legal status remains a barrier to earning a livelihood in the city.

Mayor Booker created the African Commission, a volunteer body aimed at raising awareness of African culture and African immigrants in Newark. In the 2014 mayoral election that brought Ras Baraka into the mayor's office, immigration was not featured in candidates' policy agendas. However, in the summer of 2015, Baraka and the council adopted the Municipal ID program for city residents, available regardless of immigrant status. Baraka also created the Office of International Relations and Diaspora Affairs and has spoken of the needs of English-language-learners in the city's schools. During his 2017 State of the City address, he spoke in Spanish to praise the city's diversity.

Ottawa, Ontario

Queen Victoria selected Ottawa as Canada's capital city in 1857, a choice that has driven the city's growth and economic base—it is a government town, housing Parliament and much of the federal bureaucracy.[23] The entire metropolitan area of Ottawa is home to about 812,000 people, although the area inside the Greenbelt and constituting the city prior to amalgamation in 2000 is home to about 487,000. About 244,000 more people live in the outlying areas still considered part of the urban center, whereas 80,000 more live in the rural areas included in the Ottawa borders.[24] Foreign-born people constitute 22 percent of the city's population, and 19 percent of city residents are members of census-designated "visible minority" groups. Most immigrants (nearly 70 percent) live inside the Greenbelt, with most of the others living in the outlying urban centers rather than the rural areas. Three central wards house 20 percent of the city's immigrants.[25]

Most of the city's immigrants are from Asia, the Middle East, Europe, and Africa. The top ten source countries are China, India, Somalia, Iran, the United States, the Russian Federation, former Yugoslavia, Pakistan, and Bangladesh.[26] The 2006 census found the largest visible minority groups to be black, Chinese, South Asian, and Arab.[27] Through the first half of the twentieth century, immigrants to Ottawa came from Ireland, Germany, and Italy, and the city also attracted Jewish and Polish immigrants. Since the 1970s, Jamaicans, Portuguese, Chinese, and South Asians began to settle in Ottawa, and the 1990s brought Somalians and people from both the former Yugoslavia and the former Soviet Union.[28] The majority of immigrants are "prime working age of 18–49," and about half are economic immigrants. The city received the highest percentage of immigrants with university degrees, and recent immigrants were earning higher salaries than in other Canadian cities.[29] About 20 percent of Ottawa's immigrant stream is refugees, among the highest rates in Canadian cities.[30]

Ottawa's location at the border between Ontario and Quebec and the presence of the federal government, which operates bilingually, means that there is a strong presence of French language and culture in the city and a long-standing Francophone community living in the city. One neighborhood, Rideau-Vanier, is the historic and current heart of the Francophone community and also one of the top three neighborhoods where immigrants live.

Visible minorities and immigrants are underrepresented among elected officials in the city, though members of some groups, such as Somali migrants and Muslim residents, have begun to run for office.[31] Representation of interests occurs through various municipal planning processes and the efforts of community organizations. For example, the Equity and Diversity Advisory Committee was formed to work to eliminate discrimination during negotiations for the city's amalgamation in 2000.[32] And the Community Police Action Committee was formed in the aftermath of several police shootings of black men in Ottawa.[33] The city's development of its Human Services Plan included consultation with immigrant and minority communities.[34] The city government has worked in collaboration with immigrant organizations to integrate immigrant issues and needs into city services and to develop an official integration strategy. The city's website features data on the city's immigrants and directs newcomers in how to find help.

Local Politics of Immigrant Integration

In both Ottawa and Newark, NGOs carry out much of the work of supporting immigrants as they make their place in these cities. Ottawa-based NGOs partner with government and private-sector stakeholders to meet the needs of new immigrants and to educate these partners about such needs, in keeping with the national policy's identification of immigrants as clients of programs that will bring about integration, including labor-market participation. Newark-based NGOs engage in a range of activities, defining integration as they do their work, in the absence of national policy. They articulate alternative images of immigrants, depending on NGO mission.

Ottawa

In Ottawa, local government agencies work closely with nonprofit organizations to determine and meet immigrants' socioeconomic needs. NGOs receive funding from the federal government to offer an array of services to immigrants, who are the clients of their organizations. In this way, immigrants are similar to clients of other types of government services. NGOs referred to as settlement organizations provide integration services funded primarily by national and provincial ministries of immigration and offer services such as language training and assistance in finding and securing housing, finding jobs, enrolling children in school, and enrolling in the national health system. Settlement organizations vary in terms of which immigrants they primarily serve; for instance, the largest organizations are general, while smaller organizations often serve specialized populations such as particular ethnic or national-origin groups, women, or Francophone immigrants.

Related to public investment in programs for immigrants and to national discourse describing immigrants as essential to the Canadian economy are the federal dollars for academic research about immigrant settlement success and challenges. A search of Social Sciences and Humanities Research Council (SSHRC) awards indicated 60 awards between 2000 and 2015 made to academic research related to immigration and settlement and more than 1,000 awards for research more generally related to immigration. In conjunction with the federal agency Immigration, Refugees and Citizenship Canada, the SSHRC announced $600,000 in short-term grants awarded to twenty-five projects in September 2016 on issues that affect the settlement and integration of Syrian refugees. These projects focused on "issues such as employment, social integration, youth, housing, mental health and the impact on local support systems," according to the press release. "Social sciences and humanities researchers help us to understand issues affecting our daily lives and provide evidence for sound policy-making. This initiative is vital to supporting the successful integration of refugees into Canadian society," stated Minister of Science Kirsty Duncan.

Though clients of service organizations and subjects of research, immigrants also are understood and behave as active participants in the quest for improvements in settlement outcomes. Partly from a history of consultative practices at City Hall for many demographic groups within Ottawa and partly from the "push" of federal funding to support local integration partnerships, immigrants do influence local government. For example, the Ottawa Local Immigration Partnership (Partenariat Local pour l'Immigration Ottawa, OLIP) is the city's largest and most ambitious local partnership program in the area of immigrant integration. OLIP was cofounded in 2009 by the city and the Local Associations Serving Immigrants (LASI) coalition as part of the broader program that emerged from the 2005 Canada-Ontario Immigration Agreement. In 2008 and 2010, Citizenship and Immigration Canada solicited proposals for the development of local partnerships. Federal funding was available to form a partnership council and to carry out a community-wide strategic planning process for immigrant settlement so as to develop a strategy and then plan for its implementation. The intent was that strong broad-based cross-sector relationships would be forged that ultimately would integrate newcomer needs into a city's community planning and service delivery. OLIP-type partnerships were to be convening bodies, not direct service providers.[35]

From October 2009 to March 2011, OLIP engaged in the start-up and planning phase of the partnership, creating a council of stakeholders and undertaking a yearlong broad consultative process about the state of immigrant integration in Ottawa and what was needed to improve integration experiences and outcomes. Hundreds of people were involved in the forums and meetings, including staff members and directors of key city and provincial organizations and NGOs. The result was a detailed and comprehensive integration strategy that was adopted by the city council. The strategy covers areas including economics, initial settlement needs, health, language, and capacity development.[36] Now OLIP works to support the implementation of the strategy by fostering collaboration through its council, tracking implementation progress, and continuing to promote the message that, according to a recent OLIP report, "Ottawa's success depends on immigration."[37] OLIP is an extremely lean organization, with only three staff members, and is housed within one of the city's large settlement organizations. Its accomplishments are built on the willingness of staff members and organization directors across the sectors as well as volunteers from various Ottawa communities to take part on an ongoing basis.

This most recent collaboration built upon a collaborative habit among settlement organizations. Settlement organizations came together in 1989 to create the LASI coalition. Directors of six settlement organizations meet to share concerns and to coordinate with one another when soliciting funding. The group aims to foster an environment of cooperation as opposed to competition, trying to think rationally about divisions of labor and avoid service duplication so that all organizations might prosper. This aim is not always realized in practice, especially during recent years when federal funding has contracted. In 1997 LASI created World Skills, an organization focused on employment related services for newcomers. Each member becomes involved in providing these services, and World Skills employs staff to design and deliver them. LASI enabled the settlement sector to speak collectively with federal agencies about integration program needs.

Newark

In Newark, a wide variety of NGOs work on behalf of immigrants and in doing so spread ideas about immigrant identities as legitimate and rights-bearing members of the city and the country. Interactions with local government tend to be through channels of elected officials. In addition, NGOs directly resist the enforcement activities of the federal government as they are implemented locally. Immigrant advocates make claims that hinge on building an image of immigrants in line with their organizational goals: as city workers deserving a right to earn a living, as city residents deserving a seat at the table and responsive policies, and as human beings deserving of the broad rights that native-born residents enjoy. Some advocates seek alliances with the racial and ethnic groups that have been politically empowered by winning elected office in Newark.

Immigrant advocates seek to build alliances with groups by highlighting shared identities. For example, NGOs that serve African immigrants have sought to emphasize notions of shared culture with the city's African Americans to thereby interest this majority group in its own African roots as a basis for alliance. On the other hand, other immigrant advocates put forth alternative ideas, seeing themselves as politically salient—despite their inability to vote—because of their close ties to voting Newarkers by dint of being in mixed-status families, including having American-born children, and because they work alongside Newarkers who can vote.

The American Friends Service Committee (AFSC) is one of several organizations in Newark directly contesting the US discourse of immigrants as criminals. The AFSC's general framing of undocumented immigrants is captured in the slogan "No Human Being is Illegal," which features prominently on the organization's website and appears on AFSC posters and literature used at rallies and events. The AFSC uses this narrative as its staff lawyers represent detainees in immigration courts, and its organizers work with families of detainees in efforts to lobby for national policy change. The group interacts most often with the national government, including the court system and the immigration enforcement system. It also aims to build support among national legislators for policy change. As such, building local and state allies (including state government agencies) and mobilizing local residents of the Newark metro area are part of the work of lobbying for national change.

A second type of discourse depicts immigrants as integral parts of the local workforce who should be treated lawfully regardless of their immigration status. In Newark, the local branch of a statewide group called New Labor takes on this task. Staff and members describe immigrants as seeking to support their families no differently than other US workers and as being entitled to treatment similar to that of other workers and with the same protections. New Labor interacts most often with state and city government agencies whose purview includes worker protection and licensing as well as with local elected officials. New Labor works to reduce the exploitation of informal laborers and, more generally, to advance the well-being of immigrants in the workplace. Its staff and members canvass workers to learn about issues and develop programs or campaigns to address them. Examples are direct-action campaigns against wage theft, the provision of English and computer classes, and health and safety training programs. One major undertaking by New Labor in Newark was to organize flower and ice cream vendors to lobby City Hall for changes to business licensing and treatment by local police. The resulting Union de Vendedores did not achieve its policy goal, but the effort did result in giving members experience and training in practices of lobbying, organizing, and making claims on local officials.

Newark's immigrants navigate a competitive political arena with a history of cycles of ethnic and racial group empowerment and displacement. Immigrant groups aiming to gain political capital find themselves fitting into existing racial and ethnic categories for purposes of political action. For example, as Central and South American immigrants increase in numbers, they serve to increase Newark's Latino population. This demographic trend constitutes in part a threat to what has been for decades a majority-black and black-empowered city. In addition, new immigrants from Latin and Central America and their children implicitly challenge the Puerto Rican political dominance. African and black Caribbean immigrants likewise fit tenuously into the city's black population, though their numbers may not yet constitute as much of a threat to African American political dominance as Latin American immigrants pose to local Latino politics.

A third discourse about Newark's immigrants depicts them as city residents entitled to political voice. This discourse manifests in several ways. The African Commission and the African Community Engagement initiative each seek to assert the presence of African immigrants in the city in part through events that bring African culture to city spaces, with the aim to build community across immigrants from different African countries, so as to assert a presence in part to justify claim making on the city. For example, the chair of the African Commission hopes to create a community center for African immigrants that would provide programs and services. But these groups also hope to underline the shared cultural heritage with African Americans. La Movida, a small youth-based organization focused on schools, was founded to serve Dominican immigrants and families but now also aims to include other Latin American groups in its leadership and its youth programs. Its founders are aware of the balance of power in the city and how this intersects with race and ethnicity. Any aspirations for political empowerment rest on connecting to other groups, especially long-standing racial and ethnic groups; these young leaders have heard from elders that it is important to "wait their turn."

NGOs know that to gain attention from city government, they need to show the ability to turn out a vote. Staff at the Ironbound Community Development Corporation explained their uneven support from City Hall with reference to the large immigrant population in their neighborhood, which translates into low levels of citizenship and low voter turnout. Because of immigrants, then, "we are the least powerful community," one staff member said. A similar difficulty in asserting political voice to elected officials occurred with New Labor's flower and ice cream vendors, many of whom are undocumented immigrants. Recognizing that local elected officials viewed them as a nonvoting constituency, hurting their chances of securing support for changes to licensing practices, they started to describe themselves as being integrated into the fabric of the city's political life. They talked about their own children and family members who were US citizens as well as their friends. These connections, they argued, put them in a position to communicate political information and to influence political views of voters. They argued that they deserved government responsiveness because they lived and worked in the city and had family and friends right in Newark. Many were parents to US-citizen children. But these frames did not help to persuade officials to change licensing practices.

Conclusion

How do the local cases of immigrant integration politics reflect or differ from national ideas about immigrants? In Ottawa there is largely convergence, whereas in Newark there is divergence. Without examining cases of other Canadian and US cities to see whether this pattern holds, one cannot assert that this stems from national policy exclusively. However, national funding and oversight provisions certainly shape the activities of local NGOs in Canada;[38] local NGOs do interact with federal agencies to seek to influence the content of integration programs, and they do develop strategies to try to address gaps in nationally funded services.[39] The lack of integration policy in the United States leaves the policy space open for local definitions. And in light of the highly negative image of immigrants fostered by national US policy, local immigrant advocates develop alternative images to challenge these policies and characterizations. In Newark, multiple ideas about immigrants coexist.

Modes of immigrant politics also differ across the two cases. In Ottawa, a bureaucratic mode of citizenship emerges from understanding immigrants as clients and objects of research. Immigrants consult with government about policy implementation and programs. In Newark, an electoral mode of citizenship emerges from the local political dynamics, ranging from local resistance to federal criminalization, and to the opportunity to define integration that exists without a national policy in place. Though different, each mode of citizenship connotes a particular way of asserting a "right to the city."

Besides employing an ideational perspective to examine local immigrant politics and highlighting the role of NGOs in local political processes and development, I offer a few additional arguments about studying urban politics. First is the assertion that national policies other than specifically urban policies do shape local politics. Second is the assertion that there is a need to bring work on immigrants centrally into our conceptions of urban politics rather than seeing immigrants as parts of the racial and ethnic politics long studied. While immigrants may "fit into" existing racial and ethnic groups contesting for political power, they also may not. Whether and how they incorporate is a question to examine. Their presence in cities affects and is affected by a range of government institutions and policies from education, economic development, and police and public safety to electoral processes. While other disciplines including urban sociology and urban geography have theorized and studied immigrants, urban political scientists are more recently doing so.[40] Historical analysis of urban political machines is perhaps the primary context in which immigrants have been centrally analyzed as key players in urban politics. This chapter is also a call for more study.

CHAPTER 11

"Trying Out Our Ideas"

Enterprise Zones in the United States and the United Kingdom

Timothy P. R. Weaver

In early 1980s Britain Geoffrey Howe, the first chancellor of the exchequer of Margaret Thatcher's Conservative government, launched the enterprise zone program. With their emphasis on reducing or eliminating taxes and government regulations in urban areas, enterprise zones were the quintessential place-based articulation of neoliberal ideas. Curiously, while property developers and the real estate industry were set to be the key beneficiaries of the program, the selection and introduction of enterprise zones was not driven by business interests. The same was true in the United States, where actors such as the Heritage Foundation went to great lengths to convince business to support them. Instead, as Howe made clear, urban areas in the United Kingdom were selected for enterprise zone designation as a means of "trying out our ideas" in the hope that their success would help persuade people of the efficacy of free-market ideology more broadly.[1]

Ideas provided the motive for enterprise zones, but it was the centralized and powerful institutions of the national state and the relative weakness of local state institutions that provided the opportunity for their rapid introduction in the United Kingdom. By contrast, the American institutional matrix—the separation of powers, divided government, and federalism—hindered national-level ideologically motivated policy entrepreneurs in the United States. American policy entrepreneurs thus pursued enterprise zones at the state and local levels, which became the basis for empowerment zones under Bill Clinton, Promise Zones under Barack Obama, and Opportunity Zones under Donald Trump. As a result, the pace, character, and extent of neoliberalization differed, even with respect to the same policy approach.

Ideas, Institutions, and Interests in Urban Political Development

Much of the most influential urban analysis affords a central role to organized interests, particularly businesses interests.[2] This is for good reason: any city government is centrally concerned with raising revenue, which means being sensitive to the concerns of investors in order to promote prosperity. In this sense, business unquestionably enjoys a measure of "systemic power."[3] The expectation is therefore that cities, especially in the American context, will adopt a progrowth business-friendly framework in order to maintain a healthy tax base. However, it is far too glib to assume that cities will simply capitulate to businesses demands, nor should one assume a unity city "interest."[4] As Logan and Molotch's classic study reminds us, certain elements of the "growth machine" are at odds when it comes to attempts to maximize "exchange value."[5] At a minimum, convincing accounts of urban politics need to deal with the problem of clashing interests.

A further potential weakness of interest-based accounts of urban politics is an undue material bias. That is, while urbanists such as Peterson, Harvey, and Logan and Molotch discuss the importance of ideology, they rarely afford ideas any motive force in driving change. This is especially true when ideas and material interests diverge. In these cases, material interests are expected to win out; when ideas take the lead it is because they do not contradict material interests. Yet as I argue below, this account leaves unexplained the emergence of policies that are contrary to or not advanced by the interests of capital.

In part as a response to Peterson's overly reductionist approach, there developed a line of research that emphasized the variability in political responses to business pressure[6] and sought to recover the role of political agency in the construction of "urban regimes."[7] This meant bringing institutions back into the analysis, although early efforts to do so left institutions rather undertheorized. More recently, however, scholarship on urban politics has highlighted the centrality of institutions, drawing most recently from some of the insights of historical institutionalism and American political development.[8] In so doing, scholars have begun to pay explicit attention not simply to the quotidian operation of urban *politics* but also to urban political *development*.

For instance, in recent work, Stone has refined his conceptualization of regime analysis by deploying the notion of an "urban political order," a conceptual frame informed by the work of Karen Orren and Stephen Skowronek, who have done much to advance institutional analysis through the American political development subfield.[9] The adoption of the urban political order(s) framework is especially attractive because it enables one to grapple analytically with the "intercurrent" operation of multilayered processes operating through time simultaneously. For Stone, this approach better captures more accurately contemporary urban development characterized by the waning of "collective business leadership," the emergence of a range of key actors (the "meds and eds," nonprofits, and grassroots organizations), and phenomena such as immigration and gentrification.[10]

Finally, Joel Rast has argued convincingly that urban scholarship might enjoy greater vibrancy and wider relevance through the application of analytical tools wielded by historical institutionalists, comparative sociologists, and students of American political development.[11] These include concepts such as "path dependence," "periodization, "policy feedback," "drift," and "sequencing."[12] In particular, Rast suggests that studies of urban political development can be enhanced through an examination of the ways institutions work variously to constrain change on the one hand and provide "resources for strategic action" on the other. That is, following Mahoney, Rast suggests that convincing accounts of continuity and change at the urban level might emerge from a close examination of the extent to which "permissive conditions" and/or "generative causes" are present.[13] When both exist together, major change is possible, but when only permissive conditions exist, change is likely to be incremental.

The renewed attention on the historically oriented, theoretically innovative institutional approaches to urban political development has unquestionably strengthened urban analysis. That said, a central claim here is that urban analysis can be improved further through a focus on ideas. In his most recent work Rast hints at this, noting that "it is through ideas that actors can imagine a reality different from the one they currently inhabit, and it is ideas . . . that inform actors [about] 'what has gone wrong' and 'what is to be done.'"[14] But while numerous urban scholars mention ideas and ideology, there has been little work done that grapples systematically with the ways in which ideas, interests, and institutions interact to shape urban political development.

The emergent literature on ideas in social science research provides fertile ground on which to develop compelling accounts of urban development. In particular, scholars such as Rogers Smith have argued that we need to bring ideas into the frame if we are to understand institutional purposes. That is, institutions, among other things, are "carriers of ideas."[15] Therefore, it is crucial that we attend to the ideas that inform the content of institutions in addition to thinking about how and why institutions advance or place fetters on change. Furthermore, despite all the advances made by institutional scholarship in showing the conditions under which change might be possible, an ideological dimension is required to explain the direction of change. As Robert Lieberman explains, institutions explain the opportunity, but ideas provide the motive.[16]

Having laid out some of the key developments in urban research as it relates to the debate of ideas, interests, and institutions, the remainder of my chapter is devoted to a close examination of the emergence, spread, and legacy of enterprise zones. In what follows, it will become clear that this element of urban political development requires close attention to ideational factors, particularly regarding the birth of the policy. However, institutional and interest-based analysis is required to explain the variegated manner in which the policy was adopted and rolled out in the United Kingdom and then the United States. As such, I suggest that all three analytical dimensions are necessarily part of a satisfactory explanation of this case of urban neoliberalization.[17]

The Enterprise Zone Idea Emerges

Neoliberalism is "a political-economic theory and rhetorical framework that rests on the notion that freedom, justice, and well-being are best guaranteed by a political-economic system, undergirded by the state, which promotes private property (including via privatization of state assets), open markets, and free trade and which privileges the interests of financial capital above all."[18] In terms of practical policies, tax cuts and deregulation are the sine qua non of the neoliberal project. Enterprise zones, in their original formulation, were urban policy approaches that combined both. Crucially, while enterprise zones would in principle be a boon to business, close attention to the emergence, transition, and adoption of the policy in the both the United Kingdom and the United States reveals that business did not propose it and was initially ambivalent about the concept. Rather, it was policy entrepreneurs, spurred on by their own neoliberal beliefs about how best to address urban decline, who blazed the trail for enterprise zones. Only later did business back the idea. Thus, an examination of the sequence of policy development clarifies the relative influence of ideas, institutions, and interests.

While enterprise zones were introduced by the Thatcher government, the idea itself was developed by Sir Peter Hall, a planner by training who had become deeply disillusioned with the apparent failures of British social democracy during the 1970s. Aghast at the moribund state of Britain's great cities, Hall suggested in a 1977 speech that the revival of urban areas required a dose of "fairly shameless free enterprise."[19] Inspired by the rapid and seemingly successful rise of cities such as Hong Kong and Singapore, Hall's "freeport solution" involved the creation of "free zones," which would be "outside the limits of the parent country's legislation," free from taxes and regulations and where "bureaucracy would be kept to an absolute minimum."[20] Hall further envisioned that collective bargaining and minimum wages should be suspended. Noting that this approach was "very blue sky" and developed "slightly tongue in cheek," Hall "did not expect anyone to take this seriously in policy terms."[21]

However, Hall's speech soon caught the attention of none other than Sir Geoffrey Howe, shadow chancellor of the exchequer in Thatcher's shadow cabinet. Just days after Howe became aware of the speech, he wrote to Thatcher, enclosing a copy. Howe was struck by the degree to which Hall's proposed strategy chimed with his and Thatcher's radical promarket philosophy. Howe emphasized that Hall was "clearly mindful of the importance of markets, and of services, in addition to the manufacturing industry, and arrives . . . at an approach very similar to the one I suggested in my recent paper 'Liberating Free Enterprise.'"[22] In a speech that developed these themes, Howe set out a comprehensive critique of British urban policy and laid out his neoliberal alternative.[23]

For Howe, the decline of the inner cities resulted from the exorbitant levels of taxation and burdensome regulations that stifled small business activity: "The consequent lack of success is breeding social tension and threatening to destroy the framework of civilized existence. And in many areas, the burgeoning of State activity now positively frustrates healthy private initiative, widely dispersed and properly rewarded. Over-regulation is a major part of the British disease."[24] Given this diagnosis, the putative cure was to be found in one of neoliberalism's defining features, the reduction of taxes on business profits. As Howe put it, "return to economic vitality crucially depends upon the fundamental reform of our tax system. . . . We must restore the legitimacy of becoming rich by taking risks: *that* is the way to promote the creation of real jobs."[25] The other "almost equally urgent need is to set about the sensible deregulation of our economy."[26]

Moreover, for Howe the enterprise zone initiative held the promise of helping to persuade the country to support the Conservatives' comprehensive national plans for both tax relief and deregulation. He understood that Conservatives "would have to wait to get support" for the radical remaking of British economic and social policy. Enterprise zones were a "kind of trial run intended to foster support for the other possible changes, which we sought to introduce more broadly in the British economy."[27] As Howe explained in 1978,

> An "enterprise-zone" initiative would be designated to go further and more swiftly than the general policy changes that we have been proposing to liberate enterprise throughout the country. It would *not* be based upon considerations of regional policy. . . . Rather it would be set up to test market areas or laboratories in which to enable fresh policies to prime the pump of prosperity, and to establish their potential for doing so elsewhere.[28]

Thus for Howe, enterprise zones would be the spark to reignite the entrepreneurial flame that had been snuffed out by the state and would help convince others of the efficacy of neoliberal ideas and techniques more broadly.

Between 1977 and the victory of Thatcher's Conservative Party in the 1979 general election, Howe pressed the future prime minister on the need to establish enterprise zones. Thatcher ultimately agreed, and Howe introduced enterprise zones in his 1980 budget as part of his "enterprise package." Companies in the zones would enjoy 100 percent capital allowances for both industrial and commercial buildings (meaning that the total costs of new buildings could be deducted from taxable profits); complete relief from development land taxes, ratings, industrial training certificates, and levies; and a drastically simplified planning scheme.[29]

Through the Local Government Planning and Land Act of 1980 and the Finance Act of 1980, eleven ten-year zones, each of which contained high levels of unemployment caused by deindustrialization, were designated during the first round: Salford/Trafford, Swansea, Wakefield, Clydebank, Dudley, Hartlepool, Corby, Tyneside, Speke (Liverpool), Isle of Dogs (London's

Docklands), and Belfast.[30] But the reach of enterprise zones went far beyond British shores; soon they would be adopted in the United States.

Diffusion to the United States

In contrast to the common pattern of policy diffusion from the United States to the United Kingdom, in the case of enterprise zones the ideational currents flowed in the opposition direction. In addition to Peter Hall and Geoffrey Howe, the other key proponent of enterprise zones was Stuart Butler. It was he who would play a central role in adapting and introducing the idea to the American scene.

Butler first discussed the enterprise zone idea in the American context in a 1979 paper produced for the Heritage Foundation in which he proposed that "the most decayed segments of major cities to be classified as 'Enterprise Zones,' and . . . virtually all zoning employment protection, and other controls within them to be suspended—and perhaps even . . . property taxes . . . be abolished." He argued that the enterprise zone concept "should strike a chord in the United States."[31] After all, "the philosophy of experimentation and individual initiative is well rooted in the American way of life." Furthermore, Butler saw the causes of urban decay in the United Kingdom and the United States to be "sufficiently similar to allow possible solutions voiced in Britain to be given serious consideration in the United States." Indeed, Butler held that enterprise zones would go some way toward solving the American "urban crisis" that had plagued cities in various forms since the 1950s.[32]

In addition to the influence of Peter Hall and Geoffrey Howe, Butler also drew on Jane Jacobs's critique of urban renewal and on David Birch's work that suggested that the key to economic revitalization would be through the promotion of small businesses.[33] As such, "intellectually, it has Hayekian roots and American roots."[34] As Butler explained,

> My value added to this was to blend that with the Jane Jacobs vision of communities, and saying well ok we won't use this to get the bulldozers in or to have massive physical redevelopment. But we'll use the essence of the enterprise zone to get latent activity coming into fruition and then combine with that the idea that the route forward for new development, economic development, was more likely through small business activity, than through large business

> activity. I think both of those are very important in terms of the distinction of the enterprise zone philosophy, if you like, that it was going to be non-planning, in a sense, and based more on small enterprise.[35]

With the intellectual groundwork for enterprise zones laid, the policy was picked up by US House representative Jack Kemp, who was the driving force behind the transformation of the idea into concrete legislative proposals.[36] A Republican from New York state who later served as the secretary of housing and urban development under George H. W. Bush, Kemp was at the heart of plans to mold urban policy in the neoliberal image. He and his fellow enterprise zone enthusiasts introduced over twenty bills in the House and Senate during the 1980s. These bills commonly included reductions to personal and business taxes, regulatory relief, and accelerated depreciation. The proposals were given key additional support from Ronald Reagan, who promoted the idea readily. During his two terms as president, enterprise zones featured in four State of the Union addresses. In 1984, he reiterated his belief in the power of free-market initiatives to reduce urban unemployment:

> I ask your help in assisting more communities to break the bondage of dependency. Help us to free enterprise by permitting debate and voting "yes" on our proposal for enterprise zones in America. This has been before you for two years. Its passage can help high-unemployment areas by creating jobs and restoring neighborhoods.[37]

Thus, in both the British and American contexts, the enterprise zone was developed by intellectuals and politicians whose solutions to urban dereliction chimed with more general convictions about economic and social policy. For Howe and Butler in particular, the enterprise zone, if successful, promised to help convince others as to the efficacy of the promarket, or neoliberal, worldview.

From Ideas to Policy: The Mediating Effect of Institutions

With the emergence of the enterprise zone idea, urban policy was about to make a major turn in a neoliberal direction. However, the mere existence and promotion of the idea did not guarantee its adoption and institutionalization.

Rather, the institutional matrix in which enterprise zone entrepreneurs operated would determine the degree to which national-level actors could bring their ideas into fruition.

In the British context, the institutional framework strengthened Geoffrey Howe's hand. A centralized state, unitary government, and strong party discipline meant that government policy has a good chance of reaching the statute book relatively unscathed. While the United Kingdom's independent, professional civil service can sometimes cause friction,[38] Howe's position as chancellor of the exchequer—arguably the second most powerful position in government— meant that he was almost uniquely placed to successfully advance new policy initiatives. As such, enterprise zones were rolled out across British cities very rapidly after Howe created them through acts of Parliament.

In marked contrast, the American institutional web ensnared national-level actors. While Butler's institutional perch at the Heritage Foundation enabled him to launch the idea onto the political agenda, he found his idea stymied time and again in Congress. Despite giving the idea prominence in a series of State of the Union addresses and having a number of allies introduce enterprise zones in Congress, even President Reagan was at a loss. As such, no substantive enterprise zone legislation made it to his desk. The multiple veto points that characterize American political institutions coupled with divided government meant that Democratic opponents of the scheme, including Ways and Means chairman Dan Rostenkowski, were able to block it.

Despite the failure to introduce a national program, enterprise zone proponents had made major progress on two important fronts. First, within Congress the enterprise zone coalition broadened and deepened over the course of the 1980s and early 1990s due in part to the tenacity of actors such as Reagan and Kemp, who repeatedly introduced enterprise zone bills, pressed for hearings, and forced votes on the issue.[39] Outside of Congress, Butler at the Heritage Foundation—and others at the American Legislative Exchange Council, the Cato Institute, and the Sabre Foundation—continued the steady drumbeat of enterprise zone promotion. But also striking was the gradual conversion of Democrats to the policy. In the early 1980s very few Democrats supported enterprise zones, and many, such as Rostenkowski, were staunch opponents. Yet by the 1990s Democrats such as Charles Rangel—who voted against enterprise zone bills in the 1980s—introduced Democratic versions. Moreover, in 1992 the Democratic Party platform included a commitment to introduce enterprise zones. Indeed, Bill Clinton actively promoted the policy as governor of Arkansas and touted it as a presidential candidate. Remarkably,

Democratic support for enterprise zones increased despite growing evidence as to the shortcomings of the enterprise zone approach.[40]

The second key sign of major progress was the spread of enterprise zones through the states. Whereas national political institutions stopped a national enterprise zone program in its tracks, forty states had developed their own enterprise zone programs by the mid-1990s. While the state-level zones retained many of the core elements in the original vision, many of them were far less radical in practice.[41] Thus, the institutional arrangements of American federalism opened up opportunities for enterprise zone advocates. Yet as neoliberals rubbed up against remnants of the American liberal political order, some of the more radical elements of the original enterprise zone concept were eroded.

Thus, while ideas provided the "motive" for the neoliberal shift in urban political development, the British and American systems presented differing opportunity structures. As such, in the United Kingdom a new enterprise zone program, which remained largely faithful to the original enterprise zone vision, was quickly introduced. In the United States, national political institutions gave the upper hand to opponents who were able to thwart the introduction of the enterprise zone program. However, federalism provided enterprise zone advocates with an alternative pathway to change, albeit one that smoothed the most radical edges of the original concept.

The Curious Absence of Business Lobbying

Given that the benefits of enterprise zones—tax cuts and incentives and a favorable regulatory environment—promised significant benefits to business, one might have expected to find the interests of capital pushing for the adoption of the policy. If this were the case, enterprise zones would serve as a relatively "easy" case for interest based accounts. Indeed, scholars such as William Goldsmith have argued that the enterprise zone idea "has been seized upon by some (sometimes consciously, to be sure) as a weapon for business in the struggle with labor over production costs."[42] However, one of the most surprising findings of my research into enterprise zones has been the relative indifference of business toward the policy, especially in the early years. This ambivalence was evident in both the British and American contexts.

In the United Kingdom, organized business was only persuaded of the efficacy of enterprise zones over time. Although the Confederation of British

Industry came out in favor of the zones in 1981, it noted that "the ironic part of the whole scheme is that businesses outside zone boundaries not only lose out completely but have to foot the bill for the £20 million capital allowances and the £50 million rates reduction."[43] Moreover, many other business groups opposed the zones because of the comparative disadvantage that accrued to firms on the "wrong" side of the enterprise zone border. As Walter Goldsmith, director general of the business group the Institute of Directors, asserted, "The arbitrary manner in which the enterprise zone boundaries are being drawn up can mean the difference between life and death for those firms that find themselves outside the zone."[44] The director general of the British Chamber of Commerce, Sir Terrence Beckett, also expressed reservations about the policy, though he did endorse the logic of deregulation and tax reductions for businesses across the board: "if the whole country were made an enterprise zone and removed from the crippling burden of business rates and planning restrictions, then we might really be talking."[45] Moreover, in the early 1980s a number of businesspeople, including Bernard Tennant of the National Chamber of Trade, wrote to *The Times* to protest against the enterprise zone plans.[46]

When Geoffrey Howe announced plans to create eleven new enterprise zones in 1982, the *Financial Times* reported that "many developers and estate agents [were] already concerned that the benefits provided by the existing zones have not been worth the disruption caused to some local markets."[47] In fact, as Doreen Massy points out, some business groups even lobbied for the reintroduction of planning controls, which resulted in automatic permission for retail outlets being limited only to developments below a certain size.[48] Hence, there is very little evidence from the British case that shows this element of urban neoliberalization as resulting from business pressures.

A similar picture is evident in the American context, where business interests represented by organizations such as the Chamber of Commerce, the National Association of Manufacturers (NAM), and the National Federation of Independent Business either opposed enterprise zones or came to support them only after they had been promoted by politicians. Indeed, Stuart Butler recalls deep frustration about the struggle to get big business associations on board with the enterprise zone idea:

> We were desperately trying to find large interest groups that would support this . . . but to get some of the really large business organizations was just an uphill battle. The Chamber and the NAM and

> so on, they were in with the old philosophy. If you wanted a large manufacturing approach, the last thing you wanted was to have an approach that said "sorry we don't want to send the bulldozers in; you are not the answer." They didn't want to hear this. So we could never get much support in the large very active business organizations.[49]

Consistent with Mark Blyth's and Colin Hay's work on the construction of business interests, Butler's account underscores the crucial place for ideas.[50] While it is undeniable that capital has an "interest" in profit, there are likely to be competing ideas about how best to achieve it. Simply knowing that capital is likely to demand policies that will prove profitable fails to explain much about which particular policies are likely to emerge. Moreover, the case of enterprise zones shows clearly that significant areas of policy development cannot be attributed to business demands but instead spring from political sources. This finding complicates the story of urban neoliberalization that assumes a central role for capital.[51]

The Legacy of the Enterprise Zone Idea

Numerous studies of both British and American enterprise zone programs have cast serious doubts about on the ability of these programs to create net economic benefits for urban areas.[52] Yet the idea, both in pure and mutated form, continued to be popular among bipartisan elites on both sides of the Atlantic.

In the United States, the presidential victory of Democratic nominee Bill Clinton raised hopes among liberals and many on the Left that the election of a Democrat to the White House would result in a new direction in federal urban policy. Moreover, rioting in Los Angeles in the spring of 1992 seemed to demand enhanced federal support and a shift in strategy for cities that once again seemed in "crisis." However, reflecting his "New Democrat" identity, Clinton resisted many of the calls for major increases in urban spending and instead reiterated his support for a series of measures that fell within the neoliberal ambit. In a speech to the United States Conference of Mayors, Clinton called for "new incentives for the private sector, an investment tax credit, urban enterprise zones, new business tax incentives, research and development incentives and others."[53]

The enterprise zone approach loomed large in President Clinton's urban policy priorities. Indeed, the administration's only major urban policy initiative was the Empowerment Zones/Enterprise Communities (EZ/EC) program, which passed as Title XIII of the omnibus Budget Reconciliation Act of 1993. Eager to avoid association with previous Democratic initiatives, Clinton reassured observers that the empowerment zone program was "not the Great Society." This was an accurate description, since unlike the relatively big spending programs of the 1960s, the empowerment zone concept owed much to the enterprise zone concept.

With their targeted use of a series of tax incentives, ranging from those to encourage employment of zone residents to relief from property taxes and accelerated depreciation, the empowerment zones idea clearly hewed closely to the enterprise zone idea. Unlike the original enterprise zones, however, $1 billion was channeled through a Title XX Social Service Block Grant (SSBG) for direct spending in empowerment zones.[54] Yet there was also more than twice that amount provided through tax incentives. As such, the empowerment zone program in many respects resembled the intercurrence of the old liberal order and the emerged neoliberal order that the enterprise zone program so typified.

Over the course of three rounds—1994, 1998, and 2001—the federal government selected 122 cities to participate in the EZ/EC program, 30 of which received SSBG funds of $100 million for community programs. The places selected all experienced high levels of unemployment and poverty. Ultimately in light of the modest levels of investment within the zones themselves, scholars have largely concluded that the program had no more than a small measurable effect on levels of employment, poverty, or business activity.[55] In a reflection of the neoliberal bone fides of the program, when President George W. Bush entered office his administration expanded the empowerment zone program, creating 30 new urban "renewal communities" and 8 new empowerment zones.[56]

Continuing in this vein, President Obama launched the Promise Zone program in 2013. Much like enterprise zones and empowerment zones, the promise zone idea sought to address the problems of poverty and unemployment through a combination of tax incentives for business and the prioritization of needy areas for the targeting of existing federal resources. Illustrating his programmatic and ideological connection to Reagan and Clinton, Obama suggested that those in the federal government will help poor areas "not with a handout, but as partners with them, every step of the way."[57] The substance of the promise zone idea also reflected the dominance of neoliberal thinking at the heart of Obama's urban policy. Most obviously, the zones involve tax incentives and "cutting red tape," two themes central to the enterprise zone idea, but offer nothing in terms of new federal funding to cities.

A final legacy of American enterprise zone advocates is found in the Trump administration's Opportunity Zone program, which was introduced in eighteen states in 2018. In particular, the program finally delivers the elimination of capital gains tax that Ronald Reagan and Jack Kemp placed at the heart of their abortive federal enterprise zone program. Specifically, the program uses tax incentives to encourage investment in "economically distressed" urban and rural census tracts. A key provision lets participants avoid capital gains tax entirely if they hold investments in an "opportunity fund" for at least ten years.[58] As with the empowerment zones, the Opportunity Zones reflected the remarkable endurance of a policy regime that has consistently failed to produce positive results.

Meanwhile in Britain, enterprise zones have come back from the dead after being snuffed out by the central government in the 1990s. Chancellor of the Exchequer George Osborne has emulated his predecessor, Geoffrey Howe, almost identically by introducing twenty-five new enterprise zones to stimulate urban prosperity.[59] Much like Howe's original vision, businesses in Osborne's zones enjoy a 100 percent business rate (tax) discount for up to five years, "enhanced capital allowances," "radically simplified planning approaches," and assistance in the availability of "superfast broadband."[60] Thus, tax cuts and deregulation as a means to stimulate the economy are back in vogue. As was widely reiterated at the time of the announcement, the experience of the 1980s enterprise zones suggested that they would "likely . . . be ineffective at stimulating sustainable economic growth in depressed areas."[61]

The chancellor plowed on nevertheless. The British government predicted that enterprise zones would create 54,000 additional jobs. However, consistent with the enterprise zone experience in the United Kingdom and beyond, the number of jobs created fell well below expectations—by 2017, 29,000 jobs had been created. As the House of Commons Public Accounts Committee noted, such results were "particularly underwhelming."[62] Moreover, due to a lack of business interest in the scheme, the Office for Budget Responsibility, a statutory body that monitors government spending, reduced its forecast for the costs of tax relief in enterprise zones by 80 percent, from £30 million in 2015–2016 to just £6 million.[63] The lack of business take-up of tax incentives reflects a key tendency that the enterprise zone case reveals: the relative absence of business lobbying in favor of the idea. Thus, what at first glance appear to be policy developments driven by the interests of capital are often instead rooted in the ideological preferences of officeholders.

Conclusion

I have used the case of enterprise zones in the United States and the United Kingdom as evidence to suggest that satisfactory explanations of urban political development will at times require an ideational component. Most striking, given the central role for tax cuts and regulatory relief, business interests were not at the heart of policy development and had to be persuaded to support it by policy entrepreneurs, driven primarily by their own ideas about how best to address urban problems. Part of this calculation did, of course, involve assumptions about what would benefit business. However, the substance of their ideas about what would benefit business is the key. Thus, interest-based accounts are not sufficient (though far from irrelevant, to be sure). However, neither can the development of the policy be fully explained by ideas. As we have seen, in both contexts institutional arrangements gave some actors (such as those in the United Kingdom) key advantages and others (in the United States especially) key disadvantages. Therefore, this research suggests major benefits to charting the ways in which urban political development is driven by the productive clash and friction among interests, ideas, and institutions operating simultaneously across time.

PART IV

Ideas in Urban Political Development in the Global South

CHAPTER 12

Ideas, Framing, and Interests in Urban Contention

The Case of Santiago, Chile

Eleonora Pasotti

Ideas can facilitate resistance and support the accumulation of political capital in adverse settings. In pursuing their interests, different political actors can appeal to different ideas. Thus, contention can be captured as a battle over who presents the most persuasive idea and is thereby able to gain popular support. In this chapter I illustrate how a neighborhood group deployed an ideational approach and was remarkably successful in resisting redevelopment and gaining institutional influence despite a hostile political environment. The case discussed below represents one of twenty-nine campaigns across ten cities examined in my book *Resisting Redevelopment: Protest in Aspiring Global Cities*.[1] In the present chapter, the analysis traces how the neighborhood association Vecinos por la Defensa del Barrio Yungay (VDBY), founded in 2005 and still active, was able to achieve key objectives and gain influence at the municipal and national levels in Santiago.

Threatened by plans for extensive high-rise towers, the VDBY within three years was able to gain permanent protection of its neighborhood by getting it listed as a national heritage district. On the basis of its legitimacy and clout among residents, the VDBY then made important institutional gains, including the shift from mayoral appointment to competitive elections for a key municipal governing body. Moreover, the VDBY gained seats on the city council and on the national civil society council. In other words, the group succeeded in extraordinary mobilization, in long-term policy changes, and even in changing the rules of local representative government, thus altering the structural balance of power in decision making itself. The VDBY then embarked on a scaling-up process by instituting a national league of neighborhood associations and deploying its strategies to other areas, thus reshaping barrio policy at the national level.

The VDBY's strategy was based on a twofold idea: (1) the identity of the neighborhood is constituted by its architectural heritage and the sociocultural-historical heritage of its (current residential and commercial) population, and (2) the proposed redevelopment threatened this identity and should be opposed. Barrio Yungay was presented as a place of specific historical significance based on the national moment of the Battle of Yungay, which is represented in the neighborhood by the statue of a footman soldier. The statue provides a class connotation to Chilean national identity as a state built on the shoulders of commoners, such as the lower- and middle-class residents of this neighborhood.

These propositions animated a remarkably successful mobilization. The VDBY mobilized with traditional tools (signature collections, street protests, sit-ins, and teach-ins), with extensive linkages with traditional media (the press, radio, and television), and with media outlets that it could directly control, such as a website, a listserv, a glossy monthly magazine, radio programs, and even an Internet television channel. These communication tools were accompanied by an impressive and crucial series of activities and events, which defined a barrio identity that was powerful but also highly inclusive. In fact, interviews and archival analysis illustrate how the emphasis on common historical heritage facilitated the inclusion of both lower- and middle-class participants as well as people of different genders, sexual orientations, work profiles, and ages. Importantly, while the political orientation of the resistance is definitely on the Left, the association carefully avoided invoking party labels and pursued instead a pragmatic approach connecting with a variety of political actors.

In pursuing its policies and redevelopment goals, the mayoral office also used ideas. The office argued that Yungay had historical heritage of national stature, which should be harnessed as an economic resource. The conflict thus can be framed as one between use value and exchange value of the neighborhood, as articulated by Molotch and Logan,[2] in that the mayor's interests were focused on raising revenue through tourism and gentrification, while the residents' interests were focused on maintaining what seemed to them to be the "authenticity" of their neighborhood that would be lost through gentrification.

Santiago de Chile is a critical case for exploring the role of ideas in urban political development. First, the city is a historical hotbed of neoliberalism. As the next section illustrates, the regime is heavily tilted toward real estate interests. Second, Santiago is a relatively unlikely setting for successful mobilization. Multicountry surveys find in Santiago the lowest level of popular trust in associations.[3] Moreover, in a continent with often fragmented, underinstitutionalized, and personalistic parties, Chile offers instead a context whereby parties are prominent, relatively more programmatic, and less personalized.

Against these odds, the VDBY successfully managed to both mobilize supporters and coordinate with other associations quickly and effectively and without resorting to party politics. The powerful combination of both traditional and innovative mobilization tools allowed for the construction of a broad and loyal mobilization among residents and a neighborhood identity that turned the residents' heterogeneity from a weakness to an advantage.

The coming pages present the context of the case with a brief overview of local governments in Chile from a political, financial, and land-use perspective. In examining the case of the VDBY, I analyze the tools employed to build the neighborhood identity and promote a loyal following and then show how this clout was deployed in a multipronged strategy with financial, political, institutional, societal, and developmental components as well an increasingly wide network of like-minded entities—an approach that was not only successful at reaching the goals that the VDBY set for itself but also fully rearticulated the terms of the political conflict with the municipal government.

The Institutional Context: Government, Finance, and Planning

With a population ten times larger than that of Chile's second city, the province of Santiago is often referred to as the "epitome of the centralized Latin American capital city."[4] In addition to its population size, economic activities are concentrated in Santiago, which scholars estimate at 50 percent of the country's gross national product, 60 percent of consumption, and 80 percent of bank deposits.[5]

Despite this socioeconomic centralization, Santiago's government is weak (and thus less able to resist the very strong real estate lobby), due largely to a strong centralist tradition and a dispersal of power at the local level. The strong centralist tradition emerges from the lack of autonomous government at the province level. As a province, Santiago is a second-level administrative division of Chile and is governed by the intendant of the Santiago Metropolitan Region, who is appointed by the president of Chile. This regional government lacks significant powers, because national government ministries make the majority of decisions that affect Santiago as a whole. This approach undermines the emergence of policies that integrate across sectors.

In addition, the province suffers from a dispersal of power at the local level. It is divided into thirty-two communes (*comunas*), each governed by a municipality consisting of a mayor (*alcalde*) and a municipal council. The effect is significant competition among communes for influence and resources. Three municipalities within the province carry the most influence: Las Condes (population 250,000 in 2014), Santiago Centro (population 345,000 in 2014), and La Florida (population 366,000 in 2014). Las Condes derives its influence from its wealth, La Florida from its large population, and Santiago Centro from its population coupled with its traditional role as the center of cultural and political life. While mayors are mostly executors of national policy, the mayors of these three municipalities can at times become contenders in the national presidency. Until 1991 mayors were appointed. Since 1991, they are elected by municipal councils, which are in turn directly elected. This chapter focuses on politics in the municipality of Santiago Centro, which had between eight and ten councilors over the period of interest (2005–2012).

The central government collects 95 percent of all taxes. Regional governments have no revenue-raising capacity and represent a small percentage of local public expenditure. After transfers, property tax is the single largest source of local revenues and is levied at a rate of 1.5 percent of cadastral evaluations, despite very outdated assessments.[6] Property taxes are collected by the central government, and part is returned to the municipalities. A decree from 1959 exempts dwellings of less than 140 square meters from property taxes—which implies an exemption for 70 percent of residential properties—and also from taxes on rental income (the legislation was designed to promote middle-class investment in real estate, but all articles of the law have been since abrogated except the tax exemption). Since in addition the state returns 65 percent of value-added tax to builders, the effect is a fiscal approach that privileges real estate developers.[7]

Real estate developers are also favored by a set of revenue sources. In addition to property taxes, building permits constitute an important source of funding for municipalities and promote the construction of multistory buildings. Business licenses (*patente comerciales*) are also issued and collected locally and prompt municipalities to offer business-friendly conditions. Vehicle registration fees constitute a third revenue source that is closely related to urban redevelopment. These fees range from 1 percent to 4.5 percent of the value of the vehicle and foster intense competition among municipalities, because vehicles do not have to be registered in the municipality of residence of the owner. In the richest of municipalities, vehicle registrations often constitute about 20 percent of municipal revenue.[8]

Chile lacks a tradition of urban planning and has historically favored the rights of property owners and developers. In the last decades, the urban area of Greater Santiago (which includes Santiago Province) has quadrupled. Different instruments have regulated land use following its growth. The leading one is the Metropolitan Regulatory Plan for Santiago (Plan Regulador Metropolitano de Santiago, PRMS), which was passed in 1994 and subsequently modified and broadened in scope in 1997, 2003, and 2014. Individual municipalities followed up the master plan in their own respective implementation plans, the Planos Reguladores Comunales.

A key goal of the PRMS was to raise densities. Yet scholars have lamented the lack of integrated territorial development and the ways in which land liberalization fed speculation.[9] A lack of territorial coordination led to weak overall logic, or to what local residents refer to as *cosismo*. Mayors of the richest municipalities have sought signature projects to enhance their status, competing to have the tallest building, the most dramatic bridge, or the most important embassy. The built environment therefore plays not only an important function in municipal finances but also a key symbolic and political role.

Given this context, private developers play a key role in urban planning. In newly emerging neighborhoods, developers take over the task of providing amenities such as playgrounds and parks and infrastructure such as schools and shopping and health care facilities. But the private sector plays a key role also in already established neighborhoods. In upper- and medium-income neighborhoods, the private sector undertakes major infrastructure development.

Resistance to Redevelopment by the Vecinos por la Defensa del Barrio Yungay

The Yungay barrio is situated in the heart of the municipality of Santiago. Until 1835 Yungay belonged to José Santiago Portales Larraín, father of the minister Diego Portales. The family subsequently subdivided and sold the

350 hectares. In 1839 at the end of the war against the Peru-Bolivian confederation, the president signed a decree to give the barrio the name of the battle that sealed the victory: Yungay. In the same year José Zapiola composed "Hymn to the Victory of Yungay," which was used as the Chilean national anthem and further fortified the identity of the barrio. The barrio was characterized since the mid-1800s as an area of the middle classes and public employees. The demographic growth at the end of the 1800s prompted the construction of several important buildings and churches, but the symbol of Yungay became the Monument of the Common Chilean, sculpted by Virginio Arias in 1888, sealing Yungay as the barrio that carried the national identity. The barrio was portrayed in important Chilean novels, and in the 1920s elegant theaters were built on its southern side. Starting from the 1930s, the barrio experienced the out-migration of middle- and upper-middle-income residents who moved to new affluent municipalities in the east (Providencia, Nunoa, Las Condes). Yungay thus underwent a slow deterioration, with a decline in maintenance and increasing subdivision of its buildings. Until the 1950s, the barrio Yungay, like several other working-class neighborhoods in Santiago, maintained a vital community and a rich everyday life.[10] Thanks to its many low-rise buildings and quiet streets, it enjoyed a provincial air and close neighborhood relations. For that reason, traditions were kept alive, such as a famous carnival.

The 1985 earthquake deepened the deterioration of the barrio, and the pattern leading to gentrification began. Building devaluation took place through redlining as financial institutions declared the area not viable, precluding owners from maintenance and repair funds. Abandonments followed, and buildings could be bought for very low prices.[11] In 1987 the area was declared an Urban Renewal Area (Zona de Renovación Urbana), and subsidies for building renovation were granted by the central government.

The central government launched several programs to promote the renovation of deteriorated housing and the provision of affordable housing in the city center. These programs were accompanied by innovative municipal management through the Corporation for the Development of Santiago, known as Cordesan. Starting in 1985, Cordesan established an effective link between municipality, local community and real estate sector. The corporation halted the abandonment of the city center with the removal of undesirable structures (a prison and derelict transportation infrastructure), improvements in public spaces, the rehabilitation of heritage buildings, and the construction of cultural facilities and parks.[12] By serving as the bridge between government programs and real estate developers, Cordesan was able to attract public school teachers by offering them new subsidized housing. This highly successful program was extended to other aspiring residents and fed a process of gentrification.[13]

The problem was that the different levels of government failed to act in unison: "while the national state decisively promote[d] a model of inner city social housing upgrading . . . , other national- and local-level branches of the state prioritize[d] the high-rise construction."[14] In particular, redlining was due not only to financial institutions limiting credit but even more so to municipal regulation that undermined small-scale redevelopment and therefore prevented small owners from realizing the rent potential of their homes. Following this highly entrepreneurial and contradictory role of the state, real estate interests developed a keen interest in the historical center of Santiago: many old buildings were replaced with high-rises, and gentrification followed.[15]

In the municipality of Santiago, the development of subsidized apartments increased tenfold, rising from 1.1 percent of the units and 1.16 percent of the square meters offered in 1989, to a 13.8 percent of the units and 11 percent of the square meters offered in 2001 in Greater Santiago.[16] Due to special regulations, the beneficiaries of the subsidies were very large construction companies, as can be deduced from the average size of new buildings, which increased from eleven floors in 1996 to eighteen floors in 2006, while the number of apartments built per condominium also soared from 78.5 in 1991 to 207.5 in 2005.[17] The effect was an appreciation per square meter that was four times higher in the Santiago municipality than in the whole of Greater Santiago during the 1990s.[18]

In this context, the VDBY set a model for development because it sought an alternative to the common socioeconomic condition of heritage sites, in which authorities are largely geared to tourism and the economic interests of the elites, pushing out historical residents. The association instead promoted citizen participation and projects of public or affordable housing in historical centers as a sustainable and inclusive model for development.

This movement formed in the fall of 2005 when neighbors met and organized over the poor quality of their garbage collection. Over 2,000 signatures were collected and sent to the municipality, the regional executive, the secretary-general of government (Secretaría General de Gobierno) and the metropolitan health office (Servicio de Salud Metropolitano del Ambiente). Over twenty-five demonstrations were organized over the fall and winter to protest against Mayor Raúl Alaino Alcaíno. An independent of center-right leanings, the mayor was a television host with an engineering background and pursued policies typical of political branding,[19] focusing on the restoration of the historical city center and the improvement of public space, investing in education and sport facilities, and emphasizing efficiency and transparency in government through a cooperation with the Chilean chapter of Transparency International.

In May 2006 almost by chance, the founders of the VDBY attended a public hearing at the municipality, which presented the plan to modify the Plan Regulador Comunal de Santiago, Sector Parque Portales (the sector that includes the barrio Yungay). With the extension of Parque Portales, the municipality was changing the allowed building height and removing several buildings from the heritage protection list.[20] The association reacted swiftly because "once more the authorities expected to impose on us a model of city in which the community has no decision right."[21]

Quickly the narrative became one of protecting the barrio from poor management and real estate speculation. Led by Rosario Carvajal, an energetic historian who was born and resided in the neighborhood, a handful of professionals and academics in the field of architecture and law mobilized low-income residents around a twofold idea: (1) the identity of the neighborhood is constituted by its architectural heritage and the sociocultural-historical heritage of its (current residential and commercial) population, and (2) the proposed redevelopment threatened this identity and must be opposed. This idea became the glue and the catalyst for mobilization and brought together a range of participants from the lower and middle classes, with different employment profiles and of different ages. The motto of the VDBY, indicative of its strategy, was "to disseminate, to disseminate, to disseminate" (*difundir, difundir y difundir*). Organizers alerted the neighbors, held meetings, collected signatures, and, thanks to the collaboration of various professionals from the barrio, succeeded in halting the initiative to raise the building height to twenty floors.

To deliver its ideas, the VDBY deployed instruments that built on and expanded well beyond the traditional repertoire. The association started mobilizing and protesting using traditional tools such as signature collections, street protests, sit-ins, and teach-ins. The VDBY quickly established links with traditional media (the press, radio and television) and also developed media outlets that it could directly control, such as a website, a listserv, a glossy monthly magazine distributed in municipal kiosks, radio programs, and even an Internet television channel.

These communication tools were accompanied by the development of specific content about the barrio's value. The content was delivered largely through experiential tools, instruments of mobilization aimed at heightening enthusiasm by providing a memorable experience that helped participants make sense of their identity through the barrio and provided them with values with which they sought association and a new sense of worth. These experiential tools included guidebooks and tours, a photo and audiovisual archive that was assembled with the contributions of residents, and "memory workshops" in which residents came together to construct the history of the barrio and elaborate its cultural significance. The heritage registry was an especially notable invention, with the dual goal of mobilizing residents' support and stopping real estate speculation. The registry consisted of an archive of local family histories and therefore deployed cultural as well as emotional heritage to legitimize and anchor residents and small businesses in the neighborhood. Thus, the registry was essential in communicating the idea that the barrio identity was based not only on architectural heritage but also on the sociocultural heritage of its current population of residents and workers.

These experiential tools constructed a cross-cleavage narrative about the identity of the neighborhood while at the same time freezing that identity in its state of early gentrification. As a result, the experiences and events were designed to suit broad tastes and implicitly transmit highly inclusive (even catch-all) values and political messages about the neighborhood. The events organized by the VDBY were particularly effective tools for political communication and mobilization, because participants were engaged through active experiences that avoided immediate political associations. The events promoted memory and emotional linkages with the core values of the association and thus developed loyalty among residents. In addition, these events provided the occasion to present specific initiatives of the VDBY (e.g., a restored monument and a newly founded group of artisans). The events also offered the occasion for core activists to coalesce around a challenge and be energized by its success. Finally, the events mobilized previously latent residents as well as outsiders—including municipal institutions, other levels of government, and partnerships—with civil society and business sectors.

Every few months the VDBY brought residents together with a major event. In January, the Festival del Roto Chileno (Festival of the Common Chilean) commemorated the Battle of Yungay of January 20, 1839, between the Peru/Bolivian Confederation and the Peru/Chilean United Restoration Army. The victory by poor and untrained soldiers (hence the name Common

Chilean) led to the end of the Peru/Bolivian Confederation. This traditional event in Santiago enjoys renewed status thanks to the organizational input of the VDBY and in January 2010 had 13,000 attendees.

In May, the VDBY started a tradition known as the Día del Patrimonio en Yungay (Day of Yungay Heritage). In June, the association organized a council called the Cabildo de Santiago, which attracted increasingly influential participants and hundreds of residents (in June 2009 among the attendees were the ministry secretary-general of government, members of parliament, and regional and municipal councilors). Council organizers asked participants to bring photos of the neighborhood, describe the changes they hoped for, and select committees in which to volunteer.

Each September since 2007, the VDBY organizes a grand celebration for the founding of the barrio. Recently the 170th anniversary was celebrated with a communal open-air dinner for hundreds of residents and an artistic gala. Finally, each November since 2007, the barrio celebrates the Festival del Barrio Yungay, with more than two hundred artists participating in multiple locations at the same time and with a myriad of activities and attractions including dozens of bands and musicians of different genres, baby football games and other sport events, theater plays, art walks, carnival parades, and children activities. Several lectures, public readings, photo exhibitions, and arts workshops deal with representations of the barrio ranging from historical depictions to the latest graffiti.

A Multipronged Strategy

The VDBY owes its effectiveness to a multipronged strategy. First, the association pursued legal avenues to reach its primary goal of the establishment of the Zona Típica (Heritage Area). In 2009, 113 hectares of Yungay obtained the status of Zona Típica, and since then a major extension has been pursued that would enlarge the area to the entire north and west of the municipality of Santiago. There were also several petitions to extend protection to individual buildings by seeking the status of Monumento Nacional (National Monument). It is interesting to note that while the Urban Renewal Areas of 1987 established zones that promoted neoliberal development, the designation of Zona Típica was intended to slow the impact of market forces on the physical transformation of the area.

Soon after Yungay reached the status of Zona Típica and gained some political visibility, the VDBY embarked on a mission to solidify its status by pursuing financial autonomy. For example, the association established a sister foundation, Fundacion Patrimonio Nuestro (Our Heritage Foundation), because foundations have better access to public funding than associations, both nationally and internationally.

Political influence was also pursued from the very beginning by lobbying local politicians, such as municipal and regional councilors, as well as sympathizers in the national government, such as in the ministry of culture. This strategy was successful, judging from the fact that increasingly prominent politicians were recorded as attending events sponsored by the VDBY. Usually on these occasions the officials are interviewed, and both videos and transcripts are posted on the websites of the association and the foundation. However, political influence was also pursued through successful participation in electoral competition by members of the association. In October 2008 a candidate from the association gained a seat on the municipal council of Santiago (the association currently has two close supporters in the municipal council). In September 2009 after a hard fight to introduce popular elections for the Consejo Económico Social Comunal (CESCO), the association's candidate won a seat on its first competition. Finally, in November 2009 the VDBY's founding president, Rosario Carvajal, was offered a seat on the Consejo de la Sociedad Civil, recently established under the Ministerio Secretaría General de Gobierno. Hence, political influence was effectively pursued at all levels of government and accompanied the increasing prominence of the VDBY.

These initiatives, the VDBY's various committees, and the coordination of the numerous festivals required an increasing number of volunteers. Therefore, the leadership of the association pursued a continuous mobilization and education effort, aiming to build its status and legitimacy within the community. For this purpose, the association reached out to residents through traditional and Internet-based media. Over the course of 2009, the association put in place an elaborate education program articulated through workshops, seminars, conferences, and schools to continue to incorporate neighbors in the movement and management of the barrio and the VDBY. Conferences covered experiences in community participation in the defense of heritage, public policies for heritage development, and proposals for community management of heritage. Schools and courses were held in various municipalities in and around Santiago (Matta Sur, Talagante, Valparaiso, Coquimbo) with lessons in community organizing, community and cultural management, identity development as immaterial heritage, heritage media, and television.

The most significant school was inspired by a visit to Colombia in July 2009. Invited to Cartagena to present strategy and results of the association, its leaders observed a masonry school that helped at-risk teenagers by providing them with skills to repair local historical buildings and contribute to the local art and craft tradition. This workshop school, the Escuela Taller de Cartagena de Indias, was founded in 1992 and allowed about one hundred youths from disadvantaged backgrounds to follow courses for eighteen months and restore real estate in the city center. The approach innovatively addressed both unemployment and heritage conservation. As there was no such school in Chile, upon its return the VDBY began to campaign to open a similar institute, the Escuela Taller de Artes y Oficios Fermin Vivaceta, and lobbied the local authorities for funding. The initiative gained urgency with the earthquake of February 27, 2010, and the school opened its doors the following April.

On the institutional front, authority was pursued through increasingly large networks of sister movements. First, the VDBY built a coalition based on sectorial interests, with a variety of cultural agents in the neighborhood of Yungay (foundations, museums, artisan and artists' groups, heterogeneous cultural centers and movements). Subsequently, the network was extended to areas outside the neighborhood, producing *hermaniamentos* (brotherhoods) with Juntas de Vecinos and like-minded groups around Metropolitan Santiago, among them being Bellavista, Vitacura, Qilicura, Matta Sur, Lo Espejo, and Colina.

After expanding the outreach to the regional level to include groups in the area of Valparaiso, the VDBY established international links. Over the course of 2009, linkages were set up with groups in Argentina (in particular the Buenos Aires neighborhoods of San Telmo and Haedo), Montevideo, Uruguay, and Colombia. The VDBY's invitation to the Seventh Conference of Historical Centers in Cartagena, Colombia, organized by the Heritage Program of the Spanish government in 2009, is an indication of the VDBY's rising visibility. On that occasion, the association was recognized as pioneering and unique in Latin America because it managed to build a model of local development from a heritage perspective that included an important role for popular participation. It is important to note that all extensions of the model developed by the VDBY were based on the twofold idea highlighted above: asserting the social character of the neighborhood's heritage and the need for its preservation against the threat of redevelopment. This message was consistently invoked and adapted to other Santiago neighborhoods, other Chilean cities, and other neighborhoods in different countries.

Interestingly, a national network was established last, possibly because the exceptional size and influence of the city made it hard to translate and replicate the experiences of Santiago to elsewhere. In July 2009, the Chilean

Association of Neighbors and Barrio Organizations and Heritage Areas (Asociación Chilena de Vecinos y Organizaciones de Barrios y Zonas Patrimoniales) was founded with an initial membership of twenty like-minded groups. While the initial participants spanned only fifteen kilometers from the center of Santiago, the goal was to promote a national movement—with the added complexity of connecting urban and rural heritage—and by April 2010 it already had members from seven of the thirteen regions of Chile. The activities of the national association were celebrated with the first Citizen Council for Heritage (Consejo Ciudadano del Patrimonio) in January 2010, promoted via a website that posted news of meeting discussions, group actions, and rallies around initiatives of individual members (the website also covers issues of interest at home and abroad).

Thus, the VDBY took a leadership role in supporting the formation of other movements around the country with the aim of increasing its institutional authority but also the scope and scale of its initiatives. Rosario Carvajal, founding president of both the VDBY and the Asociación Chilena de Vecinos y Organizaciones de Barrios y Zonas Patrimoniales, explained that the league was critical in obtaining institutional authority and increasing the leverage of individual experiences in order to be more influential: "We sought legal status to obtain more institutional authority in negotiations. We seek to establish a system of mutual collaboration, to learn from each other's mistakes and expertise. This implies a revolution in the short term: neighbors, for the first time, will speak with one voice. They will have to be heard."[22]

In sum, the association pursued an effective multipronged strategy for which it did not follow a preexisting model. In the course of a handful of years, largely concentrated in 2009, this strategy obtained important and tangible results and catapulted the association to the forefront of Chilean civil society in the field of culture and heritage.

Barrio Identity and Political Conflict

The newly acquired prominence of course prompted political tensions. Even in the context of a highly institutionalized and overall well-functioning party system, the dynamic of political contention moved from a focus on parties and traditional cleavages to the newly introduced identity politics. A good example is the conflict of the VDBY with the mayor of Santiago, Pablo Zalaquett. A rising star in the center-right coalition, Zalaquett had previously led the mayoralty of La Florida, a large middle-class municipality in the south of Santiago, where he engaged in privatization (e.g., of waste collection) and cut crime.

Due to his reliance on mass media and his telegenic style, Zalaquett was quickly dubbed the "media mayor" (*alcalde mediatico*). The confrontation between the mayor and the VDBY is therefore interesting because it brought together two media savvy opponents. Identity politics determined the language of the confrontation, and the VDBY, having introduced a vibrant new brand for the barrio, set the tone.

Conflict revolved around two issues: garbage collection and real estate development. In August 2009 when the mayor moved to privatize waste collection in Yungay, the VDBY collected 5,000 signatures and mobilized supporters from other areas, allies in the municipal council, and union members fearful for their jobs. The VDBY framed the issue of garbage collection as one of preservation and attacked the mayor for seeking to undermine the neighborhood and its quality of life, thereby emphasizing the use value of the neighborhood. The mayor's response instead emphasized the exchange value of the neighborhood, as he argued that redevelopment in a neighborhood with such prominent heritage was financially advantageous: "We have several private projects that increase the attractiveness for tourists, promise vitality and generate a more interesting space as municipality."[23] The VDBY replied that the aim was instead to reproduce the intense gentrification that had already taken place in other neighborhoods (such as Lastarrias and Bellavista) and reacted with measures to protect squatters as well as long-term renters and owners.

What is of particular note is that the mayor—like the association—based his argument on heritage. However, his deployment of the idea of heritage was less effective. In his battle over the definition of heritage, Zalaquett shut down the Foundation Victor Jara (very close to the VDBY) and the connected cultural center Galpón over the definition of "folk art." In the opinion of the mayor, the center was being used for events that were not "true" to the folk art of the city and was therefore going beyond its license. This move brought the conflict straight to the definition of the "authentic" barrio identity—a plane in which, unsurprisingly, the association had the upper hand, given its previous work and ability to mobilize around the issue. The mayor relied on a nostalgic, highbrow, and elitist notion of authenticity for the neighborhood.[24] The VDBY instead enjoyed the political advantage of a broad definition of local heritage, which united residents who listen to traditional music with those who skate to the rhythm of hip-hop during the barrio festivals. In the discourse battle that ensued, media and public opinion sided with the VDBY, and the mayor abandoned the struggle.

The earthquake of February 27, 2010, provides a second illustration of how different ideas about barrio identity were deployed for political ends. Within a few of hours after the quake hit, despite the fear and chaos that accompanied the event, the VDBY was in motion. The media presented an image of Yungay as heavily damaged, which was interpreted as a veiled form of blockbusting, fraudulently giving the impression that the neighborhood was changing for the worse in order to induce owners to sell at a loss, the classic antecedent to redlining. The association criticized the mayor's message to the media about the state of damage in the neighborhood, which "gives public opinion the impression our neighborhood is in ruin and that it shall be demolished tomorrow . . . following the interests of real estate developers to destroy our heritage barrio."[25]

Not losing a minute in the counteroffensive, the VDBY mobilized 1,000 volunteers on the day of the quake to register 1,500 buildings and inspect 350. Within a few days the association had set up a fund for reconstruction and repair, the Fondo de Restauración Patrimonial del Barrio Yungay. Problem-solving teams walked the neighborhood to address residents' emergencies. A program godfathered damaged buildings, preparing them for repair and protecting them from demolition. The local heritage masonry school, in the plans since the VDBY's visit to Cartagena the previous August, found a boost in the urgent needs and was inaugurated less than two months later.

Conclusion: Place Identity and Participation

The lack of formal membership in the type of association examined here allows the VDBY to be flexible, low cost, and adaptable to varying levels of enthusiasm. For this reason, a key challenge for the leaders of the association was the development of powerful ideas able to mobilize and maintain a loyal and committed following in various activities ranging from protests to internal management. The key idea was the articulation of a place-based identity and the call for its protection. Various events and experiences promoted that identity and thus overcame the challenges of mobilization in a highly heterogeneous socioeconomic space. One might fear that the downside of place-based identity is insularity, as each heritage conservation association is deeply committed to its own neighborhood and might therefore be unable to sympathize or effectively cooperate with other barrio associations. This, however, is not the result that played out in Santiago. On the contrary, heritage conservation associations are mushrooming in an environment of deep mutual aid in which ideas, resources, and strategies are shared and supporters eagerly join each other's battle.

This surprising result is due to the way in which the idea of place-based identity is cast, driven by a logic that has universal aspirations and seeking justification beyond the limits and history of the barrio. The overarching identity in Yungay is based on the advocacy of art and local values in the context of a critique of the government's "misguided modernistic approach to development"[26] that is considered excessively homogenizing. Hence, heterogeneity is a key component of this identity, which as a result is open, amorphous, adaptable, and prone to network effects to be shaped depending on the specific place and circumstance. This is not a weakness but instead is a point of force of groups that share this approach, because it allows the leaders to harness the potential of place identification even in the context of diversity, both within and outside the barrio. Thanks to this approach, the VDBY was able to mobilize and coordinate despite being in a city with a powerful real estate lobby and low trust in popular associations and prominent parties. Developing an idea of place identity that sways supporters *and* is highly inclusive is not easy. But once it is achieved, almost any challenge can be recast within its terms—not only consumption and social services but also redistributive policies and technical issues such as land use.

CHAPTER 13

Ideas, Politics, and Urban Development in China

William Hurst

Throughout history, civilization has bloomed on the fertile ground of urbanization. Agrarian societies have been most influential in their production of sufficient caloric surpluses to allow for an increasing division of labor and the growth of most concentrated population centers in which critical masses of humanity could focus on pursuits other than farming, hunting, or gathering—from industrial labor to literature, baking to banking, pottery to politics, and services to science. At least that is the classical perspective, shared by a diverse collection of scholars from Herodotus and Thucydides to Veblen and Marx (even if a few dissenters, such as Hesiod and William Morris, piped up occasionally and a few others, such as Virgil and Simmel, remained conflicted in their views). Seen through this lens, the industrial revolution and its aftermath across Europe, North America, and then other parts of the globe could appear coherent and universal. Economic and technological change produced demand for urban labor and capital aggregation; at the same time, farmers were becoming increasingly idle as agriculture gained in efficiency. This confluence of factors brought laborers and money into cities just as their factories boomed and provided needed jobs, which then produced more capital that could be reinvested. Only the post-World War II problems of urbanization in the developing world—especially in Latin America, South, and Southeast Asia, but also in Africa and elsewhere—called this march of progress consensus into question.

As traditional, colonial, and imperial orders began to disintegrate, the rapid growth of rural populations squeezed many farmers off the land. Stagnating incomes and persistent poverty across the countryside also lured many villagers into cities, which swelled to immense size. This explosive growth of cities took place without any concomitant development of employment or infrastructure, however. New urbanites were increasingly clustered into slums and shantytowns at the margins of urban economies and societies.[1]

Urbanization without industrialization thus became the order of the day in the late twentieth century across much of the developing world.[2] Cities grew without the economic foundations that many assumed were needed to support them and have had difficulty grappling with the resulting upheaval ever since. Moreover, just as cities were beginning to come to terms with their expanded populations, largely informally employed or unemployed, and neighborhoods, the era of mass employment in manufacturing was drawing to a close. The small-scale and largely nonregulated economic activities of the slum had become a mainstay of the urban economy, even as many in the formal sector were being displaced or saw their livelihoods begin to stagnate.[3] The city had become an organic creation that existed mostly beyond the reach of the state or the discipline of formal institutions of the market. In fact, it had come to exist almost despite the state, even as it had outgrown the formal market and officially governed society that the state had privileged.

Neither of these has been China's experience, however. Instead, China has followed a path almost entirely distinct from those of either early or late developers. This journey has been shaped by China's unique historical experience but also guided by a Chinese Communist Party (CCP) with a very specific view of cities as both threats and utopias. For the CCP and especially for Mao Zedong, cities were seen not only as critical nodes of all that was wrong with capitalism but also as weak points of socialism in which dangerous tendencies such as "bureaucratism" (官僚主义) were especially likely to take hold and sap the spirit and vigor of the revolution. At the same time, China's planned economy focused on cities as centers of industrialization and innovation that had to be protected from being overrun by masses of rural residents who might threaten the new communist urban order. As CCP priorities and ideological currents shifted, however, the party and the state influenced China's cities and urbanization in markedly different ways during different periods.

A very powerful Chinese state thus forestalled comprehensive urbanization for roughly fifty years after the CCP's rise to power in 1949. But the same state has more recently been very much behind trends in the past couple of decades that have seen more than 400 million people transition from rural to urban citizenship, even as formal urban employment has become increasingly scarce across much of the country. Finally, the Chinese state has adopted unique strategies and faced special challenges in its efforts to adapt its institutions to the new urbanization of space and people.

There are thus three aspects of China's urbanization that stand out from the rest of the world: its timing, its motivation, and its particular blend of distinct forms of urbanization of space, people, and governance structures. I will focus on these critical idiosyncrasies of Chinese urbanization to discuss its roots in the communist past and the rationale for its augmented speed in the present, the role of the state and the party in both delaying urbanization earlier and promoting it now, and the distinctive ways that land, people, and institutions are being urbanized in China today.

China's Urban Politics in the Maoist Era, 1949–1978

Upon their takeover of Chinese politics in 1949, CCP leaders inherited a mélange of loosely governed and incoherent urban politics and policies. Little was standardized nationally, and even less was enforced. The boundaries of who and what locations should be considered urban were far from fixed. The CCP set out adroitly and expeditiously to change this, establishing cities as distinct redoubts separated from the countryside[4] through a new conception of citizenship that divided urban from rural residents.

What resulted was a system of household registration, *hukou* (户口), modeled somewhat on the "internal passports" used in the Soviet Union, that was introduced in 1951. The primary rationale was to monitor and keep track of population movements as well as prevent the unregulated clustering of impoverished masses into cities or informal settlements. Families were assigned either "agricultural" or "nonagricultural" status. The former were entitled to agricultural land but were required to remain in the countryside. The latter were permitted to live in cities and were entitled to a variety of social benefits reserved for urbanites. By keeping each family in its place both spatially and socially, the *hukou* system enabled the CCP to control the world's most populous country with a still-incipient government bureaucracy and to prevent the very sort of unchecked expansion of slums and shantytowns that marked urbanization in many other developing countries at the same historical moment. The resulting "right to the city"—in many ways quite the opposite of how Henri Lefebvre[5] would use the term two decades later—was restricted to a small minority, but with it came numerous other social rights: to a job, health care, housing, and the like.

Later, when more workers were required in cities for massive infrastructure projects during the Great Leap Forward (1958–1962), tens of millions were brought in temporarily from the rural hinterlands, only to be sent back when their services were no longer required. When the specter of unemployment loomed for the children of China's boom urban generation (born in the 1950s), millions of youths were summarily sent to the countryside in the late 1960s and 1970s. Many of these "rusticated youths" found their life chances irrevocably altered when they finally made it back to the city (often five, ten, or even fifteen years later). But the state was able to extend the reach of the command economy to regulate the supply of labor into urban manufacturing and services, tapping peasants as temporary workers when needed and consigning an entire generation of urban youths to internal exile in villages when demand was insufficient.

Overall, the Maoist order kept most of China's population in the countryside. According to the World Bank, more than 82 percent of Chinese citizens were classified as rural as late as 1978.[6] By establishing urban areas as redoubts of an inclusive socialist social contract from which rural residents were excluded, the CCP succeeded at building socialism in its cities essentially on the backs of its villagers, from whom the extraction of the agricultural surplus (through "price scissors" and grain requisitions from collectivized communes) served as the primary locus of state-society interaction across the countryside and a critical means of state fiscal support. By denying most citizens access to the city, the CCP offered urban workers far more benefits—and in far more orderly and controlled environments—than would have been possible otherwise given China's low per capita gross domestic product (GDP) and the general global conditions of the time.

Creeping Urbanization of People, Sudden Urbanization of Places, 1978–2011

Almost as soon as Mao died, however, this system of urban-rural segregation began to erode. Along with rusticated youths returning to their urban homes, millions of rural workers began to stream into Chinese cities as early as the 1980s.[7] Many came on formal short-term contracts with urban enterprises in relatively organized groups. But by the end of the decade, small streams became more substantial flows that only increased through to the end of the century.[8] Two essential reforms underpinned this: the decollectivization of agriculture and the establishment of (largely informal) markets for urban goods and services beyond the allocation of the formal planned economy.

Beginning in 1979, the CCP acted to reverse the agglomeration of villages into township-level communes (人民公社) that had taken place in 1958 as part of the Great Leap Forward.[9] After two decades of using collectivized agriculture to maximize the state's ability to extract the rural surplus, leaders and planners became convinced that the cost of administering the system outweighed the benefits. That is, there were both bottom-up[10] and top-down[11] logics motivating reform that centered around ideas of allowing rural producers to share more in the harvest to improve efficiency and of releasing the state from the infrastructural capacity demands of overseeing critical components of the planned economy. Though this was not universally welcomed and did not everywhere produce great economic or social gains,[12] the aggregate effect at the national level was to increase the overall efficiency of agriculture and thus free many farmers and rural laborers to look for work outside of the immediate tasks of cultivation. By the mid-1980s, many of these erstwhile farmers began to seek opportunities in cities.

At the same time, informal markets were permitted, on which grain, produce, and other rural goods could be bought and sold for the first time in more than twenty years. Gradually, a generalized framework known as the dual-track system (双轨制) was established to allow urban firms and other producers to sell any goods or services not required by the plan to any willing buyer on the open market. Quickly, the new market grew up alongside the plan, providing opportunities for profit and also the procurement of goods and services without the need for rationing coupons or formal state allocations.[13] Workers who moved from the countryside to the city thus could avail themselves of opportunities to work outside formal state-initiated contracts with state-owned enterprises, but they also were able to acquire goods and services in the city with the cash they earned. This step was critical, since before they needed to either carry their own food with them or gain access to state firms' rations.[14]

Once the dual-track system was officially ended, replaced by exclusive reliance on the market for nearly all goods and services in 1994, the streams of rural migrants coming to cities became torrents. Farmers-turned-workers were free to search out whatever opportunities they might find and could both purchase goods and remit money back to their villages with relative impunity. Though legal barriers to formal urban residency remained and migrants were often sorely mistreated in cities across the country, upwards of 150–200 million people had moved from rural to urban areas in search of work by the turn of the twenty-first century.

Administrative governance structures were also reformed during the 1980s and early 1990s in ways that changed the boundaries of urban areas, as the CCP leadership became convinced of the greater efficiency of administering and taxing "cities" and of the greater market potential they had versus rural prefectures. Prefectures (地区) were replaced throughout most of China by prefecture-level cities (地级市), each with a major urban area at its core. This integrated hundreds of millions of rural *hukou* holders into structures of urban governance and authority for the first time, facilitating their migration into cities. The replacement also resulted in much of China's landmass being reclassified as "urban" through administrative fiat, if not organic social or economic change. Indeed, by the mid-1990s a much greater proportion of China's land had been classified as urban, and evidence suggests that much more land was being put to urban uses.[15]

The conclusion of this administrative reform coincided with a thorough and disruptive fiscal reform in 1994, however. The central government garnered the lion's share of tax revenues that had previously been collected by and allocated to subnational and local governments. Specifically, nearly 80 percent of fiscal revenues had accrued to subnational governments before the reform, with only a little over 20 percent flowing to the center. These percentages reversed in the wake of the changes, with Beijing claiming more than two-thirds of fiscal revenues a few years later. This changed incentives and constraints markedly at the local level.

The first response was to raise money by whatever means local governments had at their disposal. This frequently meant the imposition of fees and levies beyond official budgetary limits or procedures.[16] The so-called peasant burdens that these produced were shouldered by China's rural masses but also ensured that at least a minimum of basic social services and government functions could be carried out across the country's 1,400 counties. But the peasant burdens also created new incentives for rural residents to move to cities in search of opportunities to earn cash. Farmers who might be calorie-rich were still often cash-poor, which made it difficult to pay fees, taxes, and levies. Remittances helped bridge this gap, and the need for liquid money pushed millions to migrate.

When President Hu Jintao and Premier Wen Jiabao announced a crackdown against many forms of peasant burdens and extrabudgetary fees and revenues as well as an abolition of the agricultural tax, they were clearly acting in what they thought to be rural residents' best interests. These reforms were paired with the abolition of school fees for rural children and the extension of certain additional social benefits to villagers. But they also had unintended consequences for the ways local governments managed revenues and taxation.

Deprived of the fees and levies they had relied on to squeeze villagers after losing tax streams twelve years earlier, local governments turned to the sale of land-use rights as an important source of funds. Within five years of losing extrabudgetary revenue streams, local governments had replaced them with sales of land-use rights—which accounted for upwards of 70 percent of local government revenues by 2011.[17] To realize these revenues, local governments first requisitioned rural land from villagers (paying them at least some compensation, though the equity of the amount was often in dispute) and then sold the right to use the land (essentially a leasehold) to a developer (often a state-owned or sometimes private corporation), who paid the local government far more than any compensation paid to villagers. Finally, the developer would convert the land for use as housing, industrial estates, retail centers, or agribusiness—ventures that as often as not resulted in failure.

Local governments' turn to land finance in the 2000s produced a new class of landless peasants (失地农民) who had lost the basic security guarantee of land tenure but were still excluded from the social rights reserved for urbanites. This turn also facilitated an increasingly fast-paced transformation of land from cultivated resource to at least partially urbanized space. This combination of dwindling land for farmers' use and a swelling population of rural *hukou* holders unable to engage in agricultural production placed pressure on the central state to find a long-term solution. The global recession of 2008–2009 brought this to a breaking point.[18]

Faced with dramatically falling export revenues and shrinking industrial employment, the Chinese government decided to move toward implementing a new economic model with alacrity, an example of an exogenous crisis forcing a domestic reckoning of competing ideas at a critical juncture.[19] Instead of relying on export-oriented development strategies, often based on export processing manufacturing (加工出口创造业)—in which components are brought together for final assembly or processing in China but the principle value-added often remained abroad—China would seek to boost domestic demand and transition to a more consumption-focused pattern of economic growth. Key to this would be the expansion of the urban population and especially the urban middle class, who (as in most countries) tend to consume far more than their rural counterparts. Just as the CCP had held back the tide of urbanization for decades during the Maoist era, it sought to force the process ahead at full speed as China managed to weather the worst of the international crisis, emerging with its economy relatively intact by 2010.

State-Led Drive for Urbanization on an Unprecedented Scale, 2011–2020

Beginning in 2011, the CCP pressed forward with twin goals of urbanizing villages (农村城镇化) and integrating the city and countryside (城乡一体化), the idea being that urbanites consume more than villagers and that cities are more productive than rural areas (and thus China stood to gain by urbanizing peasants into city dwellers and villages into urban neighborhoods by command decision). In urbanizing village land and transforming villagers from agricultural into nonagricultural *hukou* holders, the state sought to create a new class of socially more secure and economically more affluent urbanites ready to consume and engage in more productive labor. These new city dwellers would move into apartments in new high-rises and be granted rights to health care, pensions, and urban schools for their children for the first time. The previously isolated village would also be integrated into a new urban structure that would bring road and transit infrastructure to previously rural counties that would be integrated relatively seamlessly into cities as urban districts. Physical space and populations would both become urban simultaneously, creating 100 million new workers and consumers by 2018.

This urbanization by fiat has proven less efficacious and more fraught than the CCP intended, however. While space and people have duly been converted from rural to urban official status and while hundreds of thousands of apartment towers have been built, thousands of kilometers of new subway lines have been extended, and vast sums of money have been spent on new hospitals, schools, and social benefits, jobs have not materialized for all of these new urbanites. And developers have not always been able to turn profits on building apartments or other infrastructure, leading to many failed projects. In extreme form, this has led to many "ghost cities" and "ghost districts" across much of China.[20] Even in less dire settings, unemployment and underemployment are rife in newly urbanized districts, and residents often struggle to pay the mortgages on the apartments they have been compelled to purchase.

Much of the rapid recent change in China's urban population and urbanization profile is thus an artifact not of organic social change but rather of political and administrative machinations or even sleight of hand. This sometimes left residents and institutions scrambling to adapt. In many places, newly urbanized citizens had to migrate to other localities in search of cash earnings to pay mortgages on apartments they had been obliged to purchase. Elsewhere, provision of urban social services lagged behind the urbanization of both space and people such that many thousands were left without access to the benefits they had been promised.

The change from the recent past was striking and was indeed nothing short of a radical paradigm change. Rather than holding back urbanization to preserve the command economy, the state and the CPP aggressively pressed forward with perhaps reckless urbanization in order to preserve and enhance the growth of the market. Critically, however, this was not a market-driven process. The CCP has been at the center of all politics throughout China since 1949. Even prior to its victory, the party exercised extremely precise and thorough regulation over the regions under its control. The CCP has been behind recent moves as well, calling cities and new classes of urban residents into being in order to further its interests and ensure its survival. The process has not always been one of success or triumph for the CCP, however, and has given rise to many unintended consequences with significant implications.

Institutions Struggling to Adapt

Besides the issues of disruptions to citizens' lives from in situ urbanization and lagging provision of social services and benefits, the very architecture of state institutions has been unable to cope with the pace and the degree of urbanization that has taken place in China since the late 1990s. One clear example of this is the case of cities that had been country towns but now exceed the scale and population of many international metropolises. In many such localities, no institutions of government exist below the municipal level, unlike most other prefecture-level cities that have urban districts and rural counties under their administrative purview. This can make it difficult for these newly large cities to coordinate tasks and services such as law enforcement, labor dispute resolution, sanitation, and environmental protection at the neighborhood level.

A particularly famous case of this sort is the city of Dongguan (东莞), situated between Guangzhou and Shenzhen in Guangdong Province. Dongguan has served as a paragon of China's export-oriented manufacturing success and a prime example of that model's unintended consequences and negative externalities. After being upgraded to a prefecture-level city in 1988, Dongguan's nonagricultural population was only 361,400 by 1996 (which was still a marked increase over roughly 60,000 a decade earlier). By 2016 Dongguan's population was roughly as large as New York City's,[21] and Dongguan had become home to an estimated more than 5 million migrants, mostly from rural areas around the country. Also by 2016, its GDP had risen to more than 680 billion RMB (about $97 billion at then-current exchange rates)—greater than those of Salt Lake City and New Orleans and not very much less than those of Austin and Nashville. Yet no county or district-level institutions had been created.

Dongguan became a leading exporter of all manner of consumer goods and manufactures[22] but also became a leading center of crime, corruption, and political decay. Some even claimed that up to one in ten Dongguan residents were prostitutes as of about 2010. All of this criminal activity, coupled with rampant pollution, infrastructure bottlenecks, and social disorder, flourished along with Dongguan's booming manufacturing sector in a city largely ungoverned at the street and neighborhood level. These governance problems were compounded when China's export-oriented model came under severe strain in the wake of the 2008 world financial crisis. Even if there have been some signs of redevelopment and renewal recently,[23] Dongguan will likely continue to grapple with its underdeveloped state institutions for some time.

The mismatched pacing of urbanization and institutional development has created numerous opportunities and incentives for involution, as opposed to innovation or compliance.[24] Local governments, hamstrung by the demands of burgeoning cities they cannot govern effectively, turn to the subversion of institutions for purposes of officials' or agencies' particularistic gains, sometimes at the expense of the general welfare. Dongguan is a relatively extreme and extremely well-known example. But the problem is rife across many Chinese cities beyond Beijing, Shanghai, and the various provincial capitals. It even occurs in very large cities such as Chongqing and Chengdu, especially in newly urbanized districts that only a few years ago had been rural counties.

Bringing Comparison Back In

What does all this idiosyncrasy of China mean? What does it matter if its urbanization story occurs later in the arc of its political-economic development, if urban social change is tightly bound up with the CCP, and if urbanization now occurring in situ is outpacing institutional and market development? China's strong unitary state and increasingly centralized fiscal system have contributed to a relatively more uniform pattern of urbanization than in other countries with multiple large cities such as Indonesia, where fiscal and regulatory decentralization since 2000 has given rise to disparate rates of urban population growth that are strongly correlated with factors such as locally set minimum urban wages.[25] Moreover, China's penchant for in situ urbanization and large-scale renewal and redevelopment of urban space has prevented the accumulation of competing and incongruous land-usage patterns in concentrated old city areas, as was observed to have occurred, for example, in Delhi.[26] Finally, while some have suggested that the use of urban land markets and urbanizing development for capital generation may be spreading among Southeast Asian countries,[27] such practices remain nascent and underdeveloped in comparison with what has become a virtuosic art form in contemporary China.[28]

Taken together, these distinctions mark Chinese urban politics today with three challenges that appear to be unique in the developing world. First, urbanization is self-sustaining to the point of excess. The state, especially at the local level, is dependent on revenues from the sale of land-use rights for urban development. Real estate development and construction companies depend on new stocks of land and projects to continue operations, receive credit, and drive sales to consumers. Both individuals and institutions have generally shied away from China's still nascent secondary market in real estate, preferring to use investments in newly developed properties as long-term stores of wealth. Thus, investors are hungry for new urbanization, which real estate and construction companies cannot exist without providing, and governments increasingly rely on the whole cycle continuing in order to maintain revenues in a process that drives much of China's rapid accumulation of aggregate debt and highly inefficient allocation of resources. The problem is that breaking free of this would harm numerous and powerful vested interests in the status quo.

Second, urbanization continues without powerful push or pull factors in a manner that outstrips the development of employment markets. The urbanization of vast numbers of jobless or underemployed people and unneeded space has caused a new displaced class of urban poor to emerge, alongside laid-off workers and other disadvantaged urbanites.[29] This has combined with the increasing gentrification of newly developed and redeveloped areas, pursued by local governments in search of ever greater revenue streams.[30]

Inequality (of income, housing, and benefits), unemployment, and the spiraling growth of both empty districts and underserved communities are thus all consequences of China's ongoing overurbanization.

Third, the state is at the center of all aspects of these processes in a way entirely different from any other developing country's experience. This means that the state has great power to affect change or implement policy decisions but also faces much more direct criticism or blame when things do not turn out as planned. Also, being so tightly bound up with urbanization and all its consequences restricts the state's ability to maneuver toward any new political equilibrium. For all its capacity, the CCP and China's state bureaucracy are largely trapped in a cage of their own making, dependent on a pattern and pacing of urbanization that many leaders recognize as being highly suboptimal.

Conclusion

China has at times been held up as a model of development and urbanization success. Yet, precisely the attributes that make it appealing—a strong role of the state in directing urbanization and planning, rapid urbanization and aggregate GDP growth, and avoidance of the most glaring problems of rapid urbanization in the recent pasts of other developing countries—also have roots in causal factors and patterns that conspire to make China's present and road ahead uniquely challenging. That this has not been recognized more widely is probably due to China specialists' tendency to avoid comparison and broader comparativists' general lack of knowledge or insight into China's internal politics and contemporary history.

Future research therefore ought to begin with comparison as its goal but must also not seek deductively to force China's proximate experience into a procrustean conceptual bed fashioned in nineteenth-century Europe or mid-twentieth-century Latin America or India. China's urbanization in the reform era, which we are still witnessing unfold today, is indeed a third pattern. Not driven by industrialization and a regulatory state or taking place against the backdrop of flight from rural poverty and a lack of state coordination, the burgeoning growth and transformation of China's cities demands the world's attention. It is happening at precisely the moment of deindustrialization, called into being by a deceptively weak state dependent on revenues generated from it, and with the effect of creating vast (if somewhat hidden) new disadvantaged classes and inefficiently allocated tracts of land. It is far from clear that a similar pattern could be replicated in a different country. But if it should become more common, China's model of urbanization will likely look more similar to those critiqued by many analysts in the 1960s and 1970s than those praised by others in the early 1900s.

What will likely remain unique to China's experience, however, are the ideational shifts and peculiarities that have prevented or inspired urbanization at specific moments and in particular forms. The CPP's ideology and its conceptions of citizenship, class, development, and urbanity are important not just for its own internal debates or domestic propaganda. The party's direct influence and the processes it helps shape structure not only Chinese citizens relationship to the state but also the relations between local, regional, and national institutions of governance in the world's largest polity. As China transitions from communist agrarianism to a new kind of postindustrial urbanism, it will remain both global exemplar and, across many dimensions, sui generis.

CHAPTER 14

Politics of Dwelling

Divergent Ideas of Home in Kolkata

Debjani Bhattacharyya

Speculative urbanization is neither new nor like a bubble. Yet after 2008, speculative urbanization increasingly captured our imagination as if it were a novelty. What was striking perhaps was the simultaneity with which empty skyscrapers were shooting up in the cities of India, unoccupied towns were sprawling in China, and ghost estates were proliferating in Ireland while houses were foreclosed and vacated across the United States. This sudden building boom in one part of the globe is connected to the massive foreclosures in the other part through globalized instruments of finance, new forms of real estate, and, more importantly, the proliferation of vacant homes. What made 2008 dramatic was precisely the intimate connections that yoked together the cement, concrete, and empty housing landscapes of accumulation in places such as India with the other forcefully vacated landscapes of, for instance, Los Angeles.[1] These empty landscapes of accumulation driven by derivative futures in the Global South and a regime of debt in the Global North were both spectacular and physically different manifestations of financial speculation. This chapter focuses on the long twentieth century leading up to 2008 to show how the period was also marked by a simultaneous rise of homelessness, squatting, and different forms of dwelling practices.

While financial speculations from earlier centuries were linked to urban land markets, until a decade or so ago it was not the transnational phenomenon of "residential capitalism" it has become.[2] In the past thirty years with the liberalization of credit structures and inventive forms of real estate securitization, building speculation has accelerated, resulting in massive displacements of population through gentrification, land grabs, and foreclosures. According to the last global survey of homelessness conducted by the United Nations, 100 million people are homeless worldwide, while 1.6 billion people lack adequate housing. Of these an estimated 20 million to 40 million are in urban centers.[3] This scenario is exacerbated in the Global South, where urbanization, homelessness, and squatting are on the rise. In India the number of available houses has increased, but so have the homeless and squatter populations.

In this chapter I examine the case of the Indian city of Kolkata (historical name Calcutta).[4] Beginning as a tiny colonial emporium in the marshes of eastern India at the turn of the seventeenth century, Calcutta became an iconic image of poverty in the twentieth century.[5] As described by one of its historians, "Plagued by poverty, politics, disease, and disorder, British attempts to build a city went awry."[6] Poverty tourism and sensationalist cinematic representations of human habitation spilling out into the streets have compounded the image of a failed and disorderly city. Thus, Kolkata offers a case to think about the crisis of housing and urban development. The spectacular rise of unaffordable housing through the nineteenth and twentieth centuries has resulted in the creation of various forms of dwelling conditions, from *bastis* in Calcutta, *chawls* in Mumbai, and barrios in Brasilia to tent cities in Los Angeles and squats in Amsterdam.[7] This current moment is unique in the geographic scope of real estate speculation and the expulsion of people from their homes. As Herman Schwartz and Leonard Seabrooke put it, "both financially repressed and financially liberal systems are globally interdependent and the deregulation of the national housing system has largely been a transnational phenomenon."[8]

In this chapter I ask how to dwell in these landscapes of accumulation and dispossession. My material comes from archival and ethnographic projects documenting various forms of dwelling practices that resisted the state and the market historically and continue doing so in the contemporary moment. These forms of dwelling emerge within the historical archive as legal recalcitrance and in our contemporary bureaucratic parlance as deviance. Through a close analysis of three moments in the story of Calcutta's urbanization, I seek to learn from the ground up the legal meaning and bureaucratic significance of these forms of recalcitrance.

The right to property and the right to affordable housing are always in conflict with one another, and moments of economic crisis deepen and reveal the contradiction between these two rights in a spectacular manner. Moving away from strictly legalistic analysis, I turn to those spatial ideas and practices where the contradiction between private ownership and the right to affordable housing becomes manifest in various kinds of ideas around home and dwelling within the city. I am deliberately using the phrase "politics of dwelling," as I want to recover how dwelling occurs and what ideas are embedded therein beyond the overarching rubrics of law, resistance, and rights. In order to situate these practices within the idea of deregulation of the housing system, I trace instances of a politics of dwelling in Calcutta.

My chapter rests on the premise that the act of dwelling outside the formal housing framework in postcolonial cities in the Global South—but this might also be extended to the Global North—is a political act. This then raises the questions of what dwelling is and how it is political. According to a recent study by the United Nations, about 1 billion people worldwide are living outside the frameworks of capitalist housing markets, welfare systems, or state housing.[9] This astounding figure shows that one person out of seven is either homeless or is providing for a home in what the state would mark as being beyond the pale of the law. The twentieth century has seen a striking rise in this figure as a result of the privatization of public services and spaces, the commodification of many aspects of our lives and livelihoods, the dwindling of social housing, and the emergence of residential capitalism. This necessitates that we return to the conversations around the "right to the city" from a different vantage point: the act of dwelling.[10]

Therefore, instead of asking why some acts of dwelling became recalcitrance or deviance, I ask against what larger structures and statecraft do the working poor provide for their own housing in the absence of protection, housing, and welfare systems? What ideas around home and rights might one discern in these acts of political dwelling in the interstices of what the state sees as formal and informal? That is, how do the poor in our cities *dwell*? What new ideas of housing and urbanization are generated when we explore three kinds of dwelling practices in Calcutta: *basti*, encroaching, and squatting? Housing markets are unique and especially so in Calcutta, given its speculative character. Indeed, if we begin from the premise that the right to shelter is a fundamental right as stipulated by the Indian Constitution,[11] these practices reveal real estate "speculation using housing stock as one of the worst legal behaviors within a capitalist society, since it is the origin of housing exclusion and other social inequalities."[12] In the case of Calcutta, these three moments in the history of its urbanization also reveal the collusion of state and market, where the distinction between private capital and public funds is always obfuscated.[13] At the same time, a deviant spatiality of dwelling in the city blurs the distinction between public and private spaces.

Precisely because of the obfuscation of state-market distinctions on the one hand and private-public distinctions on the other hand, displacement of the working poor has been one of the central mechanisms of urban development even when the development is pledged as an answer to the question of housing rights, as was the case in the early twentieth century.[14] Thus, it is not surprising that the urban improvements trusts that began sprouting up under the aegis of representative municipal bodies in England and its colonies at the turn of the nineteenth century were nothing but an embodiment of "strong executive action unencumbered by accountability to representatives of local self-governing institutions."[15] What these colonial urban improvement trusts embodied was not merely the principles of a developmental agenda that was urban and spatial in particular ways. They also manifested the centralization of particular legal instruments within a quasi-municipal body that facilitated unrestricted private investment in housing in the name of worker's housing rights.[16] The three stories of deviant dwelling that I narrate in the following sections are located within this complex inheritance of state-market collusion over housing.

How to House the Human?

If displacement is the other side of "residential capitalism"[17] that marks urban growth in the Global South, then its direct fallout in the form of homelessness is the other side of legal propertyhood. This then raises questions about what a home is within the larger urban property market in Calcutta, defined as it is by the simultaneity of homelessness and speculative urbanism.

Deploying the concept of politics of dwelling illuminates how the idea of illegitimate occupancy and the erasure of the human in the idea of the space of dwelling were constitutive of the classificatory regime of formal and informal housing used in the urban zoning nomenclatures starting from the colonial period. The informal spaces that we call *bastis* (slums) in India or "blight" in North America, as Sally Lawton discusses in more detail in Chapter 3 of this book, straddle both the official and nonofficial spaces of the city. Let me share a vignette from late 1980s India, a period that was beginning to see the opening up of the Indian economy to neoliberal market policies.

On February 5, 1989, the Salt Lake Development Trust of Calcutta evicted the inhabitants of a *basti* along a major highway on the outskirts of the city. This *basti* consisted of dwellings built in 1985 that were intended as housing for the urban poor. After completion these households remained vacant, for the government took no initiative to allocate the housing. Around 1987, a group of people whom official discourses labeled "squatters" were evicted from the areas surrounding the housing complex. Subsequently they moved into these vacant dwellings, by then covered in grass and weeds. For two years the people lived there, cleaned up the area, gardened and grew vegetables, and made the homes habitable. In 1989 armed police raided the area and evicted the people from these dwellings. For days on end, the evicted people sat out in the streets during the winter month of February.

Having entered the official discourse as "squatters," their practices of dwelling were deemed illegal according to the developmentalist logic of the state. How does one understand this state-sanctioned action of evicting these dwellers from housing for the urban poor, relegating them back to homelessness, and then calling these very "homeless" people encroachers? In trying to understand how slum dwellers in Kolkata continue to live and make claims for basic necessities such as water and electricity, political theorist Partha Chatterjee distinguishes between the idea of rights-bearing citizens, who comprise civil society, and the popular politics of slum dwellers, who in contrast to civil society comprise "political society." He adds that their "claims are irreducibly political. They could only be made on a political terrain, where rules may be bent or stretched, and not on the terrain of established law or administrative procedure. The success of these claims depends entirely on the ability of particular population groups to mobilize support to influence the implementation of governmental policy in their favor."[18]

Yet not all homeless are able to form a political society. Their deviant practices of dwelling on the margins of the state and the market foreclose many of the political possibilities theorized by Chatterjee, especially for the homeless in ways that are not foreclosed for slum dwellers. Thus, another way to approach this would be to return to the idea of spatial deviance and ask what initially produced them as deviant in this scenario so that it was possible to evict them from the very homes that were built to supply the working poor. If their only possibility of becoming legible to the state was as the statistical entity of the working poor of the city, why was that possibility not available to them? In order to take this approach, we must begin to historicize the space that was marked as *bastis* in the statist narratives in order to answer why the ideas that congeal around this term produce it as the deviant within urban society.

In the colonial archives, the *basti* first enters as an uncanny "rural space" within urban spaces as a consequence of the medico-moral topographies of colonial cities. In 1836 the *Medical Topography of Calcutta* singled out the "native tenement huts" as the cause of effluvia in the city, creating a so-called scientific spatial category.[19] With the repeated outbreaks of cholera in the nineteenth century and the development of germ theory in place of the miasma theory of fever, the medicalized landscape of Calcutta produced the space of the *basti* (already marked as the uncanny other of the city) as the site of decay and death.[20] Through the twentieth century as the language of science organized this division in neater, tighter lines, extending the conceptual distance between what is urban and nonurban, the *bastis* and encroachments became the economically wasted spaces of the developmental city. Underlying this classification and designation is a certain relation between the official municipal, juridical, and medical discourses and the economization of the spaces under their jurisdiction. In these discourses, the *basti* signified the failure of both scientific modernity of medicine and developmental practices of the market.

Reading the colonial archive against the grain reveals the juridically deviant space of the *basti* as a quintessentially urban space—a product of both urbanization and colonialism, coeval with modernity. Therefore, it became a site rife for social engineering throughout the twentieth century and a site to be overcome in the twenty-first century. For instance, in 1970 the Calcutta Metropolitan Planning Organization estimated that in Calcutta and its neighboring hinterland town of Howrah, about 2,000 acres of land were "locked up in *bastis*" that needed to be "recovered" and brought within the market economy. For the state, the *basti* was outside the profit-generating uses of an organized market, controlled by slumlords rather than the increasingly influential official land developers or land lobbies. It is especially interesting how the space of the *basti*, rather than its residents, became a central focus. Moreover, by deploying a notion of land being "locked up," the state made clear that the living practices of the urban poor and the laboring migrant communities were neither useful nor necessary. Accordingly, such land had to be developed and made into a resource. Procuring that land from the urban poor would unlock the land and release it to the capitalist land market.

Slum-clearance schemes—hallmarks of nineteenth-century colonialism that continue to galvanize municipal politics in the Global South and legitimize state-led evictions of the working poor from their dwellings—reveal that ever since the entry of the *basti* into the official archive as the "native village" with a "putrefying, toxic smell" in the heart of the city, the slums have not ceased being a threat.[21] The pathologized space of the *basti*, then, manifests itself today as nothing more than a site smeared by the violence of accumulation through dispossession.[22] The space of the *basti*, required for the supply of cheap labor yet derided for its threat to urbanity, challenges the easy power relationship between government institutions and the space of the inhabitants those institutions try to discipline. Precisely because profit-oriented development is embedded in the very notion of the city itself, there is no grammar for dealing with the space of the *basti* as anything other than "obsolete," "rural," a "temporal lag," and "not yet urban." In independent India, municipal bodies repeatedly attempt to rationalize these spaces through evictions and by bulldozing squatter settlements to remove encroachers. At the far end of this spectrum of informal housing are the homeless in the city. If the space of the *basti* emerges as one mired in a shadow land economy, then the homeless complicate the relation between state and market even further, as I show in the next section.

Lone Encroacher in a Crowded City

Kali Ray, a homeless woman in her midforties, had made her home—a blue tarpaulin, two pots, a brick hearth, and a bundle of clothing—in the Maidan for the past thirty years. Maidan is a vast open green space, measuring 333 acres, in the heart of Kolkata, comparable to Central Park in New York and Hyde Park in London. Ray's life in the Maidan became precarious following a 2007 ruling by the Calcutta High Court that brought an abrupt halt to any kind of temporary or makeshift buildings in the Maidan and ordered the relocation of the city's annual fairs that had been held there through much of the twentieth century.[23] This ruling came out of a decade-long citizens' environmental movement to save what they called Kolkata's "only green space." A ragpicker by profession, Ray was now known for being the "lone encroacher on the army-owned territory" where one was no longer permitted to cook or build permanent structures.[24]

The Maidan was created by land drainage and originally intended as a fortification and buffer between the colonial Fort William, built in 1781, and the city.[25] Given the Maidan's military origins, the jurisdiction of this open green space falls under the military, city police, and municipal departments. The violence of eviction is aggravated by the triple authority of the municipality, the police, and the military. Despite mounting pressure from these entities, Ray continued to live in her ten- by five-foot shack by "def[ying] the army, dodg[ing] the police, evad[ing] civic eviction and ignor[ing] rules that prohibit encroachment of the *Maidan*."[26] In 2009 the Kolkata municipality, the police, and the army accused her of flouting the Calcutta High Court's directive. Ray's only response was "I have nowhere to go, and I wish to die on the Maidan. This is my home."[27] Ray is among one of the many people who survive in or on the edges of the Maidan and make a living by cleaning and foraging in this public space; her "frictions" with the law and the police are a microcosm of the diverse and conflicting social interactions that make up this "messy and awkward" history of dwelling in the city.[28]

Like Ray, many live messily and fractiously in the city. The city is their home, and they have nowhere to go. They keep the city clean, maintain it, and, if the need arises, pay their dues. They are very similar to the fruit sellers, the vibrant hawker markets on the footpaths, the typewriter shops outside the courts and offices of the city, the tea stalls that spill onto the footpaths, and the packaging guy who runs a quick business outside post offices.[29] The state is aware of these thickets of ownership practices that make up the city. Not just footpath dwellers but also middle-class homeowners in Calcutta wage their own battles with the municipal bodies by encroaching on public roads through small gardens and balconies, which they expect to be demolished once every few years. How do we understand the definition of home held by Ray, who just wants to live and die in the Maidan? Her life is not lived as an open expression of defiance or resistance to the state and law. She does not wish to become a political message. Yet she vociferously claims her right to die in her home, the Maidan, like everyone else who wishes to die in their homes too. The only difference is that her home has neither walls nor a roof.

Kali Ray is not exactly a member of Partha Chatterjee's "political society"; she does not have the leverage to occupy a different politico-social terrain. Ray is one of the many dispersed homeless people of the city. In contrast to the strategy suggested by Chatterjee, the politics of space that the homeless exercise operates on a different register that instead of engaging policies strategically subverts them to make the state confront its own limits. I am not claiming that this deviant spatiality is some form of a romantic politics of the poor; rather, I want to expose this as a site where both state violence and the limits of urban planning coalesce. Before I conclude the chapter, let me briefly turn to another reading of the homeless to illuminate an additional aspect of this politics of dwelling that exists within the city, revealing the limits of urban political development.

Home as a Condition of Homelessness

This final ethnographic encounter brings to light a different register of ownership practice that challenges the ideas of property, land markets, and urban housing. This story, narrated to me by a member of the team with whom I was conducting ethnographic research for a project on urban homelessness in Calcutta in 2011, highlights the multitude of property and spatial relations that remain the unspoken background to the creation of a strict codification of the urban property and housing market.

In 2010 a directive from the Supreme Court of India mandated that state governments build twenty-four-hour shelters for the urban homeless in sixty-two cities, including Calcutta. In the wake of this ruling, I was invited by the School for Women's Studies at Jadavpur University and an organization called the Calcutta Samaritans to join a team of researchers to conduct interviews with the homeless population and present a draft report to the government of West Bengal detailing how the homeless population imagined shelters.[30] This was also a period when I was undertaking research on the colonial housing market in the city. When the archive shut down at 5:00 p.m. and the entire city rushed home, I and two other researchers would head to various stretches of footpath dwellings, to sites under bridges or along railway tracks, where the homeless of Kolkata had constructed makeshift tenements. Sometimes the homeless marked their homes with little more than a poster on a bare wall and a stack of small cartons of valuables. Visual markers of space need not always be tangible borders but can also consist of spoken and unspoken negotiations.[31] These cardboard tenements are found all over the world from refugee shelters to tent cities, a phenomenon that makes us confront the question of how to imagine dwelling and home when you can carry your "weightless homes" on your back.[32]

During one of the meetings my colleague told me Lalita's story,[33] an intriguing example of weightless housing. Lalita was a woman in her mid-fifties who worked as a domestic servant and lived with her three children on a footpath in the northern part of Calcutta. Nine other homeless families lived under the awning of the subway entrance that Lalita had made her home.

Not far from where they lived was the local police station. Every couple of years they would be evicted from this area. Most of the time they managed to escape the eviction drives, "lie low for a while," and return back to their homes under the awning. Life would continue, and the police would turn a blind eye, sometimes in return for sexual services, money, or upon satisfying other methods of extortion. However, one particularly brutal eviction drive took place. The police came one afternoon, rounded up Lalita and some of her neighbors, destroyed their belongings, and carted the group of people away to the Bangladesh border, over three hundred miles away. Most of the men who lived there, including Lalita's husband, were away working at the local loading and unloading station along the riverbank when this happened. By the time the group of women had walked back to Kolkata, a journey that took months to complete, Lalita's husband was not to be found. To date she has still not found him. As we learned during our research, this is a particularly common phenomenon for a mobile population such as the homeless in Kolkata.

When the time came for the marriage of her elder daughter, Lalita was deeply troubled by the possibility of eviction breaking up her daughter's family. If such a thing were to happen, then Lalita wanted her daughter to be close to her. Lalita went about searching for a place in the same stretch under the subway awning and decided to give a small patch of the footpath land, right next to hers, as a dowry to her son-in-law. She went to great lengths to secure her daughter and son-in-law's rights to that space—a small stretch of the footpath—and no one dared touch them.

How was her ownership to that stretch of footpath marked? Not through cardboard. She owned the place because she knew the exact measurements of this patch of pedestrian land. Did the police know? This seemed like a puzzling question to ask about something so ubiquitous of postcolonial urbanism. A whole host of questions remained unanswered, including how Lalita's rights were recognized and how she or her daughter would secure their rights back on that land following eviction drives. What I realized was perhaps not that my questions were unanswered but that they were modeled on a conviction in rights, documents, and a particular reality that law creates around housing. The basic premise of my questions suddenly felt misguided. In a city of overwhelming homelessness, even eviction drives meet their limit. It is at this limit that new political possibilities of home and a counterimaginary of radical spatiality emerge.

Lalita's story is not an unusual one. During this period, we encountered countless forms of claims to the city's spaces and differing registers of ownership that overlap with formal, registered property deeds. Like Lalita, the many homeless people we spoke to did not consider buying, selling, or gifting the footpath as forms of trespassing or encroachment on public property. If we were to step back from the legal reality of our spatial practices, perhaps the borders between legitimate and illegitimate forms of property relations would start to look messy. We may then take pause to ask what legitimizes speculative urbanisms that appear as gated communities without any dwellers in Kolkata, when thousands have no roof over their heads? We must also ask where we locate home and dwelling in this context.

Economizing Space

As encroachers, Lalita and Kali Ray disrupt the idea of the urban marked by planning and zoning that clearly demarcates spaces and property rights. They consider the public spaces in the city their home and nothing more. They are not bending rules of the state to make political claims for the recognition of "illegal" forms of ownership. They work and make the city, and they dwell there. So, how do we read these practices not as strategic resistance to the state but instead as opening up other possibilities. One way would be to view such ownership patterns as constitutive of the absent presence that haunts the margins of modern contractual property relations. Perhaps this absent presence of the encroachable, squattable space created the paper deed attesting to property and the contract in the first place. These practices are neither recalcitrance within the modernizing geography of the city, which shoots up glitzy skyscrapers, nor a temporal lag on the onward march of global urban progress. Rather, they are part of the landscapes of accumulation that produce both the shiny empires of Asian cities and its dispossessed. They are the invisible background to the visible (legal, contractual) text of property.

Legal principles and economics filter our knowledge about spaces and the people who live in, work in, and own those spaces. If an understanding of ownership and property marks human relations to urban spaces, then I have demonstrated those multiple registers in which spaces exist and that are lived by people who toil in and inhabit those spaces. These various assemblages of dwelling cannot always be subsumed into a propertied geography—a geography that has been equally punctured by the vacant buildings of speculative urbanism. As I have argued, the answer to understanding a multiplicity of valences of ownership is not certitude and a higher level of transparency but rather an expansive notion of what it means to dwell in, claim, and occupy spaces. Finally, once we admit the insufficiency of the juridico-economic definition of property, we will see that firmly held property lines of our urbanizing landscapes are everywhere and are all the time muddied by various forms of occupancy and dwelling. Then, the proposition for an openness to understanding what it means to dwell might not sound triumphalist or utopian but instead might mark an opening where another history begins.

CHAPTER 15

Policy Mobility and Urban Fantasies

The Case of African Cities

Vanessa Watson

Over the past century or so African cities have been shaped spatially and visually through urban planning laws and policies, first introduced by colonial governments and perpetuated by newly independent national governments and local elites. Colonially inspired ideas of "the good city" were embedded in these laws and policies. Today, significant parts of these cities are shaped by actors seeking to evade these laws and policies (through informal settlement and trade outside the reach of the costs and constraints imposed by planning), yet planning remains a central influence on urban land values and is a political tool for ruling parties and elites to marginalize or incorporate particular urban communities.

In Africa in recent years, new urban images and visions have come to the fore involving a different set of built environment professionals, namely architects, property developers, and engineers. These new ideas are diffusing through the continent, as they have in other regions of the Global South, and their impact can be seen in new land speculation, infrastructural investments, and new kinds of actor collaboration around the political power that these new images promise. Yet their outcome is likely to be even more negative than earlier planning ideas for poor and unemployed urban majorities.

In this chapter I draw on recent urban theory that explores the concept of policy mobilities as a way of understanding how new urban ideas, images, and visions are becoming influential in African cities. My contribution to the book is to show the power of ideas as images (of desirable cities) and thus as a form of "symbolic" power[1] that can shape institutions, decision-making processes, land markets, and physical outcomes. The southern location of these cities (which in themselves are highly diverse across the African continent) means that the sociopolitical and economic context in which these new ideas are attempting to root themselves is very different from the context of the Global North, and this also has a significant effect on traveling ideas.

I first explore the ideas behind the concept of policy mobilities. I then turn to the African continent to provide some background to the nature and scale of urban growth and development. Processes of new African city building and the visions and actors involved are explained as a recent phenomenon of policy transfer, showing how the power of ideas and their relationship to other drivers of urban change are having a fundamental impact on the lives of city dwellers.

Policy Mobilities

There is a long history of cross-continental borrowing of ideas and models in urban planning, primarily from the Global North to the Global South and based on assumptions that most advanced and "modern" planning models originate in "developed" countries, in effect the Euro-American context. Garden cities, Le Corbusian residential towers, urban green belts, and land-use zoning are all examples of these. More recently there have been examples of South-South borrowing, such as rapid transit bus systems from Bogota and plans drawn from the architecture and skylines of cities such as Dubai and Singapore. All these forms of borrowing have found their way into past and current plans for African cities. Geographer Tim Bunnell has put the newer evidence of borrowing into three possible types of "imaginings of urban antecedents": "the prototypical, paradigmatic city; the city which charts pathways to world city-ness; and the model or 'best' city."[2] The latter two categories have featured strongly in policy and planning transfer.

Bunnell's second category of "world" or world-class cities has been concerned with analyzing the characteristics that give a city status in a hierarchy of ranked importance (usually measured by its economic role in the global economy) as well as putting forward interventive measures that claim to be able to promote cities up the hierarchy of rankings.[3] What started as a set of measures of global economic importance is now promoted as a desirable state to which all cities should aspire and has resulted in even quite small and remote cities in various parts of the world claiming world-class status as a form of boosterism or to attract investors and tourists. The list of measures promoted by urban consultants and governments for a city to achieve world-class status usually includes urban projects such as waterfronts, conference centers and stadia, smart city technologies, and increasingly architecture regarded as "iconic"—usually high-rise glass box buildings. Quite how or why these interventions can secure economic growth to achieve world-class status is never made clear, and the dismal track record of such policies in achieving these goals does not seem to diminish their appeal.

Bunnell's third category—model or "best" cities—usually involves the labeling of particular cities as successful in a certain sphere and worthy of emulation, such as Glasgow's status as the "gold standard" of culture-led regeneration, with other former industrial cities seeking to copy the Glasgow strategy.[4] These "league tables" of success, Bunnell suggests, develop "discursive power" that is circulated through consultants, policy documents, and the media and become entrenched as policy solutions, even when adopting cities have little in common with original models. Acuto explains how Dubai has used what he calls "symbolic power" to claim world-class status but has then become a model city for many others (particularly in Africa and the East) wanting to emulate its success.[5] The exercise of symbolic power involves the production of narratives promoting the city and addressed to global elites and also implies a concern with the importance of a city in relation to other cities rather than the extent to which it functions for its citizens. Singapore[6] is also often cited as having best-city status, particularly for its housing and transport initiatives, as is Medellin in Colombia for its ability to control the drug trade partially through urban planning.[7] Yet frequently the copying of these models goes very little beyond an adoption of visual and architectural characteristics—in the cases of both Dubai and Singapore this adoption means modern tower buildings and landscaped open spaces.

Cities that emerge as success stories through any of the processes described above have been explored through a strand of research now termed "policy mobilities," which critiques and builds on earlier work on policy transfer from one part of the world to another. The policy transfer concept has been criticized for its "literalist" conception of the way ideas travel, which does not account for the ways that traveling from one place to another changes the character and content of the mobilized ideas.[8] An important element of mobilities theorizing accepts that many of these ideas travel internationally as part of a neoliberal urban transformation, sometimes through financing and lending agencies such as the World Bank, but argues that this does not have to only be an imposition "from above."[9] There can also be a demand side of neoliberal policy from city authorities who then oversee the implementation of these strategies, often drawing in professional consultants. Moreover, some of the new Global South city antecedents, such as Singapore and Seoul, are in countries with relatively strong and developmental governments that cannot be regarded as fully neoliberal. In other instances, community-based innovative urban interventions "from below," such as to improve the lives of slum dwellers, have traveled internationally through global nongovernmental organizations such as Slum Dwellers International.[10] The geographies of globally circulating urban ideas are therefore complex and multidirectional, involve a wide range of actors and institutions, and can be both top-down and bottom-up.

Skyscraper buildings have come to be closely associated with world-class and model "best" cities as a way not only of signaling modernity but also of spatially accommodating high levels of income inequality. As Acuto has argued for Dubai, its high-rise architectural icons represent modernization and power—they are intended to represent efficiency and sustainability and the presence of an advanced producer services economy.[11] Moreover, for Dubai this architecture is not intended as a copy of elsewhere but instead intends to be bigger and better than elsewhere in order to achieve the top of world-class city rankings. Acuto makes the important point that the use of these high-rise visions is not simply driven by land speculation and economic profit: exercising "symbolic power" involves the creation of a city (and national) identity intended to promote political and cultural as well as economic prominence on a "world stage."[12]

One of the few available studies on how built environment professionals play a role in and benefit from these policy mobilities has particular relevance for new megaprojects and city building on the African continent.[13] Tracking the companies that prepare "masterplans" for urban projects around the world, Rapoport notes that "they are largely conceived and designed by a small, elite group of international architecture, engineering and planning firms based in North America and Europe sometimes referred to as the global intelligence corps."[14] These projects are also strongly influenced by the requirements and demands of the client, supporting the position of mobilities theorists of interventions shaped both from "above" and "below." Many of these master-planned megaprojects fail to progress from design idea to construction, yet significant benefits will already have been derived by a host of built environment professionals during the early design stages of the project.[15] These include the fees derived by urban designers and architects, lawyers, valuers, engineers, and other built environment professionals. These professionals may not have significant financial interests in the final completion of the project and thus may not be overly concerned with whether the project is ever completed. In addition, a significant amount of infrastructure to support the project will have been designed and budgeted by a host of consultants and building companies. Finally, property owners and land speculators in and around the project will generally benefit from increased property values resulting from the improvement of municipal infrastructure and the marketing hype associated with a large project, even if it is never implemented.

In the next section I turn to the recent wave of new city and large urban project planning on the African continent to explore how Bunnell's "world city" and "best city" concepts have made themselves felt through policy mobilities.[16] Given the unique nature of sub-Saharan Africa's urban transition, the borrowed plans for new and reconfigured cities are being considered in contexts that are significantly different in regard to their regions of origin (advanced economies to the north and east). If this decreases the chances of their implementation, why then do they continue to be produced?

Distinctive Characteristics of African Urbanization

Sub-Saharan Africa is the last of the world's continents to undergo an urban transition. At the time of colonial independence most of Africa's population was rural, and it is still the least urbanized region in the world. However, sub-Saharan Africa's urban population is expected to double in the next twenty years and will be 50 percent urbanized by 2035.[17] The region already has a total urban population larger than that of North America.[18] Significantly, only a third of this urban growth is a result of rural to urban migration, with the other two-thirds resulting from the natural increase of the population already urbanized.[19] Hence, over the next ten years, 50 million people will leave the countryside to move to cities, but a further 100 million people will be added to current urban populations from the expansion of families already living in towns and cities. While politicians in Africa and even some international development agencies still sometimes refer to the need to "curb urbanization," clearly this is an impossible hope on their part, and the urban transition is being driven forward by factors well beyond the control of policy makers.

Africa's urban transition has distinctive economic characteristics. In contrast to other regions where cities exist as sites of economic production, African urbanization is driven largely by natural resource exports.[20] Those African countries that rely heavily on natural resource production suffer from a "resource curse" whereby growth is based on extracting commodities and export proceeds pay for imported consumer goods. This does not generate proportional employment within cities or anywhere else. This feature underlies a further important aspect of African cities: Where economic growth is not producing formal urban jobs, the majority of urban dwellers have little alternative but to survive off informal income-generating activities and find shelter in informal settlements. UN-Habitat estimated that 62 percent of urban populations in sub-Saharan Africa live in "slums" (compared to a much lower 43 percent in South Asia and 27 percent in Latin America) and that 70 percent earn an income through informal activity.[21]

These factors of very rapid but largely jobless urban growth serve to emphasize the very serious developmental problems faced by African cities and how this challenge will escalate in the decades to come. In cities where the majority of the population is poor, unemployed and unserviced, the hope of many African politicians and policy makers that these cities can become world class through the implementation of modernist urban plans and particular building styles is clearly not only unrealistic but also a major distraction from the real problems these cities face.

New African City Building and African Fantasy Cities

The recent wave of interest in new city building on the continent emerged in the late 2000s and could perhaps be related to the contemporaneous global financial crisis, driving both built environment professionals and property investment companies to seek new markets in those parts of the world where economic growth and demand for new urban growth continued, particularly in the Middle East, Asia, and Africa. This moment of significant change, which would certainly qualify as a critical juncture, paved the way for the penetration of new urban visions into the African continent, but other local factors were also at play. There was, for instance, renewed attention to the high rates of urbanization and a growing urban middle-class.

A number of international finance houses have been highlighted in this middle-class growth in African cities. Africa's middle class has tripled over the last thirty years and is now the fastest growing in the world. A growing urban middle class generates demand for formal housing, public facilities and amenities, retail outlets and transport routes for a growing number of car owners, and certainly potential customers for the kinds of urban environments portrayed in world-class and best-city urban fantasy plans. This class also provides a consumer market for goods and services of all kinds and hence investment in production and services buildings. A growing middle class therefore fuels demand for well-located and well-serviced urban land and development projects as well as architectural styles considered "aspirational" or "modern."

At the same time, prospective property developers may be seriously misreading the African market. The African Development Bank defines the middle class as those spending between US$2 and $20 a day and the upper middle class as those spending US$10–$20 a day. It is difficult to imagine how households with such minimal spending power can afford the luxury apartments portrayed in the fantasy plans and the vehicles needed to move around the fantasy cities.

The new wave of city plans in Africa falls into three categories: (1) those that aim to replace large parts of an entire city, such as the plan for Kigali, capital of Rwanda; (2) "edge cities" or megaprojects within existing large cities, such as Eko-Atlantic on land infill in Lagos, Nigeria; and (3) satellite cities, which are autonomous new towns beyond the edge of existing cities and supposedly aimed at redirecting urban growth away from them, such as Konza City and Tatu City, among others, outside of Nairobi, Kenya.[22] There are few countries on the continent that have not experienced this new wave of city planning, although predictably those countries that are more economically successful and politically stable have seen more of them. Further, while the category of plans varies (only Kigali and to some extent Addis Ababa, Ethiopia, are embarking on full-city makeovers, while edge and satellite cities are very common), there is a great deal of commonality in terms of the actors involved and the nature of the plans.

As Rapoport suggests, the origins of these plans is in most cases the "global intelligence corps": private-sector international real estate companies composed of engineers, architects, planners, and property developers headquartered in the United States and Europe and, increasingly, in global centers in the Middle East and Asia.[23] Companies such as Rendeavour, Surbana, Hawkwood Properties, Dar el Handasah, and others are involved. However, they very frequently partner with local African real estate companies and local finance partners, and there are usually government interests involved as well.

For example, Tatu City is a planned satellite city aiming to divert population growth from neighboring Nairobi, the capital city. The main developer is the international company Rendeavour (at one stage a subsidiary of the Russia-based company Renaissance) in partnership with local landowners, a former central bank governor, and a local businessman. In another example of how global and local factors are intertwined in the shaping of these new cities, the website plans for Hope City (a new satellite "techno" city in Ghana) consist of six linked towers that, the plans claim, will house 25,000 residents and 50,000 workers. These beehive-shaped towers, which seem to bear no relationship to their surrounding environment, were supposedly inspired by ancient mud and thatched huts arranged into a compound typical of traditional African society. It was designed by Italian architect Paulo Brescia and was to be built by RLG Communications, a Ghana-based information technology company, at an estimated cost of $10 billion. Reportedly Microsoft was a partner in this development. However, local forces have already intervened in the location of Hope City. It was shifted from the original site at Dunkunaa to the larger site at Prampram when Dunkunaa residents claimed that the project had incurred the displeasure of the gods when the developers refused to acknowledge the chiefs and elders of the area.[24] Several years on from the launch, no development has yet happened.[25]

Local political shaping of imported urban models is particularly evident in the case of Kigali, where a relatively authoritarian but also determinedly modernizing government has taken steps to transform the capital of Rwanda into a world-class city. Rwanda considers itself the Switzerland of Africa with a clear commitment to business-friendly development, and the plan reflects this vision of its government. The Kigali Conceptual Master Plan was developed by the US-based Oz Architecture Team and was adopted by the Rwandan parliament in 2008. Oz and the Singapore company Surbana developed more detailed plans. The website graphics all suggest high modernism (glass box towers, landscaped boulevards and freeways), yet the rhetoric is about sustainability.[26] Finance and construction can be linked back to global circuits of property construction, with the China Civil Engineering Construction Corporation and New Century Developments (a real estate company based in Hong Kong with a Rwanda branch) having jointly constructed and financed most of Kigali's simulated skyline. At the same time, UN-Habitat reported that 90 percent of Kigali's population lives in informal housing or with unregulated (i.e., unrecognized) land tenure.[27] Evictions in Kigali had been reported prior to the adoption of the new plan but seemingly have been stepped up to make room for the new urban projects. There has been little evidence of public resistance to these removals.

Attempts to create world-class and best cities have also called on particular built and architectural forms, most commonly glass box tower buildings (skyscrapers) of various shapes that are usually surrounded by paved and landscaped public spaces and gardens.[28] Rapoport points out how invitations from the Global South to prominent or celebrity global architects to develop such plans is seen as a useful form of branding to increase a project's profile and obtain political and investment support.[29]

Africa's new city plans are no exception. The graphics on company websites quite predictably show skylines that emulate Dubai, Singapore, or Shanghai or take on strange shapes, such as the Hope City beehives. Buildings are designed to be a combination of office and apartment blocks, often with conference centers, and some projects include high-cost suburban housing. Tower blocks show little recognition for their reliance on power sources for elevators and air-conditioning (in contexts where power outages are a very common occurrence), little recognition of the very small urban middle class expected to occupy highly priced apartments and homes,[30] and little recognition of the small scale of the financial and services sector that might occupy expensive office space. Recently the Rwandan government issued a directive to Kigali businesses to move into new high-rise office blocks, which had been standing empty due to high rental costs (typically four times higher per square meter than in older blocks).[31] Most of these new city plans also show landscaped and paved open public spaces devoid of the usual congestion of informal traders, pedestrians, and various forms of transport that are characteristic of African urban centers. The entire informal economy has been wished away in these designer projects and replaced with an environment that assumes an economy and society only to be found in the global financial and services centers of the world.

Many of these new city visions move beyond the use of iconic global architecture in the exercise of symbolic power and also claim to be eco cities or, more recently, smart cities. The eco-city label has been less frequently used in the new plans for African urban projects, although Lagos's Eko-Atlantic (an edge city for some 250,000 people on land infill) clearly makes this claim. Nairobi's satellite Konza ICT City and Ghana's Hope City both claim to be smart cities, suggesting that they are globally connected and infrastructurally wired and operate through technological innovations. Smart cities also often claim to be sustainable on the basis of these technologies. However, writers have increasingly pointed to ways in which these terms are used as a smokescreen for rather different agendas. Hollands has argued that it is often difficult to separate out the extent to which proposed urban projects actually intend some kind of positive technological innovation as opposed to being high-tech variations of urban entrepreneurialism or just place marketing.[32] Also problematic is the assumption that smart cities simply require information technology hardware and infrastructure to become "smart," ignoring the role of social capital and networks of trust and reciprocity that are prerequisites for innovation.

Bunnell's argument, pointing to the range of global and local actors influencing policy mobilities, is certainly supported by Africa's new city plans, but it is important to understand at what point in the process these various actors "join the party."[33] In the early stages of these projects a first piece of evidence is usually the website graphics produced by the development company, and sometimes these are also carried on government websites if political support (or initiative) has been present from the start. This is very different from earlier (and still ongoing) forms of urban planning across much of the continent, where plans were usually produced as paper documents and two-dimensional diagrams to be possibly—although not always—located for public inspection in public buildings or civic hall meetings. Essentially these new plans are speaking to a very different audience: potential global and local investors and politicians. They are clearly not speaking to local city residents. A noteworthy characteristic of most of these new plans is the complete absence of public participation that has accompanied them. Usually the first time that city residents are aware of these new plans is when a billboard is erected on or near the proposed site for the new development showing the visions that were previously on the company websites. It is often the case that months or years thereafter nothing further happens as these projects become mired in local land, infrastructure, and financial disputes. Hope City has been referred to in the popular press as joining the "long line of white elephants" of projects that have failed to move off the drawing board.

It is at this early stage in the process that city ideas, or visions, play an important rolc. However, their quality and detail appear not to be important. These new city vision graphics, whether they are branded as world class, eco, or smart (or all of these), have a remarkable similarity in the type of architecture and forms of the built environment. Website graphics of these plans are often hard to distinguish from each other and may well have been cut and pasted from various architectural diagram supply sites. They also for the most part bear no relation to the context in which they are located—either physically or socioeconomically. They are essentially advertisements for a possibility that may or may not happen. Rapoport's research shows some interesting reasons for this.[34] Global intelligence corps companies describe the "planning side of the business" as a "loss leader" that generates little in fees and is allocated a small proportion of the overall budget. However, such "visioning" activities are useful at securing a foothold in the project, as this master planning stage can help secure lucrative commissions to design iconic or signature buildings. Low-budget planning means that ideas and graphics are recycled across multiple master plans over short periods of time. An interviewee described producing plans for cities of 1 million or more in just eight weeks, giving little time to develop new ideas (or presumably understand the context in which the plan is to be located).[35] She notes that this repeated referencing to the same ideas and precedents helps to create an impression that there is some kind of global consensus of what is good and sustainable urbanism.

Understanding policy mobilities in the context of Africa's new city plans hence gives rise to some new perspectives on how ideas shape urban development. Understanding the global production and circulation of ideas for new cities is clearly important but needs to be combined with the responses of local actors in government, in civil society, and in the market. Also necessary is understanding how different actors play roles at different points in time from the start of the project and into its phases of implementation. These can have a major impact on how ideas diffuse across space and how they warp and change as they begin to land in different contexts. Important as well is understanding how many of these factors operate both globally and locally. For example, profit plays a major motivating role in the global uniformity of urban plans and visions as a cost-cutting and branding exercise, but those motivations also influence land and infrastructure development and who finally gains access to such developments or is impacted by them.

Traditionally, urban planning has been regarded as a state-driven activity undertaken in the interests of the "public good." Colonial planning in the African context has shown how urban planning can also be used as a tool for social control. But the most recent wave of city planning shifts ideas into the realm of the market in very new ways and undoubtedly with new effects, which I will discuss in the following section in which I argue that the form of policy mobility and idea diffusion discussed here is not just of academic interest but is also impacting the lives and livelihoods of African urban residents in startling new ways.

How Africa's New Fantasy Plans Shape Urbanization

While new urban development will have to take place, given the rate of urban expansion in Africa, the location and form of this development can significantly impact urban inequalities. The impact on poorer urban dwellers will be felt most directly where new urban master plans and projects attempt comprehensive urban renewal to remake the city in the image of somewhere else considered world class. Kigali and Addis Ababa (Ethiopia) are currently subject to these kinds of makeovers, and their extensive shack populations are being systematically moved to make way for the new projects. Usually relocations are to the urban periphery or beyond, and in the process social networks and economic livelihoods are destroyed and significant new costs are imposed on poor households, where new formal housing and transport costs have to be absorbed.

In most cities, however, developers and governments find it easier to avoid the difficulties of removal in dense urban areas and look to development on the urban edge or in the rural areas beyond. Around African cities, periurban areas have been growing very rapidly as poor urban dwellers look for a foothold in the cities and towns where land is more easily available, where they can escape the costs and threats of urban land regulations, and where there is a possibility of combining urban and rural livelihoods. These are the areas usually earmarked for development by new urban extension projects. The Cité le Fleuve' project on land infill on the edge of Kinshasa[36] will affect large tracts of land along the Congo River that have been converted into productive rice fields to supply Kinshasa's markets, although more recently pressures of urban growth have seen some of these areas used as shack lands. In the case of new satellite cities, their location is often justified as being located on "empty land," but it is rare that land around larger cities is empty, and if such land is not within an environmentally protected area, then it is very likely to be actively farmed. In the eviction processes that attend development, landowners rarely hold land title, and full compensation for land, shelter, and livelihoods is unlikely.

Beyond these immediate impacts there are a number of further outcomes that can be anticipated with a degree of confidence. State spending on large-scale infrastructure (transport, sanitation, power) is likely to be skewed in the direction of support for new cities and projects and away from meeting the basic service and housing needs of the much larger poor urban populations. Should the middle classes and higher-end investors retreat to these new elite enclaves (and this after all is their target market), then their tax base and spending power will be lost to the exiting city, thus exacerbating urban decline. This is exactly what happened in the case of the new Chinese-built Kilamba City outside of Luanda in Angola, where the government had to extensively subsidize apartments to make them affordable for the middle class.[37] The hope that these new cities and developments will be self-contained and able to insulate themselves from the disorder and chaos of the existing cities is remote. Satellite cities are frequently unable to sustain all the job and service requirements of their populations and tend to generate large volumes of movement and traffic as their residents find themselves having to travel back to more established centers. Wealthy enclaves are also usually unable to function without low-income service providers (e.g., domestic workers, gardeners, and construction workers), and inevitably an informal city grows up around the edges of the formal city.

And where are the street traders, the informal transport operators, and the shack dwellers in these new fantasy plans? Would traders ever be allowed to set up business on the pristine boulevards? Could the poor (or even the middle class) afford the glass box apartments or even have the kinds of jobs that would get them access to the towering office blocks? How do people move around on foot, as most city dwellers do, through these wide-open spaces and car-oriented routes? The answer is clearly that all such urban citizens have been swept out of sight in these grand visions. In a range of ways the utopian dreams of these urban fantasies are unlikely to materialize, yet the efforts to achieve them will have profound effects on lives and livelihoods. While those with a degree of power and resources may well be able to benefit in various ways, given the overwhelming dominance in African cities of those with very little, a widening and deepening of inequality is inevitable.

Conclusion

African cities have long been on the receiving end of urban plans and policies from elsewhere. These mobile ideas, whether colonial, postcolonial, or driven by property development speculation, as they are now, have always had to engage in various ways with local forms of resistance or opportunism and have always shaped or been shaped by them. These engagements have gone well beyond the built environment that they have produced and have also drawn in political and institutional maneuvers to control or promote them and, particularly of late, large-scale and global market actors keen to profit from urban land. The concept of urban ideas diffusing through time and space is clearly complex and brings together global and regional as well as local factors.

What the African new towns example has shown is just how intertwined and complex these ideas may be but also the importance of unpacking further which actors are involved with what kinds of motivations at various stages of the urban development cycle. At the same time and while the visions of these new plans appear to homogenize across the continent (as well as in parts of Asia and the Middle East), there is no doubt that the landing of these ideas will be very particular to context. The huge diversity of the African continent and its cities and towns make this inevitable. It is also important not to generalize about the likely impact of these plans on issues of urban inequality, as this as well is highly dependent on context and particularly on the strength and capacity of state institutions to undertake sound future planning.

NOTES

Chapter 1

1. Exceptions to this include Mara S. Sidney, "Critical Perspectives on the City: Constructivist, Interpretive Analysis of Urban Politics," in *Critical Urban Studies: New Directions*, ed. Jonathan S. Davies and David L. Imbroscio (Albany: State University of New York Press, 2010), 23–39; Joel Rast, "Urban Regime Theory and the Problem of Change," *Urban Affairs Review* 51, no. 1 (2015): 138–49; Neil Bradford, "Ideas and Collaborative Governance: A Discursive Localism Approach," *Urban Affairs Review* 52, no. 5 (2016): 659–84; Timothy P. R. Weaver, *Blazing the Neoliberal Trail: Urban Political Development in the United States and the United Kingdom* (Philadelphia: University of Pennsylvania Press, 2016).

2. As Judith Goldstein has commented, "The choice from a range of possible strategies to realize economic interests may be as important, perhaps more important, in explaining political behavior than are 'objective' material interests themselves." Judith Goldstein, *Ideas, Interests, and American Trade Policy* (Ithaca, NY: Cornell University Press, 1993), 2, quoted in Joel Rast, "How Policy Paradigms Change: Housing Reform in Chicago, 1930–1947," paper presented at the annual meeting of the American Political Science Association, Washington, DC, August 28–31, 2014.

3. John A. Rawls, *A Theory of Justice* (Cambridge, MA: Belknap Press of Harvard University Press, 1971).

4. For the classic account of regime theory, see Clarence N. Stone, *Regime Politics: Governing Atlanta, 1946*–1988 (Lawrence: University Press of Kansas, 1989). In a 1981 review essay, Stone commented that "after nearly three decades of controversy, the community power debate shows no sign of abating." See Clarence Stone, "Community Power Structure—A Further Look," *Urban Affairs Quarterly* 16 (June 1981): 505. Yet by the time *Regime Politics* was published the debate had most certainly abated.

5. John R. Logan and Harvey Luskin Molotch, *Urban Fortunes: The Political Economy of Place* (Berkeley: University of California Press, 1987), esp. 85 on the "ideology of value free development" as a kind of false consciousness. For similar arguments, see David Harvey, *A Brief History of Neoliberalism* (Oxford: Oxford University Press, 2005).

6. Theda Skocpol, "Bringing the State Back In: Strategies of Analysis in Current Research," in *Bringing the State Back In*, ed. Peter B. Evans, Dietrich Rueschemeyer, and Theda Skocpol (Cambridge: Cambridge University Press, 1985), 3–37. See also Karen Orren and Stephen Skowronek, *The Search for American Political Development* (Cambridge: Cambridge University Press, 2004).

7. Ted Robert Gurr and Desmond S. King, *The State and the City* (Chicago: University of Chicago Press, 1987), 9.

8. Robert C. Lieberman, "Ideas, Institutions, and Political Order: Explaining Political Change," *American Political Science Review* 96 (2002): 697–712. See also James Mahoney and Kathleen Thelen, "A Theory of Gradual Institutional Change," in *Explaining Institutional Change: Ambiguity, Agency, and Power*, ed. James Mahoney and Kathleen Thelen (New York: Cambridge University Press, 2010), 7–10; B. Guy Peters, Jon Pierre, and Desmond King, "The Politics of Path Dependency: Political Conflict in Historical Institutionalism," *Journal of Politics* 67 (November 2005): 1275–1300.

9. Rogers M. Smith, "Which Comes First, the Ideas or the Institutions?," in *Rethinking Political Institutions: The Art of the State*, ed. Ian Shapiro, Stephen Skowronek, and Daniel Galvin (New York: New York University Press, 2006), 108. See also Rogers M. Smith, "Ideas and the Spiral of Politics: The Place of American Political Thought in American Political Development," *American Political Thought* 3, no. 1 (March 2014): 127–28.

10. Vivien Schmidt, "Discursive Institutionalism: The Explanatory Power of Ideas and Discourse," *Annual Review of Political Science* 11 (2008): 303–26.

11. Smith, "Ideas and the Spiral of Politics," 127–28.

12. Sheri Berman, "Ideational Theorizing in the Social Sciences Since 'Policy Paradigms, Social Learning, and the State,'" *Governance* 26, no. 2 (2013): 223.

13. Ibid.

14. Ibid., 223–24.

15. Vivien Schmidt, "Discursive Institutionalism: The Explanatory Power of Ideas and Discourse," *Annual Review of Political Science* 11, no. 1 (2008): 305.

16. Daniel Béland and Robert Henry Cox, "Introduction: Ideas and Politics," in *Ideas and Politics in Social Science Research*, ed. Daniel Béland and Robert Henry Cox (Oxford: Oxford University Press, 2011), 3–4.

17. Weaver, *Blazing the Neoliberal Trail*, 5.

18. William H. Riker, "Implications from the Disequilibrium of Majority Rule for the Study of Institutions," *American Political Science Review* 74, no. 2 (June 1980): 432–46.

19. For a range of accounts that examine the relationship between ideas and interests, see Kathleen R. McNamara, *The Currency of Ideas: Monetary Politics in the European Union* (Ithaca, NY: Cornell University Press, 1999); Mark Blyth, *Great Transformations: Economic Ideas and Institutional Change in the Twentieth Century* (Cambridge: Cambridge University Press, 2002); Béland and Cox, "Introduction"; Berman, "Ideational Theorizing in the Social Sciences Since 'Policy Paradigms, Social Learning, and the State,'" 217–37; Colin Hay, "Ideas and the Construction of Interests," in Béland and Cox, eds., *Ideas and Politics in Social Science Research*.

20. Paul Peterson, *City Limits* (Chicago: University of Chicago Press, 1981), 21.

21. On the use of the notion of the situated subject specifically in reference to institutionalist studies, see Colin Hay and Daniel Wincott, "Structure, Agency and Historical Institutionalism," *Political Studies* 46, no. 5 (1998): 951–57. For a more general though related discussion, see David Stern, "The Return of the Subject? Power, Reflexivity and Agency," *Philosophy and Social Criticism* 26 (2000): 109–22.

22. Agency is typically defined by synonyms such as "willfulness," "intentionality," "rationality," and "motivation." Two review essays that suggest the great range of definitions of agency are Laura Ahearn, "Language and Agency," *Annual Review of Anthropology* 30 no. 1 (2001): 109–37; Xabier Barandiaran, Ezequiel Di Paolo, and Marieke Rohde, "Defining Agency: Individuality, Normativity, Asymmetry and Spatio-Temporality in Action," *Adaptive Behavior 17*, no. 5 (October 2009): 367–86.

23. Orion Lewis and Sven Steinmo, "How Institutions Evolve: Evolutionary Theory and Institutional Change," *Polity* 44, no. 3 (2012): 314–39.

24. United Nations, "World's Population Increasingly Urban with More Than Half Living in Urban Areas," United Nations, July 10, 2014, http://www.un.org/en/development/desa/news/population/world-urbanization-prospects-2014.html.

25. Karen Orren and Stephen Skowronek, *The Search for American Political Development* (Cambridge: Cambridge University Press, 2004), 123.

26. Jack Lucas, "Urban Governance and the American Political Development Approach," *Urban Affairs Review* 53, no. 2 (March 2017): 338–61.

27. Ibid., 113.

28. Jeremy Wallace, *Cities and Stability: Urbanization, Redistribution, and Regime Survival in China* (Oxford: Oxford University Press, 2014).

29. Neil Brenner, "Is There a Politics of 'Urban' Development?," in *The City in American Political Development*, ed. Richardson Dilworth (New York: Routledge, 2009), 121–40.

30. Mike Davis, *Planet of Slums* (New York: Verso, 2006).

31. Blyth, *Great Transformations*, 30–37. For a more recent summary of the literature on the relationship between ideas and critical junctures, see John Hogan and David Doyle, "The Importance of Ideas: An A Priori Critical Juncture Framework," *Canadian Journal of Political Science* 40, no. 4 (December 2007): 883–910; John Hogan and Brendan K. O'Rourke, "The Critical Role of Ideas: Understanding Industrial Policy Changes in Ireland in the 1980s," in *Policy Paradigms in Theory and Practice: Discourses, Ideas and Anomalies in Public Policy Dynamics*, ed. John Hogan and Michael Howlett (London: Palgrave MacMillan, 2015), 167–88.

32. Kathryn Newman, "Organizational Transformation During Institutional Upheaval," *Academy of Management Review* 25, no. 3 (July 2000): 602–19.

33. Béland and Cox, "Introduction," 4.

34. Hay, "Ideas and the Construction of Interests," 67.

35. Gerald Frug, "The City as a Legal Concept," *Harvard Law Review* 93 , no. 6 (1980): 1079, 1121.

36. On the long-standing discussion of "diffusion" studies, see Everett Rogers, *Diffusion of Innovations*, 4th ed. (New York: Free Press, 1995); Elihu Katz, Martin Levin, and Herbert Hamilton, "Traditions of Research on the Diffusion of Innovation," *American Sociological Review* 28, no. 2 (April 1963): 237–52. Possibly the best-known article in political science on diffusion is Jack Walker, "The Diffusion of Innovations Among the American States," *American Political Science Review* 63 (September 1969): 880–99.

Use of the term "flux" to describe the aftermath of critical junctures comes from similar usage of the term by Hogan and Doyle, "The Importance of Ideas," and by Giovanni Capoccia and R. Daniel Kelemen, "The Study of Critical Junctures: Theory, Narrative, and Counterfactuals in Historical Institutionalism," *World Politics* 59, no. 3 (April 2007): 341–69.

37. Bradley Rice, "The Galveston Plan of City Government by Commission: The Birth of a Progressive Idea," *Southwestern Historical Quarterly* 78, no. 4 (April 1975): 365. For a more contemporary discussion of the spread of similar city government reforms, see H. George Frederickson, Gary Alan Johnson, and Curtis Wood, "The Changing Structure of American Cities: A Study of the Diffusion of Innovation," *Public Administration Review* 64, no. 3 (May–June 2004): 320–30.

38. Rice, "The Galveston Plan of City Government by Commission," 365.

39. See, e.g., Kevin Fox Gotham and Miriam Greenberg, *Crisis Cities: Disaster and Redevelopment in New York and New Orleans* (Oxford: Oxford University Press, 2014).

40. Timothy P. R. Weaver, "Urban Crisis: The Genealogy of a Concept," *Urban Studies* 54, no. 9 (2017): 2039–55

41. Richardson Dilworth, "Infrastructure Politics: Implications for a Cohesive National Transportation Policy in the 21st Century," in *U.S. Infrastructure: Challenges and Directions for the 21st Century*, ed. Aman Kahn and Klaus Becker (New York: Routledge, 2019), 297–310.

42. John Chin and Clement Burge, "Twelve Days in Xinjiang: How China's Surveillance State Overwhelms Daily Life." *Wall Street Journal*, December 19, 2017.

43. Daniel Drenzer, *The Ideas Industry: How Pessimists, Partisans, and Plutocrats Are Transforming the Marketplace of Ideas* (Oxford: Oxford University Press, 2017).

Chapter 2

Author's note: This chapter includes material from my book *The Origins of the Dual City: Housing, Race, and Redevelopment in Twentieth-Century Chicago* (Chicago: University of Chicago Press, 2019). My thanks to the University of Chicago Press for allowing this material to be published as part of this chapter.

1. Peter A. Hall, "Policy Paradigms, Social Learning, and the State: The Case of Economic Policymaking in Britain," *Comparative Politics* 25, no.3 (1993): 275–96; John L. Campbell, "Institutional Analysis and the Role of Ideas in Political Economy," *Theory and Society* 27, no. 3 (1998): 377–409; Grace Skogstad, ed., *Policy Paradigms, Transnationalism, and Domestic Politics* (Toronto: University of Toronto Press, 2011); Mark Blyth, "Paradigms and Paradox: The Politics of Economic Ideas in Two Moments of Crisis," *Governance* 26, no. 2 (2013): 197–215.

2. Marcus Carson, Tom R. Burns, and Dolores Calvo, eds., *Paradigms in Public Policy: Theory and Practice of Paradigm Shifts in the EU* (Frankfurt: Peter Lang, 2010), 17.

3. Hall, "Policy Paradigms, Social Learning, and the State," 279.

4. Ibid., 285.

5. Thomas S. Kuhn, *The Structure of Scientific Revolutions*, 2nd ed. (Chicago: University of Chicago Press, 1970), 24.

6. Hall, "Policy Paradigms, Social Learning, and the State," 278.

7. Ibid., 291.

8. Kathleen R. McNamara, *The Currency of Ideas: Monetary Politics in the European Union* (Ithaca, NY: Cornell University Press, 1998); Judith Goldstein, *Ideas, Interests, and American Trade Policy* (Ithaca, NY: Cornell University Press, 1993), 13–14; Sheri Berman, "Ideas, Norms, and Culture in Political Analysis," *Comparative Politics* 33, no. 2 (2001): 234; Mark Blyth, *Great Transformations: Economic Ideas and Institutional Change in the Twentieth Century* (Cambridge: Cambridge University Press, 2002).

9. John L. Campbell, "Ideas, Politics, and Public Policy," *Annual Review of Sociology* 28, no. 1 (2002): 23.

10. Karen Orren and Stephen Skowronek, "Beyond the Iconography of Order: Notes for a 'New Institutionalism,'" in *The Dynamics of American Politics: Approaches and Interpretations*, ed. Lawrence C. Dodd and Calvin Jillson (Boulder, CO: Westview, 1994), 311–30; Karen Orren and Stephen Skowronek, "Institutions and Intercurrence: Theory Building in the Fullnesss of Time," in *Political Order: Nomos XXXVIII*, ed. Ian Shapiro and Russell Hardin (New York: New York University Press, 1996), 111–46; Karen Orren and Stephen Skowronek, *The Search for American Political Development* (Cambridge: Cambridge University Press, 2004).

11. Stephen Skowronek, *Building a New American State: The Expansion of National Administrative Capacities, 1877–1920* (Cambridge: Cambridge University Press, 1982); Theda Skocpol,

Protecting Soldiers and Mothers: The Political Origins of Social Policy in the United States (Cambridge, MA: Harvard University Press, 1992), 54–57.

12. See especially Margaret Weir and Theda Skocpol, "State Structures and the Possibilities for 'Keynesian' Responses to the Great Depression in Sweden, Britain, and the United States," in *Bringing the State Back In*, ed. Peter B. Evans, Dietrich Rueschemeyer, and Theda Skocpol (Cambridge: Cambridge University Press, 1985), 107–63.

13. Robert C. Lieberman, "Ideas, Institutions, and Political Order: Explaining Political Change," *American Political Science Review* 96, no. 4 (2002): 702.

14. Skocpol, *Protecting Soldiers and Mothers*, 59. On the feedback effects of public policies, see also E. E. Schattschneider, *Politics, Pressures, and the Tariff* (New York: Prentice Hall, 1935), 288; Paul Pierson, "When Effect Becomes Cause: Policy Feedback and Political Change," *World Politics* 45, no. 4 (1993): 595–628; Jacob S. Hacker, *The Divided Welfare State: The Battle over Public and Private Social Benefits in the United States* (Cambridge: Cambridge University Press, 2002); Evelyne Huber and John D. Stephens, *Development and Crisis of the Welfare State: Parties and Policies in Global Markets* (Chicago: University of Chicago Press, 2001).

15. Vivien A. Schmidt, "Ideas and Discourse in Transformational Political Economic Change in Europe," in *Policy Paradigms, Transnationalism, and Domestic Politics*, 42. See also Grace Skogstad and Vivien Schmidt, "Introduction: Policy Paradigms, Transnationalism, and Domestic Politics," in *Policy Paradigms, Transnationalism, and Domestic Politics*, 9–10.

16. For a more comprehensive discussion of the role of endogenous factors in paradigm change, see Joel Rast, *The Origins of the Dual City: Housing, Race, and Redevelopment in Twentieth-Century Chicago* (Chicago: University of Chicago Press, 2019).

17. Robert Hunter, *Tenement Conditions in Chicago* (Chicago: City Homes Association, 1901).

18. Edith Abbott, *The Tenements of Chicago, 1908–1935* (Chicago: University of Chicago Press, 1936), 62; Thomas Lee Philpott, *The Slum and the Ghetto: Immigrants, Blacks, and Reformers in Chicago, 1880–1930* (Belmont, CA: Wadsworth, 1991), 104–5.

19. "The Slums Landlord," *Chicago Tribune*, April 24, 1903, 12.

20. D. Bradford Hunt, *Blueprint for Disaster: The Unraveling of Chicago Public Housing* (Chicago: University of Chicago Press, 2009), chap. 1.

21. "Builders Act to End Slums," *Chicago Tribune*, December 14, 1938, 1; "Slum Clearing Bill Is Given Final Touches," *Chicago Tribune*, February 9, 1941, D5; "Redevelopment Ordinance Bill Is Passed by State," *Chicago Tribune*, November 15, 1941, 10.

22. Arnold R. Hirsch, *Making the Second Ghetto: Race and Housing in Chicago, 1940–1960* (Chicago: University of Chicago Press, 1983), chap. 4; Hunt, *Blueprint for Disaster*, chap. 3.

23. "Lake Meadows Development a Show Piece," *Chicago Tribune*, May 13, 1957, 3.

24. "Vast Project Changes Face of South Side," *Chicago Tribune*, June 4, 1959, S6.

25. "1st Hospital Apartment Opens Here Today," *Chicago Sun-Times*, June 4, 1958, 20; "Prairie Shores Skyscrapers to Go in Service," *Chicago Tribune*, June 2, 1958, A1.

26. "Daley Calls for 6 Billion to End Slums," *Chicago Tribune*, February 1, 1959, 1; "Daley Asks U.S. Help to Rebuild Chicago," *Chicago Sun-Times*, February 1, 1959, 3.

27. "Daley Pledges End of Slums in 5 or 6 Years," *Chicago Tribune*, March 22, 1962, 4; "Daley, Aids Set Goal: End Chicago's Slums," *Chicago Tribune*, April 1, 1962, 1.

28. "City Finance Group OK's Vote on Bonds," *Chicago Tribune*, April 29, 1966. See also "Council Unit Approves Big Bond Issue," *Chicago Sun-Times*, April 29, 1966, 32; "Out of Step on

Bond Issue," *Chicago Sun-Times*, April 29, 1966, 47; "2 Aldermen Delay Council in Bond Vote," *Chicago Sun-Times*, April 30, 1966, 3.

29. Chicago City Missionary Society, "A Proposal for Moderate-Income Housing Development in the Hyde Park–Kenwood Urban Renewal Area," Chicago, 1964, Metropolitan Planning Council Records, University of Illinois at Chicago, Special Collections (hereafter MPC Records), box 527, folder 4452.

30. Jack Meltzer, *Selected Aspects of Urban Renewal in Chicago: An Annotated Statistical Summary* (Chicago: Center for Urban Studies, University of Chicago, 1965), 49.

31. "Lake Meadows Development a Show Piece," *Chicago Tribune*, May 13, 1957, 3.

32. Martin Anderson, *The Federal Bulldozer: A Critical Analysis of Urban Renewal, 1942–1962* (Cambridge, MA: MIT Press, 1964); "Urban Renewal: Running Hard, Sitting Still," *Architectural Forum*, April 1962, 101; John J. Egan to Morris Hirsh, May 7, 1964, MPC Records, box 13, folder 2.

33. Hirsch, *Making the Second Ghetto*, chap. 1; Muriel Beadle, "The Hyde Park–Kenwood Urban Renewal Years: A History to Date" (Chicago: Self-published, 1964), 9; Meltzer, *Selected Aspects of Urban Renewal in Chicago.*

34. Chicago City Missionary Society, "A Proposal for Moderate-Income Housing Development," 5.

35. Committee on Urban Progress, Subcommittee on Urban Renewal, Draft report, 1965, 8, MPC Records, box 540, folder 4569.

36. On the combined importance of ideas, interests, and institutions in political development, see Lieberman, "Ideas, Institutions, and Political Order"; Orren and Skowronek, *The Search for American Political Development*; Rogers M. Smith, "Which Comes First, the Ideas or the Institutions?," in *Rethinking Political Institutions: The Art of the State*, ed. Ian Shapiro, Stephen Skowronek, and Daniel Galvin (New York: New York University Press, 2006), 91–113; Timothy P. R. Weaver, "By Design or by Default: Varieties of Neoliberal Urban Development," *Urban Affairs Review* 54, no. 2 (2018): 238.

37. Hugh Heclo, *Modern Social Politics in Britain and Sweden: From Relief to Income Maintenance* (New Haven, CT: Yale University Press, 1974), 305–6.

Chapter 3

1. I use "rebellion" where others might choose "riot." This is because while "riot" emphasizes the violence on the part of protestors, "rebellion" gestures to the pent-up frustrations of institutional racism.

2. Ron Cassie, "Leaders Announce $94 Million Plan to Demolish Vacant Buildings," *Baltimore Magazine*, January 5, 2016, baltimoremagazine.net.

3. Wendell E. Pritchett, "The 'Public Menace' of Blight: Urban Renewal and the Private Uses of Eminent Domain," *Yale Law & Policy Review* 21, no. 1 (2003): 1–52.

4. Rachel Weber, "Selling City Futures: The Financialization of Urban Redevelopment Policy," *Economic Geography* 86, no. 3 (July 2010): 251–74.

5. Robert M Fogelson, *Downtown Its Rise and Fall, 1880–1950* (New Haven, CT: Yale University Press, 2001).

6. Deborah A. Stone, *Policy Paradox: The Art of Political Decision Making* (New York: Norton, 2002).

7. Robert C. Lieberman, "Ideas, Institutions, and Political Order: Explaining Political Change," *American Political Science Review* 96, no. 4 (December 2002): 697–712; Paul Pierson,

"Not Just What, but When: Timing and Sequence in Political Processes," *Studies in American Political Development* 14, no. 1 (April 2000): 72–92; Peter A. Hall and Rosemary C. R. Taylor, "Political Science and the Three New Institutionalisms," *Political Studies* 44, no. 5 (December 1996): 936–57; Karen Orren and Stephen Skowronek, *The Search for American Political Development* (Cambridge: Cambridge University Press, 2004); Stephen Skowronek, *Building a New American State: The Expansion of National Administrative Capacities, 1877–1920* (Cambridge: Cambridge University Press, 1982).

8. James, Scott C., "Historical Institutionalism, Political Development, and the Presidency," in *The Oxford Handbook of the American Presidency*, ed. George C. Edwards and William G. Howell (Oxford: Oxford University Press, 2009), 51–81; Hall and Taylor, "Political Science and the Three New Institutionalisms."

9. Marie Gottschalk, *The Prison and the Gallows: The Politics of Mass Incarceration in America* (Cambridge: Cambridge University Press, 2006); Skowronek, *Building a New American State*; Daniel P. Carpenter, *The Forging of Bureaucratic Autonomy: Reputations, Networks, and Policy Innovation in Executive Agencies, 1862–1928* (Princeton, NJ: Princeton University Press, 2001); Richard Franklin Bensel, *The Political Economy of American Industrialization, 1877–1900* (Cambridge: Cambridge University Press, 2000).

10. Lieberman, "Ideas, Institutions, and Political Order"; Timothy P. R. Weaver, *Blazing the Neoliberal Trail: Urban Political Development in the United States and the United Kingdom* (Philadelphia: University of Pennsylvania Press, 2016).

11. Orren and Skowronek, *The Search for American Political Development.*

12. Clarence N. Stone, *Regime Politics: Governing Atlanta, 1946–1988* (Lawrence: University Press of Kansas, 1989).

13. Paul E. Peterson, *City Limits* (Chicago: University of Chicago Press, 1981).

14. Jennifer S. Light, *The Nature of Cities: Ecological Visions and the American Urban Professions, 1920–1960* (Baltimore: Johns Hopkins University Press, 2009).

15. Ibid., 46–47.

16. State of Maryland, Baltimore City, "Official Ballot, Presidential General Election, Question A," November 8, 2016 (my emphasis).

17. Stone, *Policy Paradox*, 9.

18. Ibid., 148–49.

19. Pritchett, "The 'Public Menace' of Blight."

20. Colin Gordon, "Blighting the Way: Urban Renewal, Economic Development, and the Elusive Definition of Blight," *Fordham Urban Law Journal* 31, no. 2 (2003–2004): 306.

21. Tom Tresser, "TIF Off the Rails: Public Policy Problems with TIFs in Chicago," YouTube, July 23, 2015), https://youtu.be/sJp1EFPW2PU?list=PLZIy2ASrieUjFhvMsf7cEH3Bzx8YTdExk.

22. Gordon, "Blighting the Way." Indeed, the majority opinion in *Kelo vs. City of New London* lays out all of these criteria for using blight.

23. Mabel L Walker, *Urban Blight and Slums: Economic and Legal Factors in Their Origin, Reclamation, and Prevention* (Cambridge, MA: Harvard University Press, 1938).

24. John Paul Stevens, *Kelo vs. City of New London*, No. 04–108 (United States Supreme Court June 23, 2005), 15.

25. Pritchett, "The 'Public Menace' of Blight."

26. Walker, *Urban Blight and Slums*, 3.

27. Ibid., 7, 11, 15.

28. Fogelson, *Downtown Its Rise and Fall*, 349.

29. Eliel Saarinen, *The City: Its Growth, Its Decay, Its Future* (New York: Reinhold Publishing, 1943), 16.

30. Fern Shen, "Neighborhood Leaders from Across Baltimore Decry Liquor Board Inaction," Baltimore Brew, April 26, 2016, https://www.baltimorebrew.com/2016/02/18/neighborhood-leaders-from-across-baltimore-decry-liquor-board-inaction/.

31. *Young v. American Mini Theatres, Inc.*, 427 U.S. 50 (U.S. Mich. 1976).

32. Garrett Power, "Apartheid Baltimore Style: The Residential Segregation Ordinances of 1910–1913," *Maryland Law Review* 42 (1983): 289–328.

33. Andor Skotnes, *A New Deal for All? Race and Class Struggles in Depression-Era Baltimore* (Durham, NC: Duke University Press, 2013), 12–14.

34. Ibid., 13.

35. "Baltimore City Code, 1946," 18 §25 (n.d.).

36. "Baltimore City Code," §21-17 (n.d.).

37. "Baltimore City Code," VII §70 (1946).

38. John Paul Stevens, *Kelo vs. City of New London.*

39. Power, "Apartheid Baltimore Style."

40. Pritchett, "The 'Public Menace' of Blight"; Fogelson, *Downtown Its Rise and Fall.*

41. "Redevelopment Commission," Pub. L. No. 18, § 25 (1946).

42. Adolph Grant, "A Catechism of Zoning" (New Rochelle Chamber of Commerce, 1925), George E. Hooker Collection, University of Chicago Library Special Collections.

43. "NAREB 1951 Panel Discussion of the NAREB City Planning and Zoning Committee," National Association of Realtors Library, 1951.

44. "Inventory of Residential Blight" (Baltimore: Baltimore Urban Renewal and Housing Agency, October 1964), MCC S4, B15, Langsdale Library Special Collections.

45. City of Baltimore, "Baltimore Model Cities Neighborhood: Application to the Department of Housing an Urban Development for a Grant to Plan a Comprehensive City Demonstration Program" (City of Baltimore, April 26, 1967), Enoch Pratt Free Library Maryland Room.

46. Light, *The Nature of Cities.*

47. Herbert U. Nelson, "Letter to the Directors, NAREB," January 31, 1940, ULI Archivists Notes, National Association of Realtors Library.

48. Urban Land Institute, "ULI News Bulletin No. 8" (Urban Land Institute, August 1, 1942), ULI Early History, National Association of Realtors Library.

49. "To Map Policy on Blighted Areas of City," *Baltimore Evening Sun*, May 10, 1937, Vertical Files Housing—Baltimore Slum Clearance, Enoch Pratt Free Library Maryland Room.

50. "To Map Policy on Blighted Areas of City."

51. Clarissa Rile Hayward, *How Americans Make Race: Stories, Institutions, Spaces* (Cambridge: Cambridge University Press, 2013).

52. Mel Scott, *American City Planning Since 1890: A History Commemorating the Fiftieth Anniversary of the American Institute of Planners* (Berkeley: University of California Press, 1971); John Short, *Alabaster Cities: Urban U.S. Since 1950* (Syracruse, NY: Syracuse University Press, 2006); Raymond A. Mohl, "Planned Destruction: The Interstates and Central City Housing," in *From Tenements to the Taylor Homes: In Search of an Urban Housing Policy in Twentieth-Century America*, ed. J. F. Baumen, R. Biles, and K. Szylvian (University Park: Pennsylvania State University Press, 2000), 26; Sara Kathryn Stevens, "Developing Expertise: The Architecture of Real Estate, 1908–1965" (PhD diss., Princeton University, 2012).

53. Marc Weiss, "The Origins and Legacy of Urban Renewal," in *Federal Housing Policy and Programs: Past and Present*, ed. P.J. Mitchell (New Brunswick, NJ: Rutgers University, Center for Urban Policy Research, 1985), 260.

54. "Threatened Negro Blight Alarms Flatbush Residents," *Baltimore Sun*, April 22, 1907.

55. "Realtors Call Dark People 'Blights,'" *Afro-American*, January 31, 1948.

56. Commission on Governmental Efficiency and Economy, "Some Physical and Population Characteristics of Baltimore: An Analysis and Graphic Presentation of Factors to Guide in Sound City Planning and in Dealing with the Menace of Urban Blight" (Baltimore, MD, August 1943), 25, MD XHT168.B2 C617, Enoch Pratt Free Library Maryland Room.

57. Samuel Kelton Roberts Jr., *Infectious Fear: Politics, Disease, and the Health Effects of Segregation* (Chapel Hill: University of North Carolina Press, 2009).

58. Light, *The Nature of Cities*, 22–28.

59. *Planning with You* (The Architectural Forum, n.d.), MCC S4, B15, Langsdale Library Special Collections.

60. See, e.g., "Hundreds Throng Court House to Protest Against Saloons." *Afro-American*, March 8, 1913; Sally, "Flapper Reporter Sees Things on Pennsylvania Avenue," *Afro-American*, December 13, 1924; "Clean Block Campaign Closes as Month Ends," *Afro-American*, September 28, 1935.

61. This is of course not always the case. See Preston H. Smith, *Racial Democracy and the Black Metropolis: Housing Policy in Postwar Chicago* (Minneapolis: University of Minnesota Press. 2012). Smith observes that black homeowners in Chicago favored racial over class democracy, meaning more prosperous blacks sought access to the housing market in a way that skirted issues of need for poorer blacks.

62. Skotnes, *A New Deal for All?*, 37–39.

63. "Baltimore Neighborhood Heritage Project," Maryland Historical Society, http://www.mdhs.org/baltimore-neighborhood-heritage-project-1978-1982.

64. "Clean Block Campaign Closes," *Afro-American*, September 28, 1935.

65. William Perkins, 1979-07-12, Baltimore Neighborhood Heritage Project, Interview #84, Baltimore Regional Studies Archives.

66. "Avenue Quiet on Sunday Morning," *Afro-American*, June 26, 1926.

67. David Schleicher, "City Unplanning," *Yale Law Journal* 122 (2012): 1670–2720.

Chapter 4

Author's note: This chapter includes some significantly revised portions taken from Chapter 4 of my book *Black Citymakers: How The* Philadelphia Negro *Changed Urban America* (Oxford: Oxford University Press, 2013). Thanks to Oxford University Press for allowing those portions to be used here.

1. This agency, which still exists as of this writing, is now known as the Philadelphia Redevelopment Authority.

2. "City Honors Housing Activist," *Philadelphia Tribune*, January 20, 1989.

3. "Where You Live: A South Philadelphia Oasis Stands the Test of Time," *Philadelphia Tribune*, October 23, 1991; "Alice Lipscomb, 87, Phila. Activist," *Philadelphia Inquirer*, October, 10, 2003.

4. Kirk Petshek, *The Challenge of Urban Reform: Policies and Programs in Philadelphia* (Philadelphia: Temple University Press, 1973), 19.

5. Citizens' Council on City Planning, "A Chronological History of the CCCP," Citizens' Council on City Planning Papers, Temple University Urban Archives; "Dorothy Schoell Montgomery to Mrs. William Wurster (Catherine Bauer)," October 30, 1947, Housing Association of Delaware Valley Papers, Temple University Urban Archives; see also Citizens' Council on City Planning, *Annual Reports*, 1941-1970, Temple University Urban Archives; John Bauman, *Public Housing, Race, and Renewal: Urban Planning in Philadelphia, 1920–1974* (Philadelphia: Temple University Press, 1987).

6. See "Lombard Street Re-Development Project," Urban Traffic Committee, Housing Association of the Delaware Valley Papers, Temple University Urban Archives, Division of Land Planning, map "Redevelopment Areas," certified January 9, 1948, Philadelphia City Planning Commission Papers, City Archives; "Redevelopment Area No. 9 ("Southeast Central")," certified January 9, 1948, Philadelphia City Planning Commission Papers, City Archives; "Chronology of Significant Events in Relation to the Crosstown Expressway 1947 to 1970," Housing Association of Delaware Valley Papers, Temple University Urban Archives; Bauman, *Public Housing, Race, and Renewal.*

7. Ibid.

8. Matthew J. Countryman, *Up South: Civil Rights and Black Power in Philadelphia* (Philadelphia: University of Pennsylvania Press, 2006), 45.

9. Ibid., 3.

10. "Chronology of Significant Events in Relation to the Crosstown Expressway 1947–1970," Housing Association of Delaware Valley Papers, Temple University Urban Archives; "Planning Assistance: Crosstown Expressway Summer 1967," Citizens' Committee to Preserve and Develop the Crosstown Community, Philadelphia City Planning Commission Papers, City Archives; *Philadelphia Tribune*, April 15, 1967; "Crosstown Expressway Described As 'Carbon Monoxide' Curtain," *Philadelphia Tribune*, April 29, 1967; "Crosstown Rally Set For Saturday," *Philadelphia Tribune*, November 4, 1967; "Housing Association Urges Phila. To Abandon New Expressway Plan," *Philadelphia Tribune*, April 16, 1968.

11. Bauman, *Public Housing, Race, and Renewal*, 170.

12. "Chronology of Significant Events in Relation to the Crosstown Expressway 1947–1970," Housing Association of Delaware Valley Papers, Temple University Urban Archives. For a history of Delaware and Schuylkill Expressways, see "Delaware Expressway: Historical Overview," Philly Roads, http://www.phillyroads.com/roads/delaware/; "Schuylkill Expressway: Historical Overview," Philly Roads, http://www.phillyroads.com/roads/schuylkill/. For background on roots of the interracial coalition efforts, see "The Crosstown Community Development Corporation—Its Background Program and Financial Needs," The Crosstown Community Development Corporation, Philadelphia City Planning Commission Papers, City Archives; "Planning Assistance: Crosstown Expressway Summer 1967," Citizens' Committee to Preserve and Develop the Crosstown Community, Philadelphia City Planning Commission Papers, City Archives; "3 Expressways Will Be Built Here by State," *Philadelphia Inquirer*, January 18, 1966.

13. Bauman, *Public Housing, Race, and Renewal*, 170.

14. Marcus Anthony Hunter, *Black Citymakers: How The* Philadelphia Negro *Changed Urban America* (Oxford: Oxford University Press, 2013), 147.

15. Ibid.

16. See "Chronology of Significant Events in Relation to the Crosstown Expressway 1947–1970," Housing Association of Delaware Valley, Temple Urban Archives; "Planners Assailed," *Philadelphia Tribune*, April 15, 1967.

17. "25 Groups Blast Crosstown Xway," *Philadelphia Tribune*, April 26, 1969.

18. Hunter, *Black Citymakers*, 151.

19. Ibid., 160.

20. "Chronology of Significant Events in Relation to the Crosstown Expressway 1947–1970"; "Letter to Mayor James H. Tate," April 13, 1967, Philadelphia Anti-Poverty Action Committee, Philadelphia City Planning Commission Records, City Archives; "Letter to Albert Greenfield," July 23, 1956, Armstrong Association of Philadelphia, Housing Association of Delaware Valley Papers, Temple University Urban Archives; "Memo to The Crosstown Business Committee," June 29, 1967, 1, The Citizens Committee to Preserve and Develop the Crosstown Community, Philadelphia City Planning Commission Records, City Archives; Benedict Anderson, *Imagined Communities* (New York: Verso, [1983] 1991); "Planners Assailed," *Philadelphia Tribune*, April 15, 1967; "Black Leaders Rap New Expressway as Negro Removal Fear 'Burma Road' for South Philadelphia Residents; Easy Street for Whites," *Philadelphia Tribune*, March 18, 1969.

Chapter 5

Author's note: Brief portions in this chapter, including Tables 5.3 and 5.4, appeared previously in Jason Hackworth, "Defiant Neoliberalism and the Danger of Detroit," *Tijdschrift voor Economische en Sociale Geografie* 107 (2016): 540–51.

1. Michael D. Tanner, "Government, Not Globalization, Destroyed Detroit," Cato Instutute, July 24, 2013, http://www.cato.org/publications/commentary/government-not-globalization-destroyed-detroit. Cato, of course, refers to itself as a "libertarian" think tank. I use the term "conservative" to refer to the broader movement of which it is a part. There is no single source for the conservative movement. It is composed of a variety of ideational sources and is represented by a number of institutions. Since the 1950s, there has been a organized attempt by conservatives to "fuse" these factions into a political machine. One of many devices used to find common ground has been a narrative of Detroit described in this chapter. I derive my understanding of the American Right from a number of sources, including Sara Diamond, *Roads to Dominion: Right-Winged Movements and Political Power in the United States* (New York: Guilford, 1995); Jason Stahl, *Right Moves: The Conservative Think Tank in American Political Culture Since 1945* (Chapel Hill: University of North Carolina Press, 2016).

2. Hackworth, "Defiant Neoliberalism and the Danger of Detroit"; Hadas Gold, "Detroit, the Right's Perfect Piñata," Politico, August 18, 2013, http://www.politico.com/story/2013/08/detroit-michigan-conservatives-95630.html; Emily Badger, "The Odd Republican Obsession with Detroit," *Washington Post*, August 8, 2016, https://www.washingtonpost.com/news/wonk/wp/2016/08/08/why-republicans-are-obsessed-with-detroit/.

3. I derive my understanding of "conservativism" from Corey Robin, who defines it broadly as "a meditation on—and a theoretical rendition of—the felt experience of having power, seeing it threatened, and trying to win it back." Conservatism and its advocates profit politically from the perceived loss of privilege—the notion that one's individual or group position has been undermined by social change. It includes a variety of now-powerful institutions and movements including but not limited to neoliberalism. See Corey Robin, *The Reactionary Mind: Conservatism from Edmund Burke to Donald Trump* (Oxford: Oxford University Press, 2018). For an elaboration of my own thoughts on conservatism, see Jason Hackworth, *Manufacturing Decline: Race, the Conservative Movement, and the American Rust Belt* (New York: Columbia University Press, 2019).

4. Deborah Stone, "Causal Stories and the Formation of Policy Agendas," *Political Science Quarterly* 104, no. 2 (1989): 281–300; John Campbell, "Ideas, Politics, and Public Policy," *Annual Review of Sociology* 28, no. 1 (2002): 21–38; Daniel Béland, "Ideas and Social Policy: An Institutionalist Perspective," *Social Policy and Administration* 39, no. 1 (2005): 1–18; Fred Block and Margaret Sommers, *The Power of Market Fundamentalism: Karl Polanyi's Critique* (Cambridge, MA: Harvard University Press, 2014); Timothy Weaver, *Blazing the Neoliberal Trail: Urban Political Development in the United States and the United Kingdom* (Philadelphia: University of Pennsylvania Press, 2016).

5. Mark Blyth, *Great Transformations: Economic Ideas and Institutional Change in the Twentieth Century* (Cambridge: Cambridge University Press, 2002).

6. It should be noted that "crisis" is not a fixed or universally agreed-upon construction. Two dominant conceptions of urban crisis—a conservative one pinning the malaise of places such as Detroit on a collapse of morality and a more structural one framing it as the residue of uneven development—have dominated urban theory. See Timothy Weaver, "Urban Crisis: The Genealogy of a Concept," *Urban Studies* 54, no. 9 (July 2017): 2039–55. Blyth's *Great Transformations* uses the latter conception of crisis.

7. Blyth, *Great Transformations.*

8. See, e.g., Naomi Klein, *Shock Doctrine: The Rise of Disaster Capitalism* (Toronto: Random House, 2007).

9. The Democratic Party, of course, is no puritanically left-leaning organization. Since at least the 1980s there has been a concerted attempt to marginalize progressive voices within the party. It remains a tenuous home for some progressives only by default (i.e., it is less bad than the Republican Party). See Stahl, *Right Moves.*

10. For a discussion of conservative and reactionary rhetoric, see Albert Hirschman, *The Rhetoric of Reaction: Perversity, Futility, Jeopardy* (Cambridge, MA: Harvard University Press, 1991); Hackworth, "Defiant Neoliberalism and the Danger of Detroit."

11. Tanner, "Government, Not Globalization, Destroyed Detroit."

12. Charles Tiebout, "A Pure Theory of Local Expenditures," *Journal of Political Economy* 64, no. 5 (1956): 416–24.

13. Dean Stansel, "Why Some Cities Are Growing and Others Shrinking," *Cato Journal* 31 (2011): 301.

14. Edward Glaeser, *Triumph of the City: How Our Greatest Invention Makes Us Richer, Smarter, Greener, and Happier* (New York: Penguin, 2011).

15. Steven Klepper, "The Origin and Growth of Industry Clusters: The Making of Silicon Valley and Detroit," *Journal of Urban Economics* 67, no. 1 (2010): 15–32.

16. Glaeser, *Triumph of the City,* 49.

17. Ibid., 43.

18. Stephen Walters, "Unions and the Decline of U.S. Cities," *Cato Journal* 30 (2010): 117–35.

19. Glaeser, *Triumph of the City.*

20. Marc Binelli, *Detroit City Is the Place to Be: The Afterlife of an American Metropolis* (New York: Henry Holt, 2013).

21. Glaeser, *Triumph of the City,* 50.

22. Walters, "Unions and the Decline of U.S. Cities"; Glaeser, *Triumph of the City.*

23. Paige Williams, "Drop Dead, Detroit! The Suburban Kingpin Who Is Thriving Off the City's Decline," *New Yorker,* January 27, 2014, http://www.newyorker.com/magazine/2014/01/27/drop-dead-detroit.

24. Steven Malanga, "Feral Detroit: Nature Is Reclaiming the Motor City," *City Journal*, Autumn 2009, http://www.city-journal.org/html/feral-detroit-13242.html.

25. Glaeser, *Triumph of the City*, 54.

26. Ibid., 55.

27. Edward Glaeser and Andrei Shleifer, "The Curley Effect: The Economics of Shaping the Electorate," *Journal of Law, Economics, and Organization* 21, no. 1 (2005): 1–19.

28. Ibid., 1.

29. Ibid., 2.

30. Ibid., 13.

31. Glaeser, *Triumph of the City*, 59.

32. See, among many others, Heather Ann Thompson, *Whose Detroit: Politics, Labor and Race in a Modern American City* (Ithaca, NY: Cornell University Press, 2001); Thomas Sugrue, *The Origins of the Urban Crisis: Race and Inequality in Postwar Detroit* (Princeton, NJ: Princeton University Press, 2005); William Bunge, *Fitzgerald: Geography of a Revolution* (Athens: University of Georgia Press, 2011); Jason Hackworth, "Why There Is No Detroit in Canada," *Urban Geography* 37, no. 2 (2016): 272–95.

33. Hackworth, "Defiant Neoliberalism and the Danger of Detroit."

34. "Triangle Shirtwaist: The Birth of the New Deal," *The Economist*, March 19, 2011, http://www.economist.com/node/18396085?story_id=18396085.

35. David Stradling and Richard Stradling, "Perceptions of the Burning River: Deindustrialization and Cleveland's Cuyahoga River," *Environmental History* 13, no 3 (2008): 515–35.

36. See Jason Hackworth, "The Limits to Market-Based Strategies for Addressing Land Abandonment in Shrinking American Cities," *Progress in Planning* 90 (2014): 1–37; Jason Hackworth, "Right-Sizing as Spatial Austerity in the American Rust Belt," *Environment and Planning A* 47, no. 4 (2015): 766–82; Jason Hackworth, "Demolition as Urban Policy in the American Rust Belt," *Environment and Planning A* 48, no. 11 (2016): 2201–22.

37. Diamond, *Roads to Dominion*; Jason Hackworth, *Faith Based: Religious Neoliberalism and the Politics of Welfare in the United States* (Athens: University of Georgia Press, 2012).

38. Hackworth, *Faith Based.*

39. Gold, "Detroit, the Right's Perfect Piñata"; Badger, "The Odd Republican Obsession with Detroit."

40. Badger, "The Odd Republican Obsession with Detroit."

41. Sugrue, *The Origins of the Urban Crisis;* Colin Gordon, *Mapping Decline: St. Louis and the Fate of the American City* (Philadelphia: University of Pennsylvania Press, 2009); Andrew Highsmith, *Demolition Means Progress: Flint, Michigan, and the Fate of the American Metropolis* (Philadelphia: University of Pennsylvania Press, 2015).

42. June Manning Thomas, *Redevelopment and Race: Planning a Finer City in Postwar Detroit* (Detroit: Wayne State University Press, 2013).

43. Adolph L. Reed, "The Black Urban Regime: Structural Origins and Constraints," in *Power, Community and the City: Comparative Urban and Community Research*, ed. Michael Peter Smith (New Brunswick, NJ: Transaction Books, 1988), 138–89.

44. Edward Bonilla-Silva, *Racism Without Racists: Color-Blind Racism and the Persistence of Racial Inequality in America*, 4th ed. (New York: Rowman and Littlefield, 2014).

45. Gosta Epsing-Andersen, *The Three Worlds of Welfare Capitalism* (London: Wiley, 1990).

46. Blyth, *Great Transformations.*

47. Friedrich Hayek, *The Road to Serfdom* (Chicago: University of Chicago Press, 1944).

48. Stahl, *Right Moves.*

49. Elisabeth Hinton, *From the War on Poverty to the War on Crime: The Making of Mass Incarceration in America* (Cambridge, MA: Harvard University Press, 2016).

50. I use the term "liberalism" here and elsewhere in the chapter to refer broadly to the New Deal coalition Democratic Party and its institutions. Philosophically this term refers to egalitarian liberalism rather than classical liberalism.

51. This is not to deny, of course, that Democrats themselves have not taken on neoliberal, probusiness positions. In fact, as Reed argues in "The Black Urban Regime," the first generation of black mayors routinely found themselves in a situation wherein such positions were integral for maintaining the support of the business community who viewed them with greater suspicion than their white, often more liberal predecessors.

52. Alan Greenblatt, "Beyond North Carolina's LGBT Battle: States' War on Cities," Governing, March 25, 2016, http://www.governing.com/topics/politics/gov-states-cities-preemption-laws.html.

53. Alan Greenblatt, "Rural Areas Lose People but Not Power," Governing, April 2014, http://www.governing.com/topics/politics/gov-rural-areas-lose-people-not-power.html.

54. Additionally, the close division of these states tilts Republican (and rural) because of the political geography of prison populations. Prisons are disproportionately located in rural (Republican-voting) areas of states such as Michigan and Ohio, while the prisoners are disproportionately *from* the urban (Democratic-voting) areas of the states. Though they are not permitted to vote, prisoners are counted by residence (i.e., in the prison where they currently reside). Heather Ann Thompson estimates that five (rural Republican-voting) state senate districts in Michigan alone would not exist were it not for this method of apportionment. See Heather Ann Thompson, "How Prisons Change the Balance of Power in America," *Atlantic Monthly,* October 2013, http://www.theatlantic.com/national/archive/2013/10/how-prisons-change-the-balance-of-power-in-america/280341/.

55. Joshua Akers, "Making Markets: Think Tank Legislation and Private Property in Detroit," *Urban Geography* 34, no. 8 (2013): 1070–95.

56. Hackworth, "The Limits to Market-Based Strategies for Addressing Land Abandonment in Shrinking American Cities."

57. Examples abound, but two prominent ones include the frequent state takeovers of the "fiscally incompetent" Detroit School District. In a recent version of this, the state took over the district to straighten out its finances but instead left it hundreds of millions more in debt than when the state arrived. See Binelli, *Detroit City Is the Place to Be.* And, of course, most recently the emergency manager law, imposed by the governor of Michigan, led to the poisoning of the water supply for Flint. In neither of these cases is there an electoral backlash toward those who made these decisions, because the consequences are largely felt by people who would *never* vote for them.

58. Greenblatt, "Beyond North Carolina's LGBT Battle."

59. Stahl, *Right Moves.*

60. Jamie Peck, "Liberating the City: Between New York and New Orleans," *Urban Geography* 27, no. 8 (2006): 681–783; Akers, "Making Markets"; Jamie Peck, "Framing Detroit," in *Reinventing Detroit*, ed. Michael Peter Smith and Lucas Owen Kirkpatrick (New Brunswick, NJ: Transaction Books).

61. Eric Lipton and Brooke Williams, "How Think Tanks Amplify Corporate America's Influence," *New York Times*, August 1, 2016.

62. Stahl, *Right Moves.*

Chapter 6

1. Mark Blyth, *Great Transformations: Economic Ideas and Institutional Change in the Twentieth Century* (Cambridge: Cambridge University Press, 2002); John L. Campbell, "Institutional Analysis and the Role of Ideas in Political Economy," *Theory and Society* 27, no. 3 (June 1998): 377–409; John L. Campbell and Ove Kaj Pedersen, *The Rise of Neoliberalism and Institutional Analysis* (Princeton, NJ: Princeton University Press, 2001); Peter A. Hall and David W. Soskice, *Varieties of Capitalism the Institutional Foundations of Comparative Advantage* (Oxford: Oxford University Press, 2001); Monica Prasad, *The Politics of Free Markets: The Rise of Neoliberal Economic Policies in Britain, France, Germany, and the United States* (Chicago: University of Chicago Press, 2006).

2. Paul Gilroy, ". . . We Got to Get over Before We Go Under . . . ," *New Formations* 80/81 (2013): 23–38; Stuart Hall, *Policing the Crisis: Mugging, the State, and Law and Order* (New York: Holmes & Meier, 1978); Stuart Hall, *The Hard Road to Renewal: Thatcherism and the Crisis of the Left* (London: Verso, 1988); David Harvey, *A Brief History of Neoliberalism* (Oxford: Oxford University Press, 2005); Paul A. Passavant, "The Strong Neo-Liberal State: Crime, Consumption, Governance," *Theory & Event* 8, no. 3 (2005), muse.jhu.edu/article/187839; Loïc Wacquant, *Punishing the Poor: The Neoliberal Government of Social Insecurity* (Durham, NC: Duke University, 2009).

3. Andrew Barry, Thomas Osborne, and Nikolas S. Rose, *Foucault and Political Reason: Liberalism, Neo-Liberalism and Rationalities of Government* (London: UCL Press, 1996); Graham Burchell, "Liberal Government and Techniques of the Self," in *Foucault and Political Reason: Liberalism, Neo-Liberalism and Rationalities of Government*, ed. A. Barry, T. Osborne, and N. Rose (London: UCL Press, 1996); Mitchell Dean, *Governmentality: Power and Rule in Modern Society* (London: Sage Publications, 1999); Michel Foucault, Michel Senellart, and Collège De France, *The Birth of Biopolitics: Lectures at the Collège De France, 1978–79* (Basingstoke, UK: Palgrave Macmillan, 2008); Colin Gordon, "Government as Rationality," in *The Foucault Effect: Studies in Governmentality*, ed. M. Foucault, G. Burchell, C. Gordon, and P. Miller (Chicago: University of Chicago Press, 1991); Thomas Lemke, "'The Birth of Bio-Politics': Michel Foucault's Lecture at the Collège De France on Neo-Liberal Governmentality," *Economy and Society* 30, no. 2 (2001): 190–206; Pat O'Malley, Lorna Weir, and Clifford Shearing, "Governmentality, Criticism, Politics," *Economy and Society* 26, no. 4 (1997): 501–17; Aihwa Ong, *Neoliberalism as Exception: Mutations in Citizenship and Sovereignty* (Durham, NC: Duke University Press, 2006); Nikolas Rose, "Governing by Numbers: Figuring out Democracy," *Accounting, Organizations and Society* 16, no. 7 (1991): 673–92; Nikolas Rose and Peter Miller, "Political Power Beyond the State: Problematics of Government," *British Journal of Sociology* 43, no. 2 (1992): 271–303.

4. John L. Campbell, "Institutional Analysis and the Role of Ideas in Political Economy," *Theory and Society* 27, no. 3 (June 1998): 377–409.

5. Mark Blyth, *Great Transformations: Economic Ideas and Institutional Change in the Twentieth Century* (Cambridge: Cambridge University Press, 2002).

6. Neil Brenner and Nik Theodore, "Cities and the Geographies of 'Actually Existing Neoliberalism,'" *Antipode* 34, no. 3 (2002): 349–79; Jason Hackworth, *The Neoliberal City: Governance, Ideology, and Development in American Urbanism* (Ithaca, NY: Cornell University Press, 2007); Jamie Peck, "Political Economies of Scale: Fast Policy, Interscalar Relations, and Neoliberal Workfare," *Economic Geography* 78, no. 3 (2002): 331–60; Jamie Peck, "Response: Countering Neoliberalism," *Urban Geography* 27, no. 8 (2006): 729–33; Jamie Peck and Nik Theodore, "Exporting Workfare/Importing Welfare-to-Work: Exploring the Politics of Third Way Policy Transfer," *Political Geography* 20, no. 4 (2001): 427–60; Jamie Peck and Adam Tickell, "Neoliberalizing Space," *Antipode* 34, no. 3 (2002): 380–404.

7. Joe Soss, Richard C. Fording, and Sanford F. Schram, *Disciplining the Poor: Neoliberal Paternalism and the Persistent Power of Race* (Chicago: University of Chicago Press, 2011); Timothy Weaver, *Blazing the Neoliberal Trail Urban Political Development in the United States and the United Kingdom* (Philadelphia: University of Pennsylvania Press, 2016).

8. Mark Blyth, *Great Transformations: Economic Ideas and Institutional Change in the Twentieth Century* (Cambridge: Cambridge University Press, 2002).

9. Melissa Nobles, *Shades of Citizenship: Race and the Census in Modern Politics* (Stanford, CA: Stanford University Press, 2000).

10. W. E. B. Du Bois, *Dusk of Dawn: An Essay Toward an Autobiography of a Race Concept* (New Brunswick, NJ: Transaction Books, 1992); W. E. B. Du Bois, *The Souls of Black Folk* (New York: Dover, 1994); Thomas C. Holt, *The Problem of Race in the Twenty-First Century* (Cambridge, MA: Harvard University Press, 2000); Desmond S. King and Rogers M. Smith, "Racial Orders in American Political Development," *American Political Science Review* 99, no. 1 (2005): 75–92; Melissa Nobles, *Shades of Citizenship: Race and the Census in Modern Politics* (Stanford, CA: Stanford University Press, 2000); Michael Omi and Howard Winant, *Racial Formation in the United States: From the 1960s to the 1990s*, 2nd ed. (New York: Routledge, 1994); David R. Roediger, *Class, Race, and Marxism* (London: Verso, 2017); Adolph L. Reed Jr., "Unraveling the Relation of Race and Class in American Politics," *Political Power and Social Theory* 15 (2002): 265–74; Nikhil Pal Singh, *Race and America's Long War* (Oakland: University of California Press, 2017); Rogers M. Smith, *Civic Ideals: Conflicting Visions of Citizenship in U.S. History* (New Haven, CT: Yale University Press, 1997); Debra Thompson, *The Schematic State: Race, Transnationalism, and the Politics of the Census* (Cambridge: Cambridge University Press, 2016).

11. Robert M. Entman and Andrew Rojecki, *The Black Image in the White Mind: Media and Race in America* (Chicago: University of Chicago Press, 2000); Jeff Levine, Edward G. Carmines, and Paul M. Sniderman, "The Empirical Dimensionality of Racial Stereotypes," *Public Opinion Quarterly* 63, no. 3 (Autumn 1999): 371–84; Eric Lott, *Love and Theft: Blackface Minstrelsy and the American Working Class* (Oxford: Oxford University Press, 1993); Charles W. Mills, *The Racial Contract* (Ithaca, NY: Cornell University Press, 1997); James A. Snead, Colin MacCabe, and Cornel West, *White Screens, Black Images: Hollywood from the Dark Side* (New York: Routledge, 1994).

12. Reed, "Unraveling the Relation of Race and Class in American Politics."

13. C. L. R. James, *The Black Jacobins: Toussaint L'ouverture and the San Domingo Revolution*, 2nd ed. (New York: Vintage Books, 1989); Stephanie E. Smallwood, *Saltwater Slavery: A Middle Passage from Africa to American Diaspora* (Cambridge, MA: Harvard University Press, 2007); Ned Sublette and Constance Sublette, *The American Slave Coast: A History of the Slave-Breeding Industry*, 1st ed. (Chicago: Lawrence Hill Books, 2016); Eric Eustace Williams, *Capitalism & Slavery* (London: Andre Deutsch, 1964).

14. Victoria Hattam, "Ethnicity & the Boundaries of Race: Rereading Directive 15," *Daedalus* 134, no. 1 (2005): 61–69; Clarissa Rile Hayward, *How Americans Make Race: Stories, Institutions, Spaces* (Cambridge: Cambridge University Press, 2013); King and Smith, "Racial Orders in American Political Development"; Joseph E. Lowndes, Julie Novkov, and Dorian Tod Warren, *Race and American Political Development* (New York: Routledge, 2008); Melissa Nobles, *Shades of Citizenship: Race and the Census in Modern Politics* (Stanford, CA: Stanford University Press, 2000); Rogers M. Smith, *Civic Ideals: Conflicting Visions of Citizenship in U.S. History* (New Haven, CT: Yale University Press, 1997); Hanes Walton, *Invisible Politics: Black Political Behavior* (Albany: State University of New York Press, 1985); Hanes Walton, *When the*

Marching Stopped: The Politics of Civil Rights Regulatory Agencies (Albany: State University of New York Press, 1988).

15. Joel Aberbach and Jack L. Walker, "The Meanings of Black Power: A Comparison of White and Black Interpretations of a Political Slogan," *American Political Science Review* 64, no. 2 (June 1970), 367–88; Lawrence Bobo, "Race and Beliefs About Affirmative Action," in *Racialized Politics*, ed. D. O. Sears, J. Sidanius, and L. Bobo (Chicago: University of Chicago Press, 2000); Lawrence Bobo and Devon Johnson, "A Taste for Punishment: Black and White Americans' Views on the Death Penalty and the War on Drugs," *Du Bois Review: Social Science Research on Race* 1, no. 1 (2004): 151–80; Michael C. Dawson, *Behind the Mule: Race and Class in African-American Politics* (Princeton, NJ: Princeton University Press, 1994); Jon Hurwitz and Mark Peffley, "Explaining the Great Racial Divide: Perceptions of Fairness in the U.S. Criminal Justice System," *Journal of Politics* 67, no. 3 (2005): 762–83; Vincent L. Hutchings, "Change or More of the Same? Evaluating Racial Attitudes in the Obama Era," *Public Opinion Quarterly* 73, no. 5 (2009): 917–42; Donald R. Kinder and Lynn Sanders, *Divided by Color: Racial Politics and Democratic Ideals* (Chicago: University of Chicago Press, 1996); Mark Peffley, Jon Hurwitz, and Paul M. Sniderman, "Racial Stereotypes and Whites' Political Views of Blacks in the Context of Welfare and Crime," *American Journal of Political Science* 41, no. 1 (January 1997); Steven A. Tuch and Michael Hughes, "Whites' Racial Policy Attitudes in the Twenty-First Century: The Continuing Significance of Racial Resentment," *Annals of the American Academy of Political and Social Science* 634 (2011): 134–52.

16. D. Jones Brittni, M. Harris Kelly, and F. Tate William, "Ferguson and Beyond: A Descriptive Epidemiological Study Using Geospatial Analysis," *Journal of Negro Education* 84, no. 3 (2015): 231–53; Richard S. Cooper et al., "Relationship Between Premature Mortality and Socioeconomic Factors in Black and White Populations of Us Metropolitan Areas," *Public Health Reports (1974–)* 116, no. 5 (2001): 464–73; Elizabeth Eisenhauer, "In Poor Health: Supermarket Redlining and Urban Nutrition," *GeoJournal* 53, no. 2 (2001): 125–33; Jessica Greene, Jan Blustein, and Beth C. Weitzman, "Race, Segregation, and Physicians' Participation in Medicaid," *Milbank Quarterly* 84, no. 2 (2006): 239–72; Michael R. Kramer and Carol R. Hogue, "Place Matters: Variation in the Black/White Very Preterm Birth Rate Across U.S. Metropolitan Areas, 2002–2004," *Public Health Reports (1974–)* 123, no. 5 (2008): 576–85; Michael McFarland and Cheryl A. Smith, "Segregation, Race, and Infant Well-Being," *Population Research and Policy Review* 30, no. 3 (2011): 467–93; Dara D. Mendez, Vijaya K. Hogan, and Jennifer Culhane, "Institutional Racism and Pregnancy Health: Using Home Mortgage Disclosure Act Data to Develop an Index for Mortgage Discrimination at the Community Level," *Public Health Reports (1974–)* 126, no. 3 (2011): 102–14; Rachel Morello-Frosch and Bill M. Jesdale, "Separate and Unequal: Residential Segregation and Estimated Cancer Risks Associated with Ambient Air Toxics in U.S. Metropolitan Areas," *Environmental Health Perspectives* 114, no. 3 (2006): 386–93; Emily F. Russel et al., "Metropolitan Area Racial Residential Segregation, Neighborhood Racial Composition, and Breast Cancer Mortality," *Cancer Causes & Control* 23, no. 9 (2012): 1519–27; David R. Williams and Chiquita Collins, "Racial Residential Segregation: A Fundamental Cause of Racial Disparities in Health," *Public Health Reports* 116, no. 5 (2001): 404–16.

17. Michael C. Dawson, *Not in Our Lifetime: The Future of Black Politics* (Chicago: University of Chicago Press, 2011); Michael C. Dawson and Megan Ming Francis, "Black Politics and the Neoliberal Racial Order," *Public Culture* 28, no. 1 (2016): 23–62; Fredrick Harris, *The Price of the Ticket* (Oxford: Oxford University Press, 2012); Cedric Johnson, *The Neoliberal Deluge: Hurricane Katrina, Late Capitalism, and the Remaking of New Orleans* (Minneapolis: University

of Minnesota Press, 2011); Adolph Reed Jr., "The Post-1965 Trajectory of Race, Class, and Urban Politics in the United States Reconsidered," *Labor Studies Journal* 41, no. 3 (2016): 260–91; Adolph Reed, Jr., *Stirrings in the Jug: Black Politics in the Post-Segregation Era* (Minneapolis: University of Minnesota Press, 1999); Lester K. Spence, "The Neoliberal Turn in Black Politics," *Souls* 14, no. 3–4 (2012): 139–59; Lester K. Spence, *Knocking the Hustle: Against the Neoliberal Turn in Black Politics* (New York: Punctum, 2015).

18. Mark Blyth, *Great Transformations: Economic Ideas and Institutional Change in the Twentieth Century* (Cambridge: Cambridge University Press, 2002).

19. David O. Sears and Jack Citrin, *Tax Revolt: Something for Nothing in California* (Cambridge, MA: Harvard University Press, 1985).

20. David Jacobs and Ronald Helms, "Collective Outbursts, Politics, and Punitive Resources: Toward a Political Sociology of Spending on Social Control," *Social Forces*, no. 77 (1999): 1497–1523; Jessica Trounstine "Segregation and Inequality in Public Goods," *American Journal of Political Science* 60, no. 3 (2016): 709–77.

21. Martin Gilens, *Why Americans Hate Welfare: Race, Media, and the Politics of Antipoverty Policy* (Chicago: University of Chicago Press, 1999); Robert C. Lieberman, *Shifting the Color Line: Race and the American Welfare State* (Cambridge, MA: Harvard University Press, 1998); Joe Soss, Richard C. Fording, and Sanford F. Schram, "The Color of Devolution: Race, Federalism, and the Politics of Social Control," *American Journal of Political Science* 52, no. 3 (2008): 536–53.

22. Christopher D. DeSante, "Working Twice as Hard to Get Half as Far: Race, Work Ethic, and America's Deserving Poor," *American Journal of Political Science* 57, no. 2 (2013): 342–56; Laura S. Hussey and Shanna Pearson-Merkowitz, "The Changing Role of Race in Social Welfare Attitude Formation: Partisan Divides over Undocumented Immigrants and Social Welfare Policy," *Political Research Quarterly* 66, no. 3 (2013): 572–84; Donald R. Kinder and Tali Mendelberg, "Individualism Reconsidered," in *Racialized Politics: The Debate About Racism in America*, ed. D. O. Sears, J. Sidanius, and L. Bobo (Chicago: University of Chicago Press, 2000); Donald R. Kinder and Nicholas Winter, "Exploring the Racial Divide: Blacks, Whites, and Opinion on National Policy," *American Journal of Political Science* 45, no. 2 (2001): 439–56; Mark Peffley, Jon Hurwitz, and Paul M. Sniderman, "Racial Stereotypes and Whites' Political Views of Blacks in the Context of Welfare and Crime," *American Journal of Political Science* 41, no. 1 (January 1997): 30–60.

23. Robert C. Lieberman, *Shifting the Color Line: Race and the American Welfare State* (Cambridge, MA: Harvard University Press, 1998); Joe Soss, Richard C. Fording, and Sanford F. Schram, *Disciplining the Poor: Neoliberal Paternalism and the Persistent Power of Race* (Chicago: University of Chicago Press, 2011).

24. Matthew C. Fellowes and Gretchen Rowe, "Politics and the New American Welfare States," *American Journal of Political Science* 48, no. 2 (2004): 362–73; Joe Soss, Richard C. Fording, and Sanford F. Schram, *Disciplining the Poor: Neoliberal Paternalism and the Persistent Power of Race* (Chicago: University of Chicago Press, 2011).

25. Ange-Marie Hancock, *The Politics of Disgust: The Public Identity of the Welfare Queen* (New York: New York University Press, 2004).

26. Marie Gottschalk, *Caught: The Prison State and the Lockdown of American Politics* (Princeton, NJ: Princeton University Press, 2016).

27. Michelle Alexander, *The New Jim Crow: Mass Incarceration in the Age of Colorblindness* (New York: New Press, 2010); Gottschalk, *Caught*; Amy E. Lerman and Vesla M. Weaver,

Arresting Citizenship: The Democratic Consequences of American Crime Control (Chicago: University of Chicago Press, 2014).

28. James Q. Wilson and George Kelling, "Broken Windows," *The Atlantic*, March 1982, 29–38.

29. Franklin D. Gilliam Jr. and Shanto Iyengar, "Prime Suspects: The Influence of Local Television News on the Viewing Public," *American Journal of Political Science* 44, no. 3 (July 2000): 560–73; Jon Hurwitz and Mark Peffley, "Explaining the Great Racial Divide: Perceptions of Fairness in the U.S. Criminal Justice System," *Journal of Politics* 67, no. 3 (2005): 762–83; Donald R. Kinder and Lynn Sanders, *Divided by Color: Racial Politics and Democratic Ideals* (Chicago: University of Chicago Press, 1996); Mark Peffley, Jon Hurwitz, and Paul M. Sniderman, "Racial Stereotypes and Whites' Political Views of Blacks in the Context of Welfare and Crime," *American Journal of Political Science* 41, no. 1 (January 1997): 30–60; Garrick L. Percival, "Testing the Impact of Racial Attitudes and Racial Diversity on Prisoner Reentry Policies in the U.S. States," *State Politics & Policy Quarterly* 9, no. 2 (2009): 176–203.

30. John L. Campbell, "Institutional Analysis and the Role of Ideas in Political Economy," *Theory and Society* 27, no. 3 (June 1998): 377–409.

31. Dawson, *Not in Our Lifetime*; Dawson and Francis, "Black Politics and the Neoliberal Racial Order," 23–62; Harris, *The Price of the Ticket*; Johnson, *The Neoliberal Deluge*; Reed, *Stirrings in the Jug*; Spence, "The Neoliberal Turn in Black Politics"; Spence, *Knocking the Hustle*.

32. King and Smith, "Racial Orders in American Political Development."

33. Kenneth T. Jackson, "Race, Ethnicity, and Real Estate Appraisal: The Home Owners Loan Corporation and the Federal Housing Administration," *Journal of Urban History* 6, no. 4 (1980): 419–52; Richard Rothstein, *The Color of Law: A Forgotten History of How Our Government Segregated America*, 1st ed. (New York ; London: Liveright Publishing, 2017); Louis Lee Woods, "The Federal Home Loan Bank Board, Redlining, and the National Proliferation of Racial Lending Discrimination," *Journal of Urban History* 38, no. 6 (2012): 1036–59.

34. Kevin Michael Kruse, *White Flight: Atlanta and the Making of Modern Conservatism* (Princeton, NJ: Princeton University Press, 2005); Antero Pietila, *Not in My Neighborhood: How Bigotry Shaped a Great American City* (Chicago: Ivan R. Dee, 2010); Thomas J. Sugrue, *The Origins of the Urban Crisis: Race and Inequality in Post-War Detroit* (Princeton, NJ: Princeton University Press, 1996).

35. Lizabeth Cohen, *A Consumer's Republic: The Politics of Mass Consumption in Postwar America* (New York: Knopf, 2003), 219.

36. Jamie Peck, "Political Economies of Scale: Fast Policy, Interscalar Relations, and Neoliberal Workfare," *Economic Geography* 78, no. 3 (2002): 331–60; Jamie Peck and Adam Tickell, "Neoliberalizing Space," *Antipode* 34, no. 3 (2002): 380–404; Jamie Peck, *Constructions of Neoliberal Reason* (Oxford: Oxford University Press, 2012); Jamie Peck and Nikolas Theodore, *Fast Policy: Experimental Statecraft at the Thresholds of Neoliberalism* (Minneapolis: University of Minnesota Press, 2015).

37. Timothy Weaver, *Blazing the Neoliberal Trail: Urban Political Development in the United States and the United Kingdom* (Philadelphia: University of Pennsylvania Press, 2016).

38. Jason Hackworth, *The Neoliberal City*.

39. Jason Hackworth, "Public Housing and the Rescaling of Regulation in the USA," *Environment and Planning* 35, no. 3 (2003): 531–49; Katherine T. Jones and Jeff Popke, "Re-Envisioning the City: Lefebvre, Hope VI, and the Neoliberalization of Urban Space," *Urban Geography* 31, no. 1 (2010): 114–33.

40. Hackworth, *The Neoliberal City*, 58.

41. Preston H. Smith, *Racial Democracy and the Black Metropolis* (Minneapolis: University of Minnesota Press, 2012).

42. David Harvey, *The Limits to Capital* (Oxford, UK: Blackwell, 1982); Erica Schoenberger, "The Spatial Fix Revisited," *Antipode* 36, no. 3 (2004): 427–33.

43. Adolph Reed, Jr., *Stirrings in the Jug: Black Politics in the Post-Segregation Era* (Minneapolis: University of Minnesota Press, 1999).

44. United States Department of Justice Civil Rights Division, *Investigation of the Baltimore City Police Department* (Baltimore: United States Department of Justice Civil Rights Division, 2016).

45. Justice Policy Institute, and Prison Policy Institute, *The Right Investment? Corrections Spending in Baltimore City* (Washington, DC: Justice Policy Institute, 2015).

46. Ayobami Laniyonu, "Coffee Shops and Street Stops," *Urban Affairs Review*, 54, no. 5 (2017): 898-930.

47. Wilson and Kelling, "Broken Windows."

48. Although a bit dated, see Bernard E. Harcourt, "The Broken-Window Myth," *New York Times*, September 11, 2011, A23; Bernard E. Harcourt, *Illusion of Order: The False Promise of Broken Windows Policing* (Cambridge, MA: Harvard University Press, 2002).

49. Jamie Peck and Nikolas Theodore, *Fast Policy: Experimental Statecraft at the Thresholds of Neoliberalism* (Minneapolis: University of Minnesota Press, 2015).

50. Johnson, *The Neoliberal Deluge*; Jason Hackworth, "Public Housing and the Rescaling of Regulation in the USA," *Environment and Planning* 35, no. 3 (2003): 531–49; Katherine T. Jones and Jeff Popke, "Re-Envisioning the City: Lefebvre, Hope Vi, and the Neoliberalization of Urban Space," *Urban Geography* 31, no. 1 (2010): 114–33.

51. Nicholas Lemann, *The Promised Land: The Great Black Migration and How It Changed America*, 1st ed. (New York: Knopf, 1991); Preston H. Smith, *Racial Democracy and the Black Metropolis* (Minneapolis: University of Minnesota Press, 2012).

52. John Arena, *Driven from New Orleans: How Nonprofits Betray Public Housing and Promote Privatization* (Minneapolis: University of Minnesota, 2012); Jason Hackworth and Joshua Akers, "Faith in the Neoliberalisation of Post-Katrina New Orleans," *Tijdschrift Voor Economische En Sociale Geografie* 102, no. 1 (2009): 39–54; Johnson, *The Neoliberal Deluge*; Cedric Johnson, "Gentrifying New Orleans: Thoughts on Race and the Movement of Capital," *Souls* 17, no. 3–4 (2015): 175–200.

53. Louise Seamster, "When Democracy Disappears: Emergency Management in Benton Harbor," *Du Bois Review: Social Science Research on Race* 15, no. 2 (2018): 295–322.

54. Mona Hanna-Attisha et al., "Elevated Blood Lead Levels in Children Associated with the Flint Drinking Water Crisis: A Spatial Analysis of Risk and Public Health Response," *American Journal of Public Health* 106, no. 2 (2016): 283–90; Anna Clark, "How an Investigative Journalist Helped Prove a City Was Being Poisoned by Its Own Water," Columbia Journalism Review, 2015, https://www.cjr.org/united_states_project/flint_water_lead_curt_guyette_aclu_michigan.php.

55. Johnson, *The Neoliberal Deluge*.

56. Ibid.; Spence, "The Neoliberal Turn in Black Politics," 139–59; Spence, *Knocking the Hustle*.

57. Including Oprah Winfrey. See Edward Wyatt, "In Hurricane's Aftermath, Winfrey Calls for Apology," *New York Times*, September 7, 2005, E3.

58. Michael C. Dawson, "After the Deluge," *Du Bois Review* 3, no. 1 (2006): 239–49.

59. Joel Aberbach and Jack L. Walker, "The Meanings of Black Power: A Comparison of White and Black Interpretations of a Political Slogan," *American Political Science Review* 64, no. 2 (June 1970): 367–88; Graham Cassano and Terressa A. Benz, "Introduction: Flint and the Racialized Geography of Indifference," *Critical Sociology* 45, no. 1 (2018): 25–32; David Fasenfest, "A Neoliberal Response to an Urban Crisis: Emergency Management in Flint, MI," *Critical Sociology* 45, no. 1 (2017): 33–47; Andrew R. Highsmith, *Demolition Means Progress: Flint, Michigan, and the Fate of the American Metropolis* (Chicago: University of Chicago Press, 2015); Todd Cameron Shaw, *Now Is the Time! Detroit Black Politics and Grassroots Activism* (Durham, NC: Duke University Press, 2009); Sugrue, *The Origins of the Urban Crisis.*

Chapter 7

Author's note: This is a significantly revised version of Chapter 5 of my book *Cities on the Hill: How Urban Institutions Transform National Politics* (Oxford: Oxford University Press, 2018).

Thanks to Oxford University Press for allowing me to publish this version as a chapter in this book.

Notes to epigraphs: "Punishment for the Crime of Lynching," Hearing of Subcommittee on S. 1978, Judiciary, HRG-1934-SJS-0003, 237; "Federal Fair Employment Practice Act," Hearing of Special Subcommittee on Fair Employment Standards Act, HRG-1949-EDL-0005, 8.

1. Conversation between Pres. Lyndon Johnson, Rep. John McCormack and Richard J. Daley, 3 December 1963, Miller Center Secret Recordings Archive, Tape K6312.02, PNO 14.

2. Roger Biles, *Richard J. Daley: Politics, Race, and the Governing of Chicago* (DeKalb: Northern Illinois University Press, 1995); Mike Royko, *Boss: Richard J. Daley of Chicago* (New York: Penguin, 1971) ; Richard A. Keiser, *Subordination or Employment? African-American Leadership and the Struggle for Urban Political Power* (Oxford: Oxford University Press, 1997).

3. Biles, *Richard J. Daley*; Mike Royko, *Boss: Richard J. Daley of Chicago* (New York: Penguin, 1971).

4. Letter to R. Daley from C. Mocny, April 26, 1968, "Riot Responses," Richard J. Daley Collection, University of Illinois–Chicago Library.

5. Thomas K. Ogorzalek, *The Cities on the Hill: How Urban Institutions Transformed National Politics* (Oxford: Oxford University Press, 2018), 169–71.

6. Desmond King and Rogers Smith, "Racial Orders in American Political Development," *American Political Science Review* 99 (2005): 75–92.

7. This was also true after the era of white flight, though responsiveness to these communities is less rare than it was before black empowerment and demographic shifts made complete marginalization of minority communities less electorally viable.

8. Jessica L. Trounstine, *Political Monopolies in American Cities: The Rise and Fall of Bosses and Reformers* (Chicago: University of Chicago Press, 2008).

9. Keiser, *Subordination or Employment?*; Dianne M. Pinderhughes, *Race and Ethnicity in Chicago Politics: A Reexamination of Pluralist Theory* (Urbana: University of Illinois Press, 1987).

10. For details on the ideological origins of segregation, see Carl H. Nightingale, *Segregation: A Global History of Divided Cities* (Chicago: University of Chicago Press, 2012). For the canonical account of institutional causes and effects of segregation, see Douglas S. Massey and Nancy A. Denton, *American Apartheid: Segregation and the Making of the Underclass* (Cambridge, MA: Harvard University Press, 1993). For more historically detailed accounts in mid-twentieth century American cities, see Thomas J. Sugrue, *The Origins of the Urban Crisis: Race*

and Inequality in Postwar Detroit (Princeton, NJ: Princeton University Press, 1996); Thomas J. Sugrue, *Sweet Land of Liberty: The Forgotten Struggle for Civil Rights in the North* (New York: Random House. 2008).

11. Ira I. Katznelson, *City Trenches: Urban Politics and the Patterning of Class in the United States* (Chicago: University of Chicago Press, 1982); Massey and Denton, *American Apartheid*; Trounstine, *Political Monopolies in American Cities*.

12. James Q. Wilson, "Two Negro Politicians: An Interpretation," *Midwest Journal of Political Science* 4, no. 4 (1960): 346–69.

13. Biles, *Richard J. Daley*; Trounstine, *Political Monopolies in American Cities*; Keiser, *Subordination or Employment?*; Pinderhughes, *Race and Ethnicity in Chicago Politics*.

14. This is consistent with Feinstein and Schickler's observation that the conversation on race seems to have been between two factions of the Democratic Party. See Brian D. Feinstein and Eric Schickler, "Platforms and Partners: The Civil Rights Realignment Reconsidered," *Studies in American Political Development* 22, no. 1 (2008): 1–31.

15. Until the 1930s, most black Americans who could vote still tended to support Republican candidates, a path we could follow back to Abraham Lincoln and Reconstruction. While most Republicans had weakened in their support for civil rights, Dyer and some of his fellow urban Republicans of this era are important exceptions.

16. "To Prevent and Punish the Crime of Lynching," Hearing before Subcommittee on S. 121, Senate Committee on Judiciary, February16, 1926, 4, HRG-1926-SJS-0003.

17. "Ku-Klux Klan," Hearing before House Committee on Rules, October 11, 1921, 3–6, HRG-1921-RUH-0001.

18. Nancy Burns et al., "Urban Politics in the State Arena," *Studies in American Political Development* 23, no. 1 (2009): 1–22.

19. "Ku Klux Klan," Hearing of House Committee on Rules, October 11, 1921, HRG-1921-RUH-0001.

20. "Federal Fair Employment Practice Act," Hearing before Special Subcommittee on Fair Employment Standards Act, House Committee on Education and Labor, May 10–12, 1949, 88, HRG-1949-EDL-0005.

21. "To Prohibit Discrimination in Employment," Hearing before House Committee on Labor, June 1, 1944, HRG-1944-LAH-0002, 13.

22. "Civil Rights," Hearing before House Committee on the Judiciary, Subcommittee No. 2. July 14–24, 1955, 206, HRG-1955-HJH-0007.

23. "Equal Employment Opportunity," Hearing before Special Subcommittee on Labor, House Committee on Education and Labor, May 15, 1961, HRG-1961-EDL-0029, 19.

24. "Federal Fair Employment Practice Act," Hearing of House Committee on Education and Labor, Special Subcommittee on Fair Employment Standards Act, May 10, 1949, 44, HRG-1949-EDL-0005.

25. This is akin to the mechanism that Glaeser and Steinberg identify as a path through which urban conditions promote democracy by "enhancing the effectiveness of uprisings." See Edward Glaeser and B. Millett Steinberg, "Transforming Cities: Does Urbanization Promote Democratic Change?," *Regional Studies* 51, no. 1 (2017): 58–68.

26. James J. Connolly, *An Elusive Unity: Urban Democracy and Machine Politics in Industrializing America* (Ithaca, NY: Cornell University Press, 2010).

27. See, e.g., Carl Smith, *City Water, City Life: Water and the Infrastructure of Ideas in Urbanizing Philadelphia, Boston, and Chicago* (Chicago: University of Chicago Press, 2013); Edwin

Burrows and Mike Wallace, *Gotham: A History of New York City to 1898* (Oxford: Oxford University Press, 1998); Eric Monkonnen, *America Becomes Urban: The Development of U.S. Cities and Towns, 1780–1980* (Berkeley: University of California Press, 1988).

28. Connolly, *An Elusive Unity.*

29. Ibid.

30. This is the essence of machine politics, the characteristic form of city governance in this era. Amy Bridges, *A City in the Republic: Antebellum New York and the Origin of Machine Politics* (Cambridge: Cambridge University Press, 1983); Connolly, *An Elusive Unity.*

31. Louis Menand, *The Metaphysical Club: A Story of Ideas in America* (New York: Farrar, Straus and Giroux, 2001).

32. Horace Kallen, "Democracy Versus the Melting-Pot: A Study of American Nationality," *The Nation* 100 (February 18 and 25, 1915): 190–94, 217–20.

33. Menand, *The Metaphysical Club.*

34. See, e.g., Eric J. Oliver, *The Paradoxes of Integration: Race, Neighborhood, and Civic Life in Multiethnic America* (Chicago: University of Chicago Press, 2010); Sugrue, *The Origins of the Urban Crisis.*

35. Desmond King and Rogers Smith, *Still a House Divided: Race and Politics in Obama's America* (Princeton, NJ: Princeton University Press, 2011).

36. King and Smith, "Racial Orders in American Political Development"; King and Smith, *Still a House Divided.*

Chapter 8

1. T. C. Williams Transformation Committee, "In the Matter of Transformation Meeting" [transcript], Alexandria City Public Schools, October 8, 2010, 97.

2. The federal appetite for reform ebbs and flows between aggressive intervention (e.g., No Child Left Behind) and greater state control (e.g., Ensuring Student Success Act of 2015). For an overview, see David F. Gamson, Kathryn A. McDermott and Douglas S. Reed, "The Elementary and Secondary Education Act at Fifty: Aspirations, Effects, and Limitations," *RSF: The Russell Sage Foundation Journal of the Social Sciences* 1, no. 3 (2015): 1–29.

3. Douglas S. Reed, *Building the Federal Schoolhouse: Localism and the American Education* State (Oxford: Oxford University Press, 2014).

4. *Milliken v. Bradley*, 418 U.S. 717 (1974) at 741–42.

5. Karen Orren and Stephen Skowronek, *The Search for American Political Development* (Cambridge: Cambridge University Press, 2004), 112.

6. David Tyack and Elisabeth Hansot, *Managers of Virtue: Public School Leadership in America, 1820–1980* (New York: Basic Books, 1982); Carl E. Kaestle, *Pillars of the Republic: Common Schools and American Society, 1780–1860* (New York: Hill and Wang, 1983).

7. David B. Tyack, *The One Best System: A History of Urban Education* (Cambridge, MA: Harvard University Press, 1974).

8. Kaestle, *Pillars of the Republic.*

9. Julie Roy Jeffrey, *Education for Children of the Poor: A Study of the Origins and Implementation of the Elementary and Secondary Education Act of 1965* (Columbus: Ohio State University Press, 1978); Harvey Kantor, "Education, Social Reform, and the State: ESEA and Federal Education Policy in the 1960s," *American Journal of Education* 100 (1991): 47–83.

10. Orren and Skowronek, *The Search for American Political Development*, 114.

11. Tyack and Hansot, *Managers of Virtue*, 34.

12. Frank Munger and Richard F. Fenno Jr., *National Politics and Federal Aid to Education* (Syracuse, NY: Syracuse University Press, 1962), 2–9. During the Great Depression, Congress authorized the Reconstruction Finance Corporation to loan money to distressed school districts unable to meet payrolls or to provide unemployment relief to unpaid teachers. These loans and unemployment relief generally do not meet a definition of federal aid to education.

13. Wayne J. Urban, *More Than Science and Sputnik: The National Defense Education Act of 1958* (Tuscaloosa: University of Alabama Press, 2010).

14. T. C. Williams Transformation Committee, *In the Matter of Transformation Meeting,* April 28, 2011, 144, Alexandria City Public Schools website. Quoted in Reed, *Building the Federal Schoolhouse*, 184–85.

15. Ibid, 151–52.

16. Ibid, 171.

17. Ibid, 172. Maxey, Yamashiro, and Balas are all also quoted in Reed, *Building the Federal Schoolhouse*, 184–85.

18. Conrado Gómez and Margarita Jiménez-Silva, "Mexican American Studies: The Historical Legitimacy of an Educational Program," *Association of Mexican American Educators Journal* 6, no. 1 (2013): 16.

19. *Fisher-Mendoza v. Tucson Unified School District* (1978). The desegregation order was upheld in *Mendoza v. Tucson Sch. Dist. No. 1*, 623 F.2d 1338, 1341 (9th Cir. 1980).

20. Gómez and Jiménez-Silva, "Mexican American Studies," 17.

21. Garcia served as Kansas City superintendent from 1987 to 1991 and as the TUSD's superintendent from 1991 to 2000.

22. Gómez and Jiménez-Silva. "Mexican American Studies," 21–22.

23. Tom Horne, "An Open Letter to the Citizens of Tucson." Arizona Department of Education, Phoenix, June 11, 2007.

24. *Fisher v. Arizona*, 594 F. App'x 917 (9th Cir. 2014).

25. "House Bill 2281," Arizona State Legislature, 2010, https://www.azleg.gov/legtext/49leg/2r/bills/hb2281s.pdf.

26. No student was ever required to take MAS courses; traditional history and literature courses were also available. But MAS courses—because they were aligned with state content standards—satisfied state course requirements for graduation. Stegeman's proposal meant that students wanting to take the MAS curriculum would have to take two sets of history and literature courses in order to graduate, something that was impossible for many students without room in their schedules for a double dose of history and literature.

27. Nolan Cabrera, Eliza L. Meza, and Roberto Cintli Rodriguez, "The Fight for Mexican American Studies," *NACLA Report on the Americas* 44, no. 6 (November–December 2011): 20–24.

28. *Arce v. Huppenthal*, slip op. at 11.

29. Now codified as ARS sec. 15–112.

30. At the 2017 federal trial, Huppenthal later stated that the ten percent figure represented "all the liquidity" of the TUSD's operating budget, rendering it, in effect, unable to operate.

31. *Gonzalez v. Douglas*, slip op. at p.26. Case 4:10-cv-00623-AWT, issued August 22, 2017.

Chapter 9

1. Peter Dreier, "The Future of Community Reinvestment: The Challenges and Opportunities in a Changing Environment," *Journal of the American Planning Association* 69 (2003):

341–53; Richard D. Marisco, "Subprime Lending, Predatory Lending, and the Community Reinvestment Act Obligations of Banks," *New York Law School Journal of Human Rights* 19 (2003): 365–78.

2. Anthony D. Taibi, "Banking, Finance, and Community Economic Empowerment: Structural Economic Theory, Procedural Civil Rights, and Substantive Racial Justice," *Harvard Law Review* 107, no. 7 (May 1994): 1463–545.

3. Timothy Bates and Alicia Robb, "Has the Community Reinvestment Act Increased Loan Availability among Small Business Operating in Minority Neighborhoods?," *Urban Studies* 52, no. 9 (2015): 1702–21; Bhutta, Neil, "Mortgage Lending to Lower Income Borrowers and Neighborhoods," *Journal of Law and Economics* 54, no. 4 (November 2011): 953–83; Taibi, "Banking, Finance, and Community Economic Empowerment," esp. 1489–90.

4. Robert C. Lieberman, "Ideas, Institutions, and Political Order: Explaining Political Change," *American Political Science Review* 96 (2002): 701.

5. Ibid., 702.

6. Ibid.

7. Karen Orren and Stephen Skowronek, *The Search for American Political Development* (Cambridge: Cambridge University Press, 2004), 113, 108.

8. Ibid., 113.

9. For example, John Campbell, "Ideas, Politics, and Public Policy," *Annual Review of Sociology* 28 (2002): 22–29.

10. Donald B. Rosenthal, *Urban Housing and Neighborhood Revitalization: Turning a Federal Program into Local Projects* (Westport, CT: Greenwood, 1988), 28.

11. Peter Dreier, John Mollenkopf, and Todd Swanstrom, *Place Matters: Metropolitics for the Twenty-first Century* (Lawrence: University Press of Kansas, 2001), 125; Rosenthal, *Urban Housing*, 28.

12. Federal Financial Institutions Examination Council (FFIEC), Community Reinvestment Act, http://www.ffiec.gove/cra/.

13. Ibid.

14. Senate Committee on Banking, Housing, and Urban Affairs (SCBHUA), *Community Credit Needs Hearing, March 23, 24, and 25, 1977* (Washington, DC: US Government Printing Office, 1977), 54.

15. Community Reinvestment Act of 1977 (CRA), Public L. 95-128, Title VIII of the Housing and Community Development Act of 1977.

16. CRA §2905.

17. House Subcommittee of the Committee on Government Operations (HSCGO), *Condominium and Cooperative Conversion: The Federal Response (Part 3-Overview Hearings Continued)* (Washington, DC: US Government Printing Office, 1981), 41.

18. Ibid., 135.

19. John P. Ross, "The FIRRE Act and Housing for Low-Income Families," *Publius* 20, no. 3 (1990): 117–30.

20. CRA §2906

21. Senate Subcommittee on Consumer and Regulatory Affairs of the Committee on Banking, Housing, and Urban Affairs (SSCRA), *Discrimination in Home Mortgage Lending Hearing, October 24, 1989* (Washington, DC: US Government Printing Office, 1989), 118.

22. Connecticut Department of Banking, "ABC's of Banking." http://www.ct.gov/dob/cwp/view.asp?a=2235&q=297892.

23. House Committee on Banking, Currency and Housing (a), *The Rebirth of the American City Hearing, September 20, 21, 22, 23, and 24, 1976* (Washington, DC: US Government Printing Office, 1976), 636.

24. HCBCH (a), *The Rebirth of the American City*, 683.

25. House Committee on Banking, Currency, and Housing (b), *The Rebirth of the American City Hearing, September 27, 28, 29, 30 and October 1, 1976* (Washington, DC: US Government Printing Office, 1976).

26. Ibid., 993.

27. Senate Subcommittee on Housing and Urban Affairs of the Committee on Banking, Housing, and Urban Affairs (SSHUA), *Current Status of the Community Reinvestment Act Hearing, September 15, 1992* (Washington, DC: US Government Printing Office, 1992), 2.

28. House Subcommittee on Consumer Credit and Insurance of the Committee on Banking, Finance, and Urban Affairs (HSCCI), *Current Status of the Community Reinvestment Act Hearing, September 15, 1992* (Washington, DC: US Government Printing Office, 1992), 17.

29. Booker A. Overby, "The Community Reinvestment Act Reconsidered," *University of Pennsylvania Law Review* 143, no. 5 (May 1995): 1431–531.

30. See for example, SSHUA, *Current Status of the Community Reinvestment Act Hearing, September 15, 1992.*

31. US Department of Housing and Urban Development, "The National Homeownership Strategy: Partners in the American Dream," Global Urban Development, May 1995, http://www.globalurban.org/National_Homeownership_Strategy.pdf (accessed August 6, 2014).

32. Often, however, rules change at the agency level, particularly those pertaining to community programs, and often require public comment periods.

33. House Subcommittee on Financial Institutions, Supervision, Regulation and Insurance of the Committee on Banking, Finance, and Urban Affairs, *Community Credit Needs Hearing, August 8, 9, and 10, 1978* (Washington, DC: US Government Printing Office, 1978), 529.

34. Javier Rojas, "The Art of the Bootstrap," Venture Beat, November 20, 2008, http://venturebeat.com/2008/11/20/the-art-of-the-bootstrap/ (accessed January 11, 2017).

35. Daniel P. Carpenter, *The Forging of Bureaucratic Autonomy: Reputations, Networks, and Policy Innovation in Executive Agencies* (Princeton, NJ: Princeton University Press, 2001).

36. Orren and Skowronek, *The Search for American Political Development*, 108.

Chapter 10

Author's note: The author would like to acknowledge the generous assistance of the Fulbright Scholar Program in the United States and Canada and the Russell Sage Foundation.

1. See, e.g., Frank R. Baumgartner and Bryan D. Jones, *Agendas and Instability in American Politics* (Chicago: University of Chicago Press, 1993); Frank Fischer and Herbert Gottweis, *The Argumentative Turn Revisited: Public Policy as Communicative Practice* (Durham, NC: Duke University Press, 2012); Dvora Yanow, "Qualitative-Interpretive Methods in Policy Research," in *Handbook of Public Policy Analysis*, ed. Frank Fischer, Gerald J. Miller, and Mara S. Sidney (Boca Raton, FL: Taylor and Francis/CRC Press, 2007).

2. Anne L. Schneider and Helen Ingram, *Policy Design for Democracy* (Lawrence: University of Kansas Press, 1997); Anne Schneider and Mara Sidney, "What Is Next for Policy Design and Social Construction Theory?" *Policy Studies Journal* 37, no. 1 (2009): 103–19.

3. Suzanne Mettler, *Soldiers to Citizens: The G.I. Bill and the Making of the Greatest Generation* (Oxford: Oxford University Press, 2005).

4. Clarence Stone and Robert Stoker, *Urban Neighborhoods in a New Era: Revitalization Politics in the Post-Industrial City* (Chicago: University of Chicago Press, 2015).

5. Traci Burch, *Trading Democracy for Justice: Criminal Convictions and the Decline of Neighborhood Political Participation* (Chicago: University of Chicago Press, 2013); Kenneth Jackson, *Crabgrass Frontier: The Suburbanization of the United States* (Oxford: Oxford University Press, 1985); John H. Mollenkopf, Peter Dreier, and Todd Swanstrom, *Place Matters: Metropolitics for the Twenty-First Century* (Lawrence: University of Kansas Press, 2013); Margaret Weir, Jane Rongerude, and Christopher K. Ansell, "Collaboration Is Not Enough: Virtuous Cycles of Reform in Transportation Policy," *Urban Affairs Review* 44, no. 4 (March 2009): 455–89.

6. Irene Bloemraad, "'Two Peas in a Pod,' 'Apples and Oranges,' and Other Food Metaphors: Comparing Canada and the United States," *American Behavioral Scientist* 55, no. 9 (2011): 1131–59.

7. Mireille Paquet and Lindsay Larios, "Venue Shopping and Legitimacy: Making Sense of Harper's Immigration Record," *Canadian Journal of Political Science* 51, no. 4 (2018): 817–36.

8. It is beyond the scope of this chapter to discuss the origins of national policies and their development and divergence. For comparative studies on US-Canadian national immigration policies, see the work of Triadafilos Triadafilopoulos, especially *Becoming Multicultural: Immigration and the Politics of Membership in Canada and Germany* (Vancouver: University of British Columbia Press, 2012) and "Global Norms, Domestic Institutions and the Transformation of Immigration Policy in Canada and the United States," *Review of International Studies* 36, no. 1 (2010): 169–93.

9. Monica Boyd and Naomi Alboim, "Managing International Migration: The Canadian Case," in *Managing Immigration and Diversity in Canada: A Transatlantic Dialogue in the New Age of Migration*, ed. Dan Rodríguez-García (Montreal: McGill-Queens University Press, 2012), 119–46.

10. Monica Boyd and Naomi Alboim, "Managing International Migration: The Canadian Case," in *Managing Immigration and Diversity in Canada*, 123–50.

11. Susana Mas, "Skilled Immigrants to Be Matched with Vacant Jobs in 2015," CBC News, January 29, 2014, www.cbc.ca/news/politics.

12. Ibid.

13. Erin Tolley, "Who Invited Them to the Party? Federal-Municipal Relations in Immigrant Settlement Policy," in *Immigrant Settlement Policy in Canadian Municipalities*, ed. Erin Tolley and Robert Young (Montreal: McGill-Queens University Press, 2011), 3–48.

14. Doris Meissner et al., *Immigration Enforcement in the United States: The Rise of a Formidable Machinery* (Washington, DC: Migration Policy Institute, 2013).

15. T. Golash-Boza, "President Obama Has Surpassed 2 Million Deportations," Social Scientists on Immigration Policy Blog, March 18, 2014, stopdeportationsnow.blogspot.com.

16. Julie Hirschfeld Davis, "Trump Calls Some Unauthorized Immigrants 'Animals' in Rant," *New York Times*, May 16, 2018, https://www.nytimes.com/2018/05/16/us/politics/trump-undocumented-immigrants-animals.html.

17. Michael Jones-Correa and Els de Graauw, "The 'Illegality Trap': The Politics of Immigration and the Lens of Illegality," *Daedalus* 142, no. 3 (2013): 185–98.

18. Irene Bloemraad and Els de Graauw, "Immigrant Integration and Policy in the United States: A Loosely Stitched Patchwork," Institute for Research on Labor and Employment, UC Berkeley, Working Paper Series, 2011, scholarship.org/uc/item/2nc0m8bm.

19. Michelle Camou, "Deservedness in Poor Neighborhoods: A Morality Struggle," in *Deserving and Entitled: Social Constructions and Public Policy*, ed. Anne L. Schneider and Helen

M. Ingram (Albany: SUNY Press, 2005), 197–222; Eva Swyngedouw, "Governing Newcomers' Conduct in the Arrival Infrastructures of Brussels," in *Arrival Infrastructures: Migration and Urban Social Mobilities*, ed. Bruno Meeus, Karel Arnaut, and Bas Van Heur (Cham, Switzerland: Palgrave Macmillan, 2019), 81–101.

20. Jennifer Robinson, "Thinking Cities Through Elsewhere: Comparative Tactics for a More Global Urban Studies," *Progress in Human Geography* 40, no. 1 (2016): 3–29.

21. Matthew Hall, Audrey Singer, Gordon F. De Jong, and Deborah Roempke Graefe, "The Geography of Immigrant Skills: Educational Profiles of Metropolitan Areas," Brookings Institution, June 9, 2011, www.brookings.edu/~/media/research/files/papers/2011/6/immigrants singer/06_immigrants_singer.pdf.

22. US census 2010.

23. John Biles and Erin Tolley, "Our Unrepresentative but Somewhat Successful Capital: Electoral Representation in Ottawa," in *Electing a Diverse Canada: The Representation of Immigrants, Minorities, and Women*, ed. Caroline Andrews, John Biles, Myer Siemiatycki, and Erin Tolley (Vancouver: University of British Columbia Press, 2008), 111–35.

24. City of Ottawa, "Ottawa Counts: The Housing Choices of Immigrants," 2010 (available from author).

25. Ibid.

26. John Biles and Erin Tolley, "Our Unrepresentative but Somewhat Successful Capital: Electoral Representation in Ottawa," 111–35.

27. "Ottawa, CV (City) [Census Subdivision], Ontario and Ontario (Province) (Table): Census Profile, 2016 Census," Statistics Canada, October 25, 2017, http://www12.statcan.gc.ca/census-recensement/2016/dp-pd/prof/index.cfm?Lang=E.

28. John Biles and Erin Tolley, "Our Unrepresentative but Somewhat Successful Capital: Electoral Representation in Ottawa," 111–35.

29. City of Ottawa, "Ottawa Counts."

30. Biles and Tolley, "Our Unrepresentative but Somewhat Successful Capital: Electoral Representation in Ottawa," 111–35

31. Ibid.

32. Ibid.

33. Ibid.

34. Ibid.

35. Neil Bradford and Caroline Andrews, "LIPS Gathering Momentum: Early Success, Emerging Challenges and Recommendations for the Future," Welcoming Communities Initiative, 2011.

36. "Ottawa Immigration Strategy: Planning Together for Prosperity, Vibrancy, and Inclusion," Ottawa Local Immigration Partnership, 2011, www.olip-plio.ca.

37. "Planting the Seeds of Progress: Ottawa's Immigration Strategy in Action," Ottawa Local Immigration Partnership, 2012, www.olip-plio.ca.

38. Nicholas Acheson and Rachel Laforest, "The Expendables: Community Organizations and Governance Dynamics in the Canadian Settlement Sector," *Canadian Journal of Political Science* 46, no. 3 (2013), 597–616; Aude-Claire Fourot, "Does the Scale of Funding Matter? Manitoba and British Columbia Before and After the Federal Repatriation of Settlement Services," *International Migration and Integration* 19, no. 4 (2018): 865–81.

39. Mara Sidney, "Settling In: A Comparison of Local Immigrant Organizations in the United States and Canada," *International Journal of Canadian Studies* 49 (2014): 105–34.

40. Els de Graauw, *Making Immigrant Rights Real: Nonprofits and the Politics of Integration in San Francisco* (Ithaca, NY: Cornell University Press, 2016); Michael Jones-Correa, *Between Two Nations: The Political Predicament of Latinos in New York City* (Ithaca, NY: Cornell University Press, 1998); Marie Provine et al., *Policing Immigrants: Local Law Enforcement on the Front Lines* (Chicago: University of Chicago Press, 2016); Monica Varsanyi, ed., *Taking Local Control: Immigration Policy Activism in U.S. Cities and States* (Stanford, CA: Stanford University Press and the Center for Comparative Immigration Studies, UCSD, 2016).

Chapter 11

1. In this chapter, I draw freely from my related book: Timothy P. R. Weaver, *Blazing the Neoliberal Trail: Urban Political Development in the United States and the United Kingdom* (Philadelphia: University of Pennsylvania Press, 2016).

2. Paul Peterson, *City Limits* (Chicago: University of Chicago Press, 1981); John R. Logan and Harvey Luskin Molotch, *Urban Fortunes: The Political Economy of Place* (Berkeley: University of California Press, 1987); David Harvey, "From Managerialism to Entrepreneurialism: The Transformation in Urban Governance in Late Capitalism," *Geografiska Annaler: Series B, Human Geography* 71, no. 1 (1989): 3–17; Michael E. Porter, "The Competitive Advantage of the Inner City," *Harvard Business Review*, June 1995, 55–71; David Harvey, *The Enigma of Capital: And the Crises of Capitalism* (New York: Oxford University Press, 2010).

3. Clarence N. Stone, "Systemic Power in Community Decision Making: A Restatement of Stratification Theory," *American Political Science Review* 74, no. 4 (December 1, 1980): 978–90.

4. Adolph L Reed, *Stirrings in the Jug: Black Politics in the Post-Segregation Era* (Minneapolis: University of Minnesota Press, 1999).

5. Logan and Molotch, *Urban Fortunes*.

6. John R. Logan and Todd Swanstrom, eds., *Beyond the City Limits: Urban Policy and Economic Restructuring in Comparative Perspective* (Philadelphia: Temple University Press, 1990); Paul Kantor and H. V. Savitch, "Can Politicians Bargain with Business?," *Urban Affairs Review* 29, no. 2 (December 1, 1993): 230–55; H. V. Savitch and Paul Kantor, *Cities in the International Marketplace: The Political Economy of Urban Development in North America and Western Europe* (Princeton, NJ: Princeton University Press, 2002); Pierre Clavel, *Activists in City Hall: The Progressive Response to the Reagan Era in Boston and Chicago* (Ithaca, NY: Cornell University Press, 2010).

7. Clarence N. Stone, *Regime Politics: Governing Atlanta, 1946–1988* (Lawrence: University Press of Kansas, 1989).

8. Richardson Dilworth, ed., *The City in American Political Development* (New York: Routledge, 2009); Joel Rast, "Why History (Still) Matters: Time and Temporality in Urban Political Analysis," *Urban Affairs Review* 48, no. 1 (2012): 3–36; Clarence N. Stone, "Reflections on Regime Politics: From Governing Coalition to Urban Political Order," *Urban Affairs Review* 51, no. 1 (2015): 101–37; Joel Rast, "Urban Regime Theory and the Problem of Change," *Urban Affairs Review* 51, no. 1 (2015): 138–49; Jack Lucas, "Urban Governance and the American Political Development Approach," *Urban Affairs Review* 53, no. 2 (March 2017): 338–61.

9. Karen Orren and Stephen Skowronek, *The Search for American Political Development* (Cambridge: Cambridge University Press, 2004).

10. Stone, "Reflections on Regime Politics."

11. Rast, "Urban Regime Theory and the Problem of Change."

12. Paul Pierson, *Politics in Time: History, Institutions, and Social Analysis* (Princeton, NJ: Princeton University Press, 2004); James Mahoney, "Path Dependence in Historical Sociology,"

Theory and Society 29, no. 4 (August 1, 2000): 507–48; James Mahoney and Kathleen Ann Thelen, "A Theory of Gradual Institutional Change," in *Explaining Institutional Change: Ambiguity, Agency, and Power*, ed. James Mahoney and Kathleen Ann Thelen (Cambridge: Cambridge University Press, 2010), 1–37.

13. Permissive conditions are weaknesses in institutional structures that make them vulnerable to rapid reconfiguration. Generative causes are "triggers that under the right conditions, can produce significant change." Rast, "Why History (Still) Matters," 22.

14. Rast, "Urban Regime Theory and the Problem of Change," 142. Rast is quoting Mark Blyth, *Great Transformations: Economic Ideas and Institutional Change in the Twentieth Century* (Cambridge: Cambridge University Press, 2002), 10.

15. Rogers M. Smith, "Which Comes First, the Ideas or the Institutions?," in *Rethinking Political Institutions: The Art of the State*, ed. Ian Shapiro, Stephen Skowronek, and Daniel Galvin (New York: New York University Press, 2006), 98.

16. Robert C. Lieberman, "Ideas and Institutions in Race Politics," in *Ideas and Politics in Social Science Research*, ed. Daniel Béland and Robert Henry Cox (Oxford: Oxford University Press, 2011), 209–27.

17. See also Timothy P. R. Weaver, "By Design or by Default: Varieties of Neoliberal Urban Development," *Urban Affairs Review* 54, no. 2 (2018): 234–66.

18. Weaver, *Blazing the Neoliberal Trail*, 11. This definition owes much to David Harvey.

19. Peter Geoffrey Hall, "Green Fields and Grey Areas," Royal Town Institute Annual Conference, Chester, UK, June 15, 1977.

20. Peter Geoffrey Hall, "Enterprise Zones: British Origins, American Adaptations," *Built Environment* 7, no. 1 (1981): 6.

21. Sir Peter Hall, interview by author, London, July 21, 2009.

22. Geoffrey Howe, letter to Margaret Thatcher, June 27, 1977, Margaret Thatcher Archives, http://www.margaretthatcher.org/archive/browse.asp?t=3.

23. Geoffrey Howe, "Liberating Free Enterprise: A New Experiment, Speech to the Bow Group, London, June 26, 1978," in *Enterprise Zones and the Enterprise Culture* (London: Bow Publications, 1988).

24. Ibid., 7; also quoted in Weaver, *Blazing the Neoliberal Trail*, 121.

25. Howe, "Liberating Free Enterprise," 9.

26. Ibid.

27. Sir Geoffrey Howe, interview by author, House of Lords, London, July 7, 2009.

28. Geoffrey Howe, "Liberating Free Enterprise," 11.

29. See Howe's 1980 Budget in Hansard, HC Deb, March 26, 1980, cc981–1439.

30. Department of the Environment, *Enterprise Zones* (London: HMSO, 1981).

31. Stuart Butler, interview by author, Heritage Foundation, Washington, DC, February 3, 2009.

32. Stuart M. Butler, "Enterprise Zone: A Solution to the Urban Crisis?" (Washington, DC: Heritage Foundation, February 29, 1979), 2, 12.

33. See Jane Jacobs, *The Death and Life of Great American Cities*, 50th anniversary ed. (New York: Modern Library, 2011); David L. Birch, "The Job Generation Process" (Cambridge, MA: MIT Program on Neighborhood and Regional Change, 1979).

34. Quoted in Daniel Stedman Jones, *Masters of the Universe: Hayek, Friedman, and the Birth of Neoliberal Politics* (Princeton, NJ: Princeton University Press, 2014), 320.

35. Stuart Butler, interview by author, Heritage Foundation, Washington, DC, February 3, 2009.

36. In the House, Representatives Robert Garcia (D-NY) and eventually Charles Rangel (D-NY) were also important, as were Rudolph Boschwitz (R-MN) and John Chafee (R-RI) in the Senate.

37. Ronald Reagan, State of the Union address to Congress, Washington, DC, January 25, 1984.

38. See, e.g., Margaret Weir, "Ideas and Politics: The Acceptance of Keynesianism in Britain and the United States," in *The Political Power of Economic Ideas: Keynesianism Across Nations*, ed. Peter A. Hall (Princeton, NJ: Princeton University Press, 1989), 53–86.

39. For details on the legislative history, see Karen Mossberger, "State-Federal Diffusion and Policy Learning: From Enterprise Zones to Empowerment Zones," *Publius: The Journal of Federalism* 29, no. 3 (June 20, 1999): 31–50; Karen Mossberger, *The Politics of Ideas and the Spread of Enterprise Zones* (Washington, DC: Georgetown University Press, 2000); Weaver, *Blazing the Neoliberal Trail.*

40. See, e.g., US General Accounting Office, "Revitalizing Distressed Areas Through Enterprise Zones: Many Uncertainties Exist" (Washington, DC: US General Accounting Office, July 15, 1982); US General Accounting Office, "Enterprise Zones: Lessons from the Maryland Experience" (Washington, DC: US General Accounting Office, 1983).

41. Mossberger, *The Politics of Ideas and the Spread of Enterprise Zones.*

42. William W. Goldsmith, "Enterprise Zones: If They Work, We're in Trouble," *International Journal of Urban and Regional Research* 6, no. 3 (1982): 441.

43. Quoted in Doreen Massey, "Enterprise Zones: A Political Issue," *International Journal of Urban and Regional Research* 6, no. 3 (1982): 431.

44. G. B. Norcliffe and A. G. Hoare, "Enterprise Zone Policy for the Inner City: A Review and Preliminary Assessment," *Area* 14, no. 4 (1982): 271.

45. John Elliot, "Beckett Call to Cut Costs for Industry," *Financial Times*, July 31, 1982, sec. 1, 24.

46. Bernard Tennant, "Development of Enterprise Zones," *The Times*, June 9, 1981, 18. See also Alan C. Hollway, "Enterprise Zones," *The Times*, August 23, 1982; Mike Brookfield, "Enterprise Zones," *The Times*, September 7, 1982, 11.

47. Andrew Taylor, "Enterprise Zones Doubts Remain," *Financial Times*, July 30, 1982, sec. 1.9.

48. Massey, "Enterprise Zones," 432.

49. Stuart Butler, interview by author, Heritage Foundation, Washington, DC, February 3, 2009.

50. See, e.g., Blyth, *Great Transformations*; Colin Hay, "Ideas, Interests and Institutions in the Comparative Political Economy of Great Transformations," *Review of International Political Economy* 11, no. 1 (February 2004): 204–26; Colin Hay, "Ideas and the Construction of Interests," in *Ideas and Politics in Social Science Research*, ed. Daniel Béland and Robert Henry Cox (Oxford: Oxford University Press, 2011), 65–82.

51. For an example of this approach, see David Harvey, *A Brief History of Neoliberalism* (Oxford: Oxford University Press, 2005); Harvey, *The Enigma of Capital.*

52. See, e.g., US General Accounting Office, "Revitalizing Distressed Areas Through Enterprise Zones"; US General Accounting Office, "Enterprise Zones"; Department of the Environment,

Monitoring Enterprise Zones (London: HSMO, 1983); Department of the Environment, *Final Evaluation of Enterprise Zones* (London: HMSO, 1995); Dan Y. Dabney, "Do Enterprise Zone Incentives Affect Business Location Decisions?," *Economic Development Quarterly* 5, no. 4 (November 1, 1991): 325–34, doi:10.1177/089124249100500404; Rodney A. Erickson and Susan W. Friedman, "Comparative Dimensions of State Enterprise Zones," in *Enterprise Zones: New Directions in Economic Development*, ed. Roy Green (Newbury Park, CA: Sage, 1991), 155–76; Sar A. Levitan, *Enterprise Zones: A Promise Based on Rhetoric* (Washington, DC: Center for Social Policy Studies, George Washington University, 1992); In contrast to most studies, Rubin and Wilder find more positive results. Barry Rubin and Margaret Wilder, "Rhetoric Versus Reality," *Journal of the American Planning Association* 62, no. 4 (Autumn 1992): 473–91, doi:10.1080/01944368908975431.

53. "The 1992 Campaign; Excerpts from Clinton's Speech on His Economic Proposals," *New York Times*, June 23, 1992.

54. Sarah F. Liebschutz, "Empowerment Zones and Enterprise Communities: Reinventing Federalism for Distressed Communities," *Publius* 25, no. 3 (July 1, 1995): 124.

55. Michael J. Rich and Robert P. Stoker, "Rethinking Empowerment: Evidence from Local Empowerment Zone Programs," *Urban Affairs Review* 45, no. 6 (July 1, 2010): 775–96.

56. Michael J Rich and Robert P Stoker, *Collaborative Governance for Urban Revitalization: Lessons from Empowerment Zones* (Ithaca, N.Y.: Cornell University Press, 2014).

57. Michael D. Shear, "Obama Announces 'Promise Zones' in 5 Poor Areas," *New York Times*, January 10, 2014, A12.

58. Timothy Weaver, "The Problem With Opportunity Zones," *CityLab*, May 16, 2018.

59. Richard Hall, "Osborne Hopes to Kick-Start Economy with Enterprise Zones," *The Independent*, August 18, 2011, http://www.independent.co.uk/news/uk/politics/osborne-hopes-to-kickstart-economy-with-enterprise-zones-2339697.html.

60. House of Commons, "Enterprise Zones," *Commons Library Standard Note, SN/EP/5942*, 13 August 2014, 3, http://www.parliament.uk/business/publications/research/briefing-papers/SN05942/enterprise-zones.

61. Andrew Sissons with Chris Brown, "Do Enterprise Zones Work?," *The Work Foundation*, February 2011, 3.

62. House of Commons, "Enterprise Zones," 6.

63. Jim Pickard, "UK Chancellor's Enterprise Zones Slow to Take Off," *Financial Times*, April 2, 2014, http://www.ft.com/intl/cms/s/0/c01ddaa4-b5c1-11e3-81cb-00144feabdc0.html#axzz3LuJMFeCC.

Chapter 12

1. Eleonora Pasotti, *Resisting Redevelopment: Protest in Aspiring Global Cities* (Cambridge:: Cambridge University Press, 2020).

2. John R. Logan and Harvey Molotch, *Urban Fortunes: The Political Economy of Place* (Berkeley: University of California Press, 2007).

3. Ruth Berins Collier and Samuel Handlin, *Reorganizing Popular Politics: Participation and the New Interest Regime in Latin America* (University Park: Pennsylvania State University Press, 2009).

4. Peter M. Siavelis, Esteban Valenzuela, and Giorgio Martelli, "Santiago: Municipal Decentralization in a Centralized Political System," in *Capital City Politics in Latin America: Democratization and Empowerment*, ed. D. J. Myers and H. A. Dietz (Boulder, CO: Lynne Rienner, 2002), 265.

5. Ibid., 268.

6. Mario Torres, "Recuperación De La Renta Urbana: Una Tarea ética Pendiente," *Revista Invi* 21, no. 58 (2006): 42–70.

7. Francisco Sabatini, "Reforma De Los Mercados De Suelo En Santiago, Chile: Efectos Sobre Los Precios De La Tierra Y La Segregación Residencial," *EURE* 26, no. 77 (2000): 49–80.

8. It should be noted that only 40 percent of the local property tax goes to the municipality, while 60 percent is contributed to the Fondo Común Municipal (FCM), a national body that redistributes resources across municipalities. In the rich communes of Santiago, Providencia, Vitacura, and Las Condes, these proportions are 35 percent and 65 percent, respectively. Similarly, business licences (*patentes comerciales*) remain entirely in the municipality except in the communes of Providencia, Vitacura, and Las Condes, where only 35 percent is of local benefit and 65 percent of the proceeds goes to the FCM, or in Santiago, where the contribution to the FCM amounts to 55 percent. On the other hand, 37.5 percent of vehicle registration proceeds remain in the municipalities. Slaven Razmilic, "Impuesto Terrirorial Y Financiamiento Municipal," *Estudios Públicos*, no. 138 (2015): 47–92.

9. Pablo Trivelli, *Sobre El Debate Acerca De La Política Urbana, La Política De Suelo Y La Formación De Los Precios De La Tierra Urbana En El Gran Santiago, Antecedentes Teóricos Y Empíricos* (Santiago: Centro De Políticas Públicas–Universidad Católica De Chile, 2006); Francisco Sabatini, "Reforma De Los Mercados De Suelo En Santiago, Chile: Efectos Sobre Los Precios De La Tierra Y La Segregación Residencial," *EURE* 26, no. 77 (2000): 47–80; Paulina Schiappacasse and Bernhard Müller, "Desarrollo Metropolitano Integrado: El Case De Santiago De Chile," *Urbano* 7, no. 10 (2004): 68–74; Jonás Figueroa Salas, "Las Leyes Del Suelo: A Propósito De La Propuesta De Modificación Y Actualización Del PRM-1994 De Santiago," *Urbano*, March 2015.

10. Manuel Castells, *The City and the Grassroots: A Cross-Cultural Theory of Urban Social Movements* (Berkeley: University of California Press, 1983).

11. Ernesto José López-Morales, "Real Estate Market, State-Entrepreneurialism and Urban Policy in the 'Gentrification by Ground Rent Dispossession' of Santiago De Chile," *Journal of Latin American Geography* 9, no. 1 (2010): 145–73.

12. Margarita Greene and Eduardo Rojas, "Housing for the Poor in the City Centre: A Review of the Chilean Experience and a Challenge for Incremental Design," in *Rethinking the Informal City: Critical Perspectives from Latin America*, ed. F. Hernández, P. Kellett, and L. K. Allen (New York: Berghahn Books, 2010), 91–115.

13. Greene and Rojas, "Housing for the Poor in the City Centre"; Pablo Trivelli, *Sobre La Propuesta De Modificación De Plan Regulador Metropolitano De Santiago* (Santiago, 2009).

14. Ernesto José López-Morales, "Real Estate Market, State-Entrepreneurialism and Urban Policy in the 'Gentrification by Ground Rent Dispossession' of Santiago De Chile," 158.

15. Millaray Navarro Ayala, "Proponen Polémico Seccional En área De Santiago Poniente," *El Mercurio*, June 12, 2006.

16. Eduardo Rojas, Eduardo Rodríguez, and Emiel Wegelin, *Volver Al Centro: La Recuperación De áreas Urbanas Centrales*, ed. División De Programas Sociales Del Departamento De Desarrollo Sustentable-Banco Interamericano De Desarrollo (Washington, DC: Banco Interamericano de Desarrollo, 2004).

17. Ernesto José López-Morales, "Real Estate Market, State-Entrepreneurialism and Urban Policy in the 'Gentrification by Ground Rent Dispossession' of Santiago De Chile," 145–73.

18. Trivelli, *Sobre El Debate Acerca De La Política Urbana.*

19. Eleonora Pasotti, *Political Branding in Cities: The Decline of Machine Politics in Bogotá, Naples, and Chicago* (Cambridge: Cambridge University Press, 2009).

20. Departamento De Urbanismo De La Dirección De Obras De La Municipalidad De Santiago, *Desafectación De Vías Comunales En El Sector Santiago Norponiente* (Santiago, 2006).

21. Rosario Carvajal, Claudia Pascual, Marcelo Arancibia Rodríguez, and José Osorio, *Estudio Del Patrimonio Arquitectónico De Santiago Poniente* (Sanitago: Vecinos Por La Defensa Del Barrio Yungay, 2008), 4.

22. "Vecinos por la Defensa del Bario Yungay," Barrio Yungay, n.d., http://www.barriopatrimonialyungay.cl/vecinos-por-la-defensa-del-barrio-yungay/.

23. Francisco Mardones, "Barrio Concha Y Toro Bajo Amenaza: Municipio Y Empresarios Quieren 'subirle El Pelo,'" *Radio Universidad De Chile*, August 2, 2009.

24. Sharon Zukin, *Naked City: The Death and Life of Authentic Urban Places* (Oxford: Oxford University Press, 2010).

25. "Vecinos por la Defensa del Barrio Yungay."

26. Ibid.

Chapter 13

1. Michael P. Todaro, "Urbanization in Developing Nations: Trends, Prospects, and Policies," Center for Policy Studies Working Papers, Number 50, The Population Council, New York, 1979.

2. Gerald Breese, *Urbanization in Newly Developing Countries* (Englewood Cliffs, NJ: Prentice Hall, 1966); Douglas Gollin, Remi Jedwab, and Dietrich Vollrath, "Urbanization With and Without Industrialization," *Journal of Economic Growth* 21, no. 1 (2016): 35–70.

3. Alejandro Portes, Manuel Castells, and Lauren A. Benton, *The Informal Economy: Studies in Advanced and Less Developed Countries* (Baltimore: Johns Hopkins University Press, 1989); Iwan Jaya Aziz, "The Increasing Role of the Urban Non-Formal Sector in Indonesia: Employment Analysis Within a Multisectoral Framework," in *Urbanization in Large Developing Countries: China, Indonesia, Brazil and India*, ed. G.W. Jones and P. Visaria (Oxford, UK: Clarendon, 1997).

4. William Hurst, "Urban China: Change and Contention," in *Politics in China: An Introduction*, ed. W.A. Joseph, 2nd ed. (Oxford: Oxford University Press, 2014).

5. Henri Lefebvre, *Le Droit à la Ville* (Paris: Anthropos, 1968).

6. World Bank, *China Systematic Country Diagnostic: Towards a More Inclusive and Sustainable Development* (Washington, DC: World Bank, 2018).

7. Dorothy J. Solinger, *Contesting Citizenship in Urban China: Peasant Migrants, the State, and the Logic of the Market* (Berkeley: University of California Press, 1999).

8. Lin You Su, "Migration and Urbanization in China."

9. David Zweig, *Freeing China's Farmers: Rural Restructuring in the Reform Era* (Armonk, NY: M. E. Sharpe, 1997).

10. See, e.g., Kate Xiao Zhou, *How the Farmers Changed China: Power of the People* (Boulder, CO: Westview, 1996).

11. See, e.g., Joseph Fewsmith, *Dilemmas of Reform in China: Political Conflict and Economic Debate* (Abingdon, UK: Routledge, 1994).

12. William Hurst, *The Chinese Worker After Socialism* (Cambridge: Cambridge University Press, 2009).

13. Barry Naughton, *Growing out the Plan: Chinese Economic Reform, 1978–1993* (Cambridge: Cambridge University Press, 1995).

14. Solinger, *Contesting Citizenship in Urban China.*

15. A. Schneider and C. M. Mertes, "Expansion and Growth in Chinese Cities," *Environmental Research Letters* 9, no. 2 (2014): 1–11.

16. Shaoguang Wang, "China's 1994 Fiscal Reform: An Initial Assessment," *Asian Survey* 37, no. 9 (1997): 801–17; Le-yin Zhang, "China's Central-Provincial Fiscal Relationships, Budgetary Decline, and the Impact of the 1994 Fiscal Reform: An Evaluation," *China Quarterly* 157 (1999): 169-200.

17. Meg E. Rithmire, *Land Bargains and Chinese Capitalism: The Politics of Property Rights Under Reform* (Cambridge: Cambridge University Press, 2015); Christian P. Sorace and William Hurst, "China's Phantom Urbanisation and the Pathology of Ghost Cities," *Journal of Contemporary Asia* 46, no. 2 (2016): 304–22.

18. William Hurst and Christian P. Sorace "Recession and the Politics of Class and Production in China" *New Political Science: A Journal of Politics and Culture* 33, no.4 (2011): 509–24.

19. Mark Blyth, *Great Transformations: Economic Ideas and Institutional Change in the Twentieth Century* (Cambridge: Cambridge University Press, 2002); Peter Gourevitch, *Politics in Hard Times: Comparative Responses to International Economic Crises* (Ithaca, NY: Cornell University Press, 1986).

20. Sorace and Hurst, "China's Phantom Urbanisation and the Pathology of Ghost Cities."

21. William Hurst, "Chinese Labor Divided," *Dissent Magazine*, Spring 2015.

22. Ibid.

23. Matthew Keegan, "Dongguan in the Spotlight: Hi-Tech Comeback for 'Factory of the World'?," *The Guardian*, February 16, 2018.

24. William Hurst and Jessica C. Teets, "Compliance, Resistance, Innovation, and Involution," in *Local Governance Innovation in China: Experimentation, Diffusion, and Defiance*, ed. J. C. Teets and W. Hurst (Abingdon, UK: Routledge, 2015), .

25. Margherita Comola and Luiz De Mello, "Fiscal Decentralization and Urbanization in Indonesia," in *Urbanization and Development in Asia: Multidimensional Perspectives*, ed. J. Beall, B. Guha-Khasnobis, and R. Kanbur (Oxford: Oxford University Press, 2012), 201–21.

26. Breese, *Urbanization in Newly Developing Countries.*

27. See, e.g., Peter J. Rimmer and Howard Dick, *The City in Southeast Asia: Patterns, Processes, and Policy* (Honolulu: University of Hawai'i Press, 2009), chap. 7.

28. Meg E. Rithmire, *Land Bargains and Chinese Capitalism: The Politics of Property Rights Under Reform* (Cambridge: Cambridge University Press, 2015).

29. Dorothy J. Solinger, "The Creation of a New Underclass in China and Its Implications," *Environment and Urbanization* 18, no. 1 (2006): 177–94; Dorothy J. Solinger, "The New Urban Underclass and Its Consciousness: Is It a Class?," *Journal of Contemporary China* 21, no. 78 (2012): 1011–28.

30. Luigi Tomba, *The Government Next Door: Neighborhood Politics in China* (Ithaca, NY: Cornell University Press, 2014); Fulong Wu, "State Dominance in Urban Redevelopment: Beyond Gentrification in Urban China," *Urban Affairs Review* 52, no. 5 (2015): 631–58.

Chapter 14

1. For a robust reading of the speculative urbanism in recent times, see Christopher Marcinkoski, *The City That Never Was* (Princeton, NJ: Princeton Architectural Press, 2016).

2. Herman M. Schwartz and Leonard Seabrooke, "Varieties of Residential Capitalism in the International Political Economy: Old Welfare States and the New Politics of Housing," in *The Politics of Housing Booms and Busts*, ed. Leobard Seabrooke and Herman Schwartz (Palgrave: London, 2009), 2.

3. United Nations, *Report of the Special Rapporteur on Adequate Housing as a Component of the Right to an Adequate Standard of Living*, E/CN.4/2005/48, March 2005.

4. In January 2001 Calcutta's name was changed to Kolkata. I use "Calcutta" to refer to the pre-2001 city and "Kolkata" to refer to the contemporary city.

5. For a history of Calcutta's land market, see Debjani Bhattacharyya, *Empire and Ecology in the Bengal Delta: The Making of Calcutta* (Cambridge: Cambridge University Press, 2018).

6. Swati Chattopadhyay, *Representing Calcutta: Modernity, Nationalism and the Colonial Uncanny* (London: Routledge, 2005), 1.

7. *Bastis*, *chawls*, and barrios are various ways that the working poor have provided for their own housing in the face of governmental indifference in both capitalistic and socialist regimes.

8. Schwartz and Seabrooke, "Varieties of Residential Capitalism in the International Political Economy," 2.

9. Robert Neuwirth, *Shadow Cities: A Billion Squatters, a New Urban World* (New York: Routledge, 2005).

10. Susan S. Fainstein, *The Just City* (Ithaca, NY: Cornell University Press, 2010); David Harvey, *Social Justice and the City* (Oxford, UK: Basil Blackwell, 1988, 1973); Henri Lefebvre, Eleonore Kofman, and Elizabeth Lebas, *Writings on Cities* (Oxford, UK: Blackwell Publishers, 1996).

11. Olga Tellis & Ors vs Bombay Municipal Corporation (1985) 1986 AIR 180, 1985 SCR Supl. (2) 51.

12. Claudio Cattaneo and Miguel A. Martinez, eds., *The Squatters' Movement in Europe: Commons and Autonomy as Alternatives to Capitalism* (London: Pluto, 2014), 7.

13. On the speculative nature of the urban housing market in Calcutta, see Debjani Bhattacharyya, "Interwar Housing Speculation and Rent Profiteering in Colonial Calcutta," *Comparative Studies of South Asia, Africa and the Middle East* 36, no. 3 (2016), 465–82.

14. Ibid., 467–79.

15. Prashant Kidambi, *The Making of an Indian Metropolis: Colonial Governance and Public Culture in Bombay, 1890–1920* (Aldershot, UK: Ashgate, 2007), 71–72.

16. Bhattacharyya. "Interwar Housing Speculation and Rent Profiteering in Colonial Calcutta," 479–80.

17. Schwartz and Seabrooke, "Varieties of Residential Capitalism in the International Political Economy," 2.

18. Partha Chatterjee, *Politics of the Governed: Reflections on Popular Politics in Most of the World* (New York: Columbia University Press, 2006), 60.

19. James Ranald Martin, *Notes on the Medical Topography: Report of the Committee Appointed by the Right Honourable the Governor of Bengal for the Establishment of a Fever Hospital and for Inquiry into Local Management and Taxation in Calcutta* (London: G. H. Huttmann, 1837); Partha Datta, *Planning the City: Urbanization and Reform in Calcutta, C. 1800–C. 1940* (New Delhi: Tulika Books, 2012), showing how important the medical topography was to planning histories; David Arnold, *Colonizing the Body: State Medicine and Epidemic Diseases in Nineteenth-Century India* (Berkeley: University of California Press, 1993), arguing that medical ideology was central to the molding of an idea of occidental cures versus oriental therapeutics.

20. Before the germ theory of disease became predominant, it was the fever theory that guided medical practitioners, public health workers, and urban sanitation reformers. Fever theory was based on the circulation of blood that was considered contagious. However, even though germ theory was gaining ground, fever theory did not disappear overnight, but both the discourses operated together for a long time in the consciousness of urban planners. In India climatic and miasmatic theory of disease causation persisted much longer than in Europe. David Arnold, "Perspectives of Indian Plague, 1896–1900," in *Subaltern Studies V*, ed. Ranajit Guha (Oxford: Oxford University Press, 1987), 60.

21. Martin, *Notes on the Medical Topography.*

22. For a powerful reading of accumulation by dispossession within the Indian context, see Kalyan K. Sanyal, *Rethinking Capitalist Development: Primitive Accumulation, Governmentality and Post-Colonial Capitalism* (London: Routledge, 2007).

23. The environmentalist Subhash Dutta and his organization Howrah Ganatantrik Nagarik Samiti (HGNS) spearheaded this citizens' movement. HGNS was founded right after the declaration of emergency in 1975, and its members are mostly middle-class Bengalis. Ideologically, HGNS is rooted in a socialist tradition and has campaigned for better civic amenities as well as against police atrocities. For more on the activities of HGNS, see Hans Dembowski, "Courts, Civil Society and Public Sphere: Environmental Litigation in Calcutta" *Economic Political Weekly* 34, nos. 1–2 (January 2–15, 1999): 49–56.

24. "Lone Intruder on the *Maidan*," *Times of India*, November 16, 2009.

25. Chattopadhyay, *Representing Calcutta.*

26. "Lone Intruder on the *Maidan.*"

27. Ibid.

28. Anna Lowenhaupt Tsing, *Friction: An Ethnography of Global Connection* (Princeton, NJ: Princeton University Press, 2004), 4–6.

29. Ritajyoti Bandyopadhyay, "Institutionalizing Informality: The 'Hawkers' Question in Post-Colonial Calcutta," *Modern Asian Studies* 50, no. 2 (2016): 675–717.

30. Debjani Bhattacharyya and Madhura Chakraborty, *Imagined Homes: Homeless People Envision Shelters* (Kolkata: Calcutta Samaritans in Association with Action Aid, 2011).

31. Carol Rose, "Seeing Property," in *Property and Persuasion: Essays on the History, Theory, and Rhetoric of Ownership* (Boulder, CO: Westview, 1994), 267–304.

32. Andrew Herscher, "Humanitarianism's Housing Question: From Slum Reform to Digital Shelter," *E-flux Journal* 66 (October 2015): 9. I borrow the idea of "weightless homes" from Mabel Wilson's talk "The Provisional Demos: Spatial Agency of Tent Cities," Concept Histories of the Urban, Columbia University, September 2016.

33. Name changed.

Chapter 15

1. Michele Acuto, "High-Rise Dubai Urban Entrepreneurialism and the Technology of Symbolic Power," *Cities* 27 (2010): 272–84.

2. Tim Bunnell, "Antecedent Cities and Inter-Referencing Effects: Learning from and Extending Beyond Critiques of Neoliberalisation," *Urban Studies* 52, no. 11 (2015): 1983–2000.

3. Bunnell, "Antecedent Cities and Inter-Referencing Effects."

4. Ibid.

5. Acuto, "High-Rise Dubai Urban Entrepreneurialism and the Technology of Symbolic Power."

6. C. B. Huat, "Singapore as Model: Planning Innovations, Knowledge Experts," in *Worlding Cities: Asian Experiments and the Art of Being Global*, ed. A. Roy and A. Ong (Malden, MA: Wiley-Blackwell, 2011), 29–54.

7. Julion D. Dávila, ed., *Urban Mobility and Poverty: Lessons from Medellín and Soacha, Colombia* (London: DPU, UCL and Universidad Nacional De Colombia, 2013).

8. Eugene McCann, "Urban Policy Mobilities and Global Circuits of Knowledge," *Annals of the Association of American Geographers* 101, no. 1 (2011): 107–30.

9. Bunnell, "Antecedent Cities and Inter-Referencing Effects."

10. Ibid.

11. Acuto, "High-Rise Dubai Urban Entrepreneurialism and the Technology of Symbolic Power."

12. Ibid.

13. Elizabeth Rapoport, "Globalising Sustainable Urbanism: The Role of International Masterplanners," *Area* 47, no. 2 (2015): 110–15.

14. Ibid., 110.

15. Ibid.

16. Bunnell, "Antecedent Cities and Inter-Referencing Effects."

17. United Nations Department of Economic and Social Affairs Population Division [UNPD], *World Urbanization Prospects: The 2012 Revision* (New York: UNPD, 2012).

18. United Nations Population Fund, *State of World Population 2007: Unleashing the Potential of Urban Growth* (New York: United Nations, 2007).

19. UN-Habitat, *The State of African Cities 2010: Governance, Inequality, and Urban Land Markets* (Nairobi: UN-Habitat, 2010).

20. See Rémi Jedwab, *Why Is African Urbanization Different? Evidence from Resource Exports in Ghana and Ivory Coast* (Paris: Paris School of Economics, 2012); Douglas Gollin, Remi Jedwab, and Dietrich Vollrath, "Urbanization With and Without Structural Transformation," paper presented to the NBER Growth Conference, San Francisco, February 7, 2013; J. Vernon Henderson, Mark Roberts, and Adam Storeygard, *Is Urbanization in Sub-Saharan Africa Different?*, Policy Research Working Paper 6481 (Washington, DC: World Bank, 2013).

21. UN-Habitat, *The State of African Cities 2008: A Framework for Addressing Urban Challenges in Africa* (Nairobi: UN-Habitat, 2008).

22. Vanessa Watson, "African Urban Fantasies: Dreams or Nightmares?," *Environment and Urbanization* 26, no. 1 (2014): 215–31.

23. Rapoport, "Globalising Sustainable Urbanism."

24. "Confusion Rocks Hope City Project," *Modern Ghana*, June 11, 2013, https://www.modernghana.com/news/468095/1/confusion-rocks-hope-city-project.html.

25. Abu Mubarak, "RLG's Hope City Joins Africa's Herd of White Elephant Projects," Pulse GH, July 5, 2016, http://pulse.com.gh/features/hope-city-project-rlg-s-hope-city-joins-africa-s-herd-of-white-elephant-projects-id5226911.html.

26. Kinyinya Subarea Master Plan," OZ, n.d., http://ozarch.com/portfolio/kinyinya-subarea-master-plan/.

27. UN-Habitat, *The State of Cities in Africa* (Nairobi: UN-Habitat, 2010).

28. See Acuto, "High-Rise Dubai Urban Entrepreneurialism and the Technology of Symbolic Power"; Lucy Hewett and Stephen Graham, "Vertical Cities: Representations of Urban Verticality in 20th-Century Science Fiction Literature," *Urban Studies* 52, no. 5 (2015): 923–37.

29. Rapoport, "Globalising Sustainable Urbanism."

30. On how this problem gave rise to Angola's "ghost cities," see Allan Cain, "African Urban Fantasies: Past Lessons and Emerging Realities," *Environment and Urbanization* 26, no. 2 (2014): 561–67.

31. "Businesses Are Being Forced to Move into Designated Properties," *The Economist*, March 2, 2017, http://www.economist.com/news/middle-east-and-africa/21717989-empty-buildings-prompt-draconian-action-businesses-are-being-forced-move?fsrc=scn/fb/te/bl/ed/ifyoubuilditttheymaynotcomebusinessesarebeingforcedtomoveintodesignatedproperties.

32. Robert G. Hollands, "Will the Real Smart City Please Stand Up?," *City* 12, no. 3 (2008): 303–20.

33. Bunnell, "Antecedent Cities and Inter-Referencing Effects."

34. Rapoport, "Globalising Sustainable Urbanism."

35. Ibid.

36. Filip De Boeck, "Spectral Kinshasa: Building the City Through an Architecture of Words," in *Urban Theory Beyond the West: A World of Cities*, ed. T. Edensor and M. Jayne (New York: Routledge, 2012), 311–28.

37. Cain, "African Urban Fantasies."

LIST OF CONTRIBUTORS

Daniel Béland is a professor of political science and the director of the McGill Institute for the Study of Canada at McGill University. He authored, with Philip Rocco and Alex Waddam, *Unfinished Fight: Federalism and the Battle over the Affordable Care Act in the States* (University Press of Kansas, 2016) and is the editor of numerous books, including, with Robert H. Cox, *Ideas and Politics in Social Science Research* (Oxford University Press, 2011).

Debjani Bhattacharyya is an assistant professor of history at Drexel University. She is the author of *Empire and Ecology in the Bengal Delta: The Making of Calcutta* (Cambridge University Press, 2018).

Robert Henry Cox is a professor of political science and the director of the Walker Institute of International and Area Studies at the University of South Carolina. He is a coeditor, with Daniel Béland, of *Ideas and Politics in Social Science Research* (Oxford University Press, 2011) and, with Gary B. Cohen, Benjamin W. Ansell, and Jane Gingrich, of *Social Policy in the Smaller European States* (Berghahn Books, 2011).

Richardson Dilworth is a professor of politics and the interim head of the Department of Politics at Drexel University. He is the author of *The Urban Origins of Suburban Autonomy* (Harvard University Press, 2005) and the editor or coeditor of nine books, with one of the most recent being *China's Urban Future and the Quest for Stability* (2019), with Rebecca Clothey.

Jason Hackworth is a professor of planning and geography at the University of Toronto. He is the author of *Manufacturing Decline: How Racism and the Conservative Movement Crush the American Rust Belt* (Columbia University Press, 2019), *Faith Based: Religious Neoliberalism and the Politics of Welfare in the United States* (University of Georgia Press, 2012), and *The Neoliberal City:*

Governance, Ideology, and Development in American Urbanism (Cornell University Press, 2007), the latter of which was nominated for the Robert Park Book Award.

Marcus Anthony Hunter is the Scott Waugh Endowed Chair in the Division of the Social Sciences, professor in sociology, and chair of the Department of African American Studies at the University of California–Los Angeles. He is the author of *Black Citymakers: How the Philadelphia Negro Changed Urban America* (Oxford University Press, 2013), the coauthor with Zandria F. Robinson of *Chocolate Cities: The Black Map of American Life* (University of California Press, 2018), and the editor of *The New Black Sociologists: Historical and Contemporary Perspectives* (Routledge, 2018).

William Hurst is professor of political science at Northwestern University. He is the author of *Ruling Before the Law: The Politics of Legal Regimes in China and Indonesia* (Cambridge University Press, 2018) and *The Chinese Worker after Socialism* (Cambridge University Press, 2009) and a coeditor, with Jessica Teets, of *Local Governance Innovation in China: Experimentation, Diffusion, and Defiance* (Routledge, 2015).

Sally Ford Lawton is a PhD candidate in political science at Johns Hopkins University. In 2017 she was named a Norton Long Scholar by the Urban and Local Politics Section of the American Political Science Association.

Thomas Ogorzalek is assistant professor of political science and urban studies at Northwestern University. He is the author of *Cities on the Hill: How Urban Institutions Transform National Politics* (Oxford University Press, 2018).

Eleonora Pasotti is an associate professor of politics at the University of California, Santa Cruz. She is author of *Political Branding in Cities: The Decline of Machine Politics in Bogotá, Naples and Chicago* (Cambridge University Press 2009) and *Resisting Redevelopment: Protest in Aspiring Global Cities* (Cambridge University Press 2020).

Joel Rast is an associate professor of political science and the director of urban studies at the University of Wisconsin–Milwaukee. He is author of *The Origins of the Dual City: Housing, Race, and Redevelopment in Twentieth-Century Chicago* (University of Chicago Press, 2019) and *Remaking Chicago: The Political Origins of Urban Industrial Change* (Northern Illinois University Press, 1999).

Douglas S. Reed is a professor of government and the director of the master's program in educational transformation at Georgetown University. He is author of *Building the Federal Schoolhouse: Localism and the American Education State* (Oxford University Press, 2014) and *On Equal Terms: The Constitutional Politics of Educational Opportunity* (Princeton University Press, 2001).

Mara Sidney is an associate professor of political science and the codirector of the global urban studies PhD program at Rutgers University–Newark. She is a coauthor, with Rodney Hero, Susan Clarke, Luis Fraga, and Bari Anhalt Erlichson, of *Multiethnic Moments: The Politics of Urban Education* (Temple University Press, 2006) and *Unfair Housing: How National Policy Shapes Community Action* (University Press of Kansas, 2003), which was named an "Outstanding Academic Title" by *Choice* magazine.

Lester K. Spence is an associate professor of political science and Africana studies at Johns Hopkins University. He is the author of *Knocking the Hustle: Against the Neoliberal Turn in Black Politics* (Punctum Books, 2015). Spence received the W. E. B. DuBois Distinguished Book Award for *Stare in the Darkness: The Limits of Hip-Hop and Black Politics* (University of Minnesota Press, 2013).

Vanessa Watson is a professor of city planning and a fellow of the University of Cape Town in South Africa. She is the Global South editor of *Urban Studies*; a coauthor, with Richard De Satgé, of *Urban Planning in the Global South: Conflicting Rationalities in Contested Urban Space* (Palgrave Macmillan, 2018); a coeditor, with Gautam Bhan and Smita Srinivas, of the *Routledge Companion to Planning in the Global South* (2018); and a coeditor, with Michael Gunder and Ali Madanipour, of the *Routledge Handbook of Planning Theory* (2018).

Timothy P. R. Weaver is assistant professor of political science at the University at Albany, State University of New York. He is the author of *Blazing the Neoliberal Trail: Urban Policy and Politics in the United States and the United Kingdom* (University of Pennsylvania Press, 2016).

Amy Widestrom is an associate professor of political science at Arcadia University. She is the author of *Displacing Democracy: Economic Segregation in America* (University of Pennsylvania Press, 2015).

INDEX

ACKNOWLEDGMENTS

This project began with some conversations and e-mails between the editors and then some initial e-mails to prospective contributors. In several instances, we did not actually know the contributors before we sent them invitations to write chapters for a book that was as yet only roughly defined and for which we had no publisher. We thank those early contributors for taking a risk with us—especially Vanessa Watson from the University of Cape Town, who had absolutely no idea who we were.

Peter Agree at the University of Pennsylvania Press was from the beginning enthusiastic about this project and provided excellent guidance over several years as we collected authors and refined our focus. And at the very end, Drexel political science major Morgan Sarao did some fast and excellent work getting the endnotes in order.

The editors would also like to thank Daniel Béland and Robert Cox for kindly agreeing to write the book's preface, not least because their own edited volume, *Ideas in Social Science Research*, laid the foundation for this project.

Several contributors dragged themselves out to conferences and workshops on behalf of this book. Doug Reed and Lester Spence showed up to present early versions of their papers at the 2015 meeting of the Social Science History Association, where Adam Sheingate provided excellent and useful feedback in his role as discussant. On Sunday morning after the 2016 meeting of the American Political Science Association, Spence, Reed, Tom Ogorzalek, Bill Hurst, Mara Sidney, Amy Widestrom, and Marcus Hunter all showed up at what turned out to be lab space at the Drexel University College of Medicine, where we all discussed our various chapters for several hours.

Several other academic fellow travelers have provided feedback and intellectual support both generally and in direct connection to this book. We are especially grateful to the conversations and debates we have had with Zack Taylor and Jack Lucas, whose work on Canadian urban political development and comparative urban political development between the United States and Canada has been especially helpful in our thinking.

Tim would like to thank Joanna for her support throughout this process, especially in stepping up to take on the role of solo parent as he skipped town to attend workshops and conferences during which the book's themes were developed. He would also like to thank his sons Benjamin and Noah who have grown up beautifully alongside this book project, always with no shortage of ideas of their own about how the world ought to work. Not to be shown up, Richard would also like to thank his wife Martha and his children, Sam and Nina, who are all very bored of hearing about urban political development.

Lightning Source UK Ltd.
Milton Keynes UK
UKHW010124010721
386446UK00001B/6